Opportunities and Challenges for the Greater Mekong Subregion

AF705270

The Mekong River is a vital and valuable resource, with huge development potential for the six states through which it flows. Given the significant asymmetry of power between those states, however, there is a real risk that some might utilise it to the detriment of others.

Without a sense of regional belonging, it is difficult to imagine that these states and their constituent communities will take regional imperatives to heart, participate in joint regulatory frameworks, or adopt behaviours for upstream-downstream and lateral cooperation over the appropriation and use of their shared resources. How effectively has closer interdependence of the Mekong countries accommodated the development of a political-social-cultural space conducive to the growth of a regional "we-ness" among not only political elites, but also the general public? The contributors to this volume approach this question from a range of directions, including the impacts of tourism, regional development programmes, the Mekong Power Grid, and Sino-US rivalry.

This edited volume presents valuable insights for scholars of international relations, Asian studies, development studies, environment studies, policy studies, and human geography.

Charles Samuel Johnston has recently retired from the School of Hospitality and Tourism at Auckland University of Technology, where he had lectured from 1998 to 2018. His main research themes focus on tourism in Asia and in cities, and on the relationship between tourism and socio-economic development.

Xin Chen is Research Fellow and Program Officer at the New Zealand Asia Institute of the University of Auckland. Her research interests focus on East Asian regional integration, China-Asia relations, and Chinese politics.

Routledge Studies on the Asia-Pacific Region

Local Political Participation in Japan
A Case Study of Oita
Dani Daigle Kida

The US-Japan Security Community
Theoretical Understanding of Transpacific Relationships
Hidekazu Sakai

Opportunities and Challenges for the Greater Mekong Subregion
Building a Shared Vision of *Our* River
Edited by Charles Samuel Johnston and Xin Chen

For more information about this series, please visit: https://www.routledge.com/Routledge-Studies-on-the-Asia-Pacific-Region/book-series/RSAPR

Opportunities and Challenges for the Greater Mekong Subregion

Building a Shared Vision of *Our* River

Edited by
Charles Samuel Johnston and Xin Chen

Routledge
Taylor & Francis Group
LONDON AND NEW YORK

First published 2020 by Routledge

2 Park Square, Milton Park, Abingdon, Oxon OX14 4RN
605 Third Avenue, New York, NY 10017

Routledge is an imprint of the Taylor & Francis Group, an informa business

First issued in paperback 2021

Copyright © 2020 selection and editorial matter, Charles Samuel Johnston and Xin Chen; individual chapters, the contributors

The right of Charles Samuel Johnston and Xin Chen to be identified as the authors of the editorial material, and of the authors for their individual chapters, has been asserted in accordance with sections 77 and 78 of the Copyright, Designs and Patents Act 1988.

All rights reserved. No part of this book may be reprinted or reproduced or utilised in any form or by any electronic, mechanical, or other means, now known or hereafter invented, including photocopying and recording, or in any information storage or retrieval system, without permission in writing from the publishers.

Notice:
Product or corporate names may be trademarks or registered trademarks, and are used only for identification and explanation without intent to infringe.

Publisher's Note

The publisher has gone to great lengths to ensure the quality of this reprint but points out that some imperfections in the original copies may be apparent.

British Library Cataloguing-in-Publication Data
A catalogue record for this book is available from the British Library

Library of Congress Cataloging-in-Publication Data
A catalog record for this book has been requested

ISBN: 978-0-367-44101-2 (hbk)
ISBN: 978-1-03-217519-5 (pbk)
DOI: 10.4324/9781003007616

Typeset in Galliard
by Taylor & Francis Books

Contents

Illustrations

Figures

Tables

Acknowledgements

The editors of this book would like to express their gratitude and appreciation to the Japan Foundation and the New Zealand Asia Institute at the University of Auckland, whose financial and institutional support made the project possible. They would also like to thank the Regional Center for Social Science and Sustainable Development of Chiang Mai University in Thailand and the Souphanouvong University in Laos for their scholarly assistance and encouragement. The editors would especially like to thank all the contributors to this book for their hard work, fresh ideas, in-depth analysis, and patience during the project.

Contributors

Bui Quang Binh is a Senior Researcher at the Institute of Regional Sustainable Development at the Vietnam Academy of Social Sciences. His research focuses on environmental issues. Being a Geographic Information System (GIS) and Geodesy specialist, Dr Binh has conducted several studies on climate change in and natural disaster risk prediction models for the Mekong Delta region.

Xin Chen is Research Fellow and Program Officer at the New Zealand Asia Institute at the University of Auckland. Her research interests focus on East Asian regional integration, China-Asia relations, and Chinese politics.

Ilpyo Hong is a Research Fellow in the Land, Water Conservation and Environment Department at the Korea Institute of Civil Engineering and Building Technology (KICT). He is widely experienced in a number of different fields with a focus on water-related risk, disasters, Integrated Water Resources Management (IWRM), water rights, the balanced allocation of water and coordinates for the High-level Experts and Leaders Panel on water and disasters (HELP) for over a decade.

Kenneth Jackson is a Research Associate at the New Zealand Asia Institute and an Honorary Research Fellow at the Centre for Development Studies at the University of Auckland. He is also an Adjunct Research Professor at the Auckland Institute of Studies. He retired in June 2012 as Director of the Centre for Development Studies at the University of Auckland, which he joined in 2003, having formerly been a long-time staff member in Economics. His. research and consultancy has covered Asia, Europe, Australia, New Zealand, and the Pacific Islands, encompassing issues related to economics, economic history, development and agriculture, trade, migration and remittances, technology and infrastructure, food supply and food security, mining and electricity-related issues.

Charles Samuel Johnston has recently retired from the School of Hospitality and Tourism at Auckland University of Technology, where he had lectured from 1998 to 2018. His main research themes focus on tourism in Asia and in cities, and on the relationship between tourism and socio-economic development.

Seungho Lee is Professor of International Development at the Graduate School of International Studies at Korea University. His current research focuses on transboundary water management with special reference to China, South Korea, Southeast Asia, in particular the Mekong River Basin, and Europe. Professor Lee often consults with government research institutions and public companies in South Korea, such as the Korea Development Institute, the Korea Economic Institute, and K-water, and international donor agencies, such as UNESCAP Bangkok, and UNESCO-Institute for Water Security and Sustainable Management, Daejeon, South Korea.

Kanokwan Manorom is Associate Professor at the Faculty of Liberal Arts at Ubon Ratchathani University in Thailand. Her research focuses on water and land governance, development and social impact assessments in Thailand and the Mekong region.

Nayeon Shin is Research Associate at the Sejong Institute in South Korea. She has earned a Master's degree in International Development and Cooperation at the Graduate School of International Studies in Korea University. Her research interests are related to transboundary river issues, in particular, those relating to hydropower and the Mekong River Basin.

Nicholas Tarling was Editor of *The Cambridge History of Southeast Asia*, and has authored and edited over 60 other books, the majority of which are on Southeast Asian history, but some cover other topics, such as theatre and opera, the history of universities, and the internationalisation of higher education. In 2012, Routledge published *The Works of Nicholas Tarling on Southeast Asia*, which comprises some 72 of his academic journal articles. The seven-volume collection was edited and introduced by Professor Ooi Keat Gin at Universiti Sains Malaysia.

Dinar Swastiningtyas Theosa is a Junior Researcher from Indonesia. She has been examining China-US strategic rivalries in the Asia-Pacific region since taking up her post-graduate studies at the Ritsumeikan Asia Pacific University in 2015.

1 Introduction

Economic growth and community construction in the Greater Mekong Subregion

Xin Chen and Charles Samuel Johnston

A nourishing and inspiring "mother"

Originating from the Tibetan Plateau and emptying into the South China Sea, the Mekong River flows through China (Yunnan Province), Myanmar, Lao PDR, Thailand, Cambodia, and Vietnam. The "Mother of Rivers", *mae khong*, [1] has not merely carved out this unique Subregion, which has a landmass the size of Western Europe and a population close to that of the US.[2] It has also provided tens of millions of the region's riparian residents with food and livelihoods.[3] The Mekong has moreover served as an essential means for intra-regional transport, social interactions, and cultural activities.[4] Being the eighth largest river in the world measured by water flow,[5] the Mekong has meanwhile endowed the region with immense resources for small-to-large-scale hydropower projects and irrigation systems.

The Mekong is often acknowledged as one of the world's last great rivers to remain mostly undammed.[6] Indeed, with few large cities, a relatively sparse population, and little industry along its course, the River is arguably the least exploited among the major rivers in the world. Decades of violent conflicts and civil strife in recent history have also resulted in much of the region being frequently referred to as undeveloped and stuck in economic stagnation. As the great majority of the 300-plus million people in the Greater Mekong Subregion (GMS) still live subsistence or semi-subsistence agricultural lifestyles, poverty is believed to be endemic.[7] With peace settling in the whole of Indochina since the early 1990s, however, the Subregion has experienced a significant turnaround. The six member states have devised a range of national, bilateral, and multilateral development schemes for banking on the rich resources of the Mekong. By the second Subregion leaders' summit held in July 2005, more than a hundred development projects had been jointly launched in energy, agriculture, transportation, telecommunications, trade and investment, tourism, environment, and human resources.[8]

Poverty reduction is a primary mission for all six governments. It thus follows that economic growth invariably dominates their domestic and foreign policy deliberations. Furthermore, they all seem to espouse the idea that harnessing the resources of the Mekong would serve as a most effective springboard for their respective economic development. This belief is put in words by Cambodia's former Minister of Transportation Khy Tainglim, who says that the Mekong "is our oil, our mines of gold, our main natural resource, and we should use our water to export and get foreign currency to develop the country".[9] Indeed, to raise living standards, the six countries in the Subregion have all been committed to promoting and facilitating infrastructure networking for hydropower development and transfer, flood control and irrigation, improved navigation channels, and easier cross-border movement of goods and people.[10]

An asymmetrical common-pool resource

Yet while the economic imperative enjoys common primacy throughout the Subregion, the six member states differ in the rates and pace of their economic and social development. The disparity and corollary power differential have unsurprisingly bred anxieties over uneven distribution of the Mekong resources and potentials among the riparian states and communities.[11] Striving to ensure an adequate measure of fair and equitable resource sharing, the six countries are actively engaged in diplomatic negotiations and joint development programmes. At the same time, however, they have also been racing to maximise their own benefits from the Mekong by pressing ahead with national hydroelectric, water diversion, and channel dredging projects on the stretches of the river or its tributaries within their respective boundaries. The fear that ever more development schemes are being introduced or implemented without sufficient region-wide consultation has led many to worry that resource rivalries may ultimately become the fault lines between the countries in the Mekong area.[12]

An international/regional river such as the Mekong perhaps projects a worst-case scenario for problems surrounding common pool resources. Not only may the use of the river by one party limit the access of others to its potential consumptive benefits, but the consequences of the former's exploitation may also "flow" with the water to the latter.[13] Meanwhile, efforts to coordinate the development in the Mekong region are often challenged by the sensitive issue of sovereignty and the "ASEAN way" of non-interference. The upstream-downstream problem in relation to the shared resources is further complicated by the fact that divergent interests and priorities of the states in the Subregion have resulted in their different reactions to controversial projects initiated by members of the community unilaterally, or through bilateral or multilateral arrangements.[14] An often cited example in this regard is the Lancang-Mekong Navigation Improvement Project signed in 2000 by China, Thailand, Lao PDR, and Myanmar. The scheme is aimed at facilitating trade and tourism by opening the route to vessels of up to 500 tons. Yet the removal of reefs, shoals, and rapids necessitated by the project reportedly has Cambodia and Vietnam down the stream worried about the impact of altered river flows on their farming and other production activities.[15] While impact studies within and without the region since 2000 have yet to reach any convincing or consoling conclusions, the 2015–25 Development Plan of the Langcang-Mekong navigation project has nevertheless been set in motion.[16]

In addition to issues of asymmetric distribution among the GMS countries of benefits and consequences from the development of the shared river, economic growth pressures, in the forms of hydroelectric dams, industrial development, intensive farming, rapid urbanisation, and navigation improvement attempts have also given rise to serious concerns about increasing environmental, ecological, social, cultural, and livelihood disturbances. Non-governmental organisations (NGOs), environmental advocates, scientists, and academics have been particularly vocal about potential adverse impacts and undesirable effects of many development initiatives that are proposed and/or already under way in the region.[17] They call into question the widespread discursive classification that reduces social, cultural, economic, ecological, and geographic specificities of the region to a homogenous lot of economic "challenges" and "opportunities".[18] They urge planners and developers to provide explicit terms of reference for the public to assess social and environmental impacts of projects with potential transboundary effects.[19] They challenge the paternalistic attitude of many political elites and institutional donors who insist on development "for" the people rather than "by" the people.[20] They argue that failing to uphold visions of, or to consult with, the affected peoples and communities in the region, development projects would only serve the interests of donor countries, international lending agencies, and/or private investors, who are vying for contracts or opportunities to exploit the vast and varied natural resources in the region.[21] They worry that local communities will be left only to deal with the economic, social, and cultural consequences such as displacement of families, removal from ancestral homeland, destruction of agricultural fields, and alienation from traditional livelihood resources.[22]

Towards an "our" river?

Yet the Subregion has to break away from poverty; and some sort of economic development will have to occur. Following this rationale, it may become more understandable that many communities along the river have pinned their hopes for prosperity on the Mekong. The same logic may also render it legitimate to argue that while it is important and necessary to scrutinise development initiatives proposed for the region and vigilantly detect detrimental impact of projects intended mainly for national self-sufficiency, it is also crucial to identify constructive means towards transforming the Mekong Subregion defined by sovereign nation states and fragmented sub-entities into a mode of coexistence and gradually reaching a strong sense of "we". Without a sense of regional belonging, it is difficult to imagine that the six states and their constituent communities would take regional, or others', imperatives to heart, participate in joint regulatory frameworks, and adopt policies of and behaviours for upstream-downstream and lateral cooperation over the appropriation and use of their shared resources. That many programmes with potential transboundary effects in the region are donor/corporate/special-interest-driven and are intended primarily for trade/investment liberalisation, market returns, or tax revenues also signifies that the impetus for coordinated and sustainable development of the Mekong River will have to come from within the region.

The sense of belonging, more than anything else, determines the precincts of a region and behaviours within it. This sense of community is not given, but socially constructed or re-invented through reflexive interactions of its members. In other words, regional socialisation is a complex but enabling evolutionary process, which may facilitate the development, or redefinition, of norms and patterns of regional relations and national positions on issues with regional consequences.[23] In the Mekong Subregion, the conversion of battlefields into market places in the 1990s has reportedly lifted the flood gates to economic and social contact among its six members. Their ever-growing interactions are, in turn, expected to help expand opportunities for them to develop informed assumptions of each other's interests. Better mutual understanding and higher level of perceived mutual predictability should arguably be conducive to confidence building among the six countries and hence the construction of a "we". Admittedly, however, the ever closer and broader interactions among the six Mekong countries occur in the context of their distinct national interests, diverse political history, varied governance structures, and different priorities in their double transitions from subsistence agricultural and centrally planned to more diversified and market-based economies.

Since the six countries share both the gifts of the Mekong and the impact of their respective actions on the river, the establishment of an integrated water resources management in the region is mainly an issue of people management. It thus follows that to realise their respective development visions and aspirations in a sustainable and equitable manner requires not only contractual arrangements at the governmental level, but, more importantly, a profound popular basis at the grassroots. Indeed, only when their peoples also share the feeling of regional "belonging", will the six nations be able to self-enforce the limits of acceptable behaviour towards the River.

In short, given that development of the Mekong is imperative for reducing poverty and improving the living standards of local communities, given that the River is subject to rivalries or even conflicts over the up-mid-down-stream water distribution for multiple uses, and given that effects of resource over-consumption and pollution will likely be devastating and asymmetrical among the riparian communities along the River, there is a pressing need for the six countries of the Subregion to align their divergent national interests and plan and work jointly for their "common benefits" and "shared prosperity". In this regard, the Mekong itself has often been described as a central thread and active bond of kinship and friendship for the various population groups in the Subregion over a long time span and over many geographical areas.[24] In other words, the River itself may be a facilitating asset for regional community building among the peoples of the six countries. In fact, burgeoning people-to-people contact along the Mekong in recent years through economic and trade relations, joint development ventures, tourism and recreation, academic exchanges, and cultural activities have already helped revive ties between people of the same ethnic groups straddling the Mekong.[25]

Yet how effectively have increased horizontal links among the people of the six member states helped awaken a sense of shared identity and a desire for regional cohesion in the Mekong development? Or how effectively has closer interdependence of the Mekong countries accommodated the development of a political-social-cultural space conducive for the growth of a regional "we-ness" among not only political elites, but also the general public? The contributors to this volume approach these questions through their analyses of the historical evolution of the Mekong as a region, the potentially vital role of the tourism sector, and the Mekong Power Grid in regional identity formation and sustainable development, the relationship between economic growth/prosperity and community construction, the impact of the US-China strategic rivalry on the Subregional geopolitical landscape, and the domestic policy deliberations and public debates respectively in Vietnam, Thailand, and China on water resources development. These thematic inquiries are intended to shed fresh conceptual and empirical light on efforts and challenges in the Mekong Subregion to bring fragmented and competitive water interests into an integrated and coordinated allocation and management framework for the ever more threatened "Mother" river.

Specifically, Nicholas Tarling traces, in the opening chapter, the history of major external and local political entities engaged in Mekong affairs, their different interests, and resultant diverse positions. The meticulously researched chapter elucidates that to refer to the "Mekong region" or "subregion" or "greater subregion" is a matter of construction rather than description. Accordingly, economic judgement in and for the region has often been moulded by political purposes or pressures.

Charles Samuel Johnston, on the other hand, observes that the designation of "Greater Mekong Subregion" is very much intended by its initiator, the Asian Development Bank, to help create a functional identity for the six countries through which the Mekong River flows. But will a common name based on a shared watercourse be sufficient to create a true sense of regional identity among the 300 million residents? Invoking theory and research on regional identity formation of another Eurasian peninsula, Europe, Johnston spells out the challenges in growing cross-border unity and cooperation along the Mekong. In that context, and given that GMS tourism marketing activities have to date demonstrated intentions to create a "single destination", the author also examines the possibilities of the Subregion to draw on the inspirational achievement of the "100% Pure New Zealand" campaign to build a "100% pure and sustainable Mekong" embraced and enjoyed by both tourists and residents.

The recent UK-EU split has, however, cast doubt on the widely accepted concept that regional economic integration is a "spill-over" process in which cooperation in one area among member states leads to the need for partnership in other areas, and ultimately to a shared willingness to accommodate each other's interests.[26] Reflecting the ongoing debate over whether and how economic liberalisation propels social convergence, Kenneth Jackson focuses his chapter on how internally and externally induced changes in the Subregion's key production processes have acted on the GMS countries, particularly in relation to their economic growth versus community construction. His findings suggest that rapid economic progress has indeed produced rising incomes and reduced poverty throughout the region. Yet the response by local communities to increased economic openness, flexibility, and migration remains more adaptive than formative. There are thus few signs that greater openness and higher growth have enhanced regional, or for that matter national, community construction in any significant way.

Further complicating the dynamic process of the Subregion's progressing from geographical to economic and social integration, argues Dinar Swastiningtyas Theosa, is the Sino-US strategic rivalry in the Mekong development. In elaborating this viewpoint, the author examines how China and America characterise their competition and what means they have adopted to attain their respective strategic objectives in the region. The inquiry concludes that while it remains anybody's guess whether China is gaining the upper hand in the region through its cross-border infrastructure investments, the "America first" doctrine and "greater burden sharing" policy certainly call into serious question Washington's commitment to its "Lower Mekong Initiative" and "Indo-Pacific" concept. The uncertainty about America's pragmatic policy drift further fuels regional anxiety over its relations with the five Lower Mekong countries, as increased volatility on that front may exacerbate ASEAN's internal cleavages in responding to regional challenges.

Daunting challenges and continuous criticism notwithstanding, Nayeon Shin, Seungho Lee, and Ilpyo Hong underscore in their chapter the success of the GMS programme in getting all the countries along the River on board. To assess how the GMS involvement impacts the setting and execution of a region-wide poverty-reduction agenda, they focus their case study on the planning and construction of the Mekong Power Grid. Carried out in the theoretical framework of benefit sharing, the research provides a well-substantiated insight into whether and how the envisioned regional open market in general and attempted cross-border energy trading system in particular may help accelerate economic growth, alleviate poverty, and narrow development gaps in and between the Mekong riparian countries.

But are the GMS countries ready to place primary and particular importance on the Subregion's economic and political unity? Bui Quang Binh's research on the Mekong Delta seems to preclude a positive answer for Vietnam. The chapter instead highlights the growing consensus among the Vietnamese that the Delta's peripheral economic status in the country points to the urgent need for immediate action to upgrade its effective, but little more than subsistence farming system. Furthermore, given the multi-faceted nature of the Delta's development, special emphasis should be placed on improving linkages among households, enterprises, supporting agencies, and government management bodies within the region as its first step in entering Subregional and global value chains.

Meanwhile, Kanokwan Manorom investigates Thailand's domestic controversies and contentions over effectively all large-scale water infrastructure projects within its borders. The chapter indicates that disputes and standoffs typically centre on the adequacy and hence reliability of hydro projects' pre-construction assessments, and on the inclusiveness of local perspectives on anticipated benefits, costs, and social consequences. As a result, considerable Thai governmental and societal efforts have been devoted to tackling internal water governance challenges. The author uses the encouraging story of the Hua Na (Weir) Irrigation scheme in Northeast Thailand to uncover particularly how the People's Impact Assessment programme contributes to the democratisation of water resource management in that region. A clear message conveyed by the research is that, though it has yet to be established or institutionalised as a standard practice in Thailand, the programme can and should be promoted as a useful tool for mitigating negative environmental and disruptive social effects of water development along the Mekong River.

By comparison, China appears more open and eager about building a "community of common destiny" in the Subregion, despite, or exactly because of, intensifying criticism, suspicion, and reservation about the dams and reservoirs straddling the upper Mekong in its Yunnan Province. Yet debates over China's hydro behaviour towards shared water resources, as illustrated by Xin Chen in the closing chapter of the volume, do not stop outside its borders. Domestically, all large dams built, launched or proposed, including those on the Lancang/Mekong River, also suffer from "popularity deficiencies" among the Chinese. Xin Chen's chapter presents and examines in detail major positions and controversies in China's internal hydro politics. Navigating through China's domestically identified and publicly debated pros and cons of its involvement with the Mekong River, the chapter concludes that the prospects are not optimistic for Beijing to change its course of action in relation to hydro development. Accordingly, the Chinese government may still have a long way to go before it can effectively reframe the prevalent China hydro-hegemonic/Mekong-choking/Subregion-encroachment "threat" accounts into a "China opportunity" narrative.

Notes

1 Nosmot Gbadamosi, "Ecologist Special Report: The battle for the 'mother of rivers'", 2017, online at https://theecologist.org/2017/may/22/ecologist-special-report-battle-mother-rivers.

2 Asian Development Bank, "Greater Mekong Subregion marks 20 years of cooperation, achievement", ADB News Release, 14 September 2012, online at https://www.adb.org/news/greater-mekong-subregion-marks-20-years-cooperation-achievement.

3 Vannarith Chheang, "Managing the Mekong River for all", *Khmer Times*, 10 February 2016, online at www.khmertimeskh.com/news/21222/managing-the-mekong-river-for-all.

4 Mekong River Commission, "Design of a master plan for regional waterborne transport in the Mekong River Basin", 2015, p. xxi, online at www.tnmc-is.org/wp-content/uploads/2016/05/Master-PlanNAP_-VOL1.pdf; S. Amnuay-ngerntra and H. Sonoda, "Developing river tourism on the Upper Mekong: Challenges and opportunities", *European Journal of Business and Social Sciences*, Vol. 1, No. 10, 2013, p. 37.

5 Andrea K Gerlak and Andrea Haefner, "Riparianization of the Mekong River Commission", *Water International*, Vol. 42, No. 7, 2017, p. 894.

6 Tanya Heikkila et al., "A study of conflict and cooperation in the Mekong River Basin: How issues and scale matter", paper presented at the FLACSO-ISA Global and Regional Powers in a Changing World Conference, Buenos Aires, Argentina, 23–5 July 2014, p. 3; Edward R. Grumbine et al., "Mekong hydropower: drivers of change and governance challenges", *Frontiers in Ecology and the Environment*, Vol. 10, No. 2, 2012, p. 91.

7 World Bank, "Rice and poverty in the Greater Mekong Sub-Region", *AEC News Today*, 2 March 2016, online at https://aecnewstoday.com/2016/rice-poverty-greater-mekong-sub-region/#axzz4p7jAQX8S; N. Matthews, "Drowning under progress: Water, culture, and development in the Greater Mekong Subregion" in Barbara Rose Johnston et al. (eds.), *Water, Cultural Diversity, and Global Environmental Change*, London and New York: Springer, p. 352; Kobkun Rayanakorn (ed.), *Climate Change Challenges in the Mekong Region*, Chiang Mai, Thailand; Chiang Mai University Press, 2011, p. back cover.

8 Xuan Hu, "Inject vitality into GMS region", *China Daily*, 7 July 2005, p. 4.

9 Cited in Evelyn Goh, "China in the Mekong River Basin: The regional security implications of resource development on the Lancang Jiang", *Working Paper*, No. 69, Institute of Defence and Strategic Studies, Singapore, 2004, p. 7.

10 Jean-Pierre A. Verbiest, "Regional cooperation and integration in the Mekong Region", *Asian Economic Policy Review*, Iss. 8, 2013, pp. 150–1.

11 Frauke Urban et al., "An analysis of China's investment in the hydropower sector in the Greater Mekong Sub-Region", *Environment, Development and Sustainability*, Vol. 15, Iss. 2, 2013, pp. 317–22.

12 Pilita Clark, "Troubled waters: The Mekong River crisis", *Financial Times*, 18 July 2014, online at https://www.ft.com/content/1add7210-0d3d-11e4-bcb2-00144feabdc0.

13 David Fullbrook, "Competing for the Mekong: A case of common-asymmetric resources?" *Global Water Forum*, 2015, online at www.globalwaterforum.org/2015/06/08/competing-for-the-mekong-a-case-of-common-asymmetric-resources/; Selina Ho, "River politics: China's policies in the Mekong and the Brahmaputra in comparative perspectives", *Journal of Contemporary China*, Vol. 23, No. 85, 2014, p. 6.

14 Gabriella Neusner, "Why the Mekong River Commission matters", *The Diplomat*, 7 December 2016, online at https://thediplomat.com/2016/12/why-the-mekong-river-commission-matters.

15 Andrea Haefner, *Negotiating for Water Resources: Bridging Transboundary River Basins*, New York and London: Routledge, 2016, pp. 63–6.

16 Nauvarat Suksamran, "Locals slam Mekong blasting plan", *Bangkok Post*, 9 January 2017, online at https://www.mekongeye.com/2017/01/09/locals-slam-mekong-blasting-plan.

17 Lilliana Corredor, "Comments on the Final Report of the MDS-IAR and the 'Ripple Effect' of Oxfam Australia's input", *Scientists for the Mekong* (blog), 2016, online at https://www.scientists4mekong.com/comments-iar-final-impacts-of-hydropower-on-mekong-river-and-the-ripple-effect-of-oxfams-input.

18 Shalmali Guttal, "Marketing the Mekong: The ADB and the Greater Mekong Sub Region – Economic Cooperation Programme" in Dorothy Guerrero (ed.), *A Handbook on the Asian Development Bank: The ADB and Its Operations in Asia and the Pacific Region*. Essen, Germany: Asienhaus, 2003, pp. 25–6.

19 Marko Keskinen et al., "Mekong at the crossroads: Next steps for impact assessment of large dams", *Ambio: A Journal of the Human Environment*, Vol. 41, Iss. 3, 2012, pp. 320–3.

20 Shalmali Guttal, "Whose lands? Whose resources?" *Development*, Vol. 54, Iss. 1, 2011, pp. 91–7.

21 Edward R. Grumbine and Jianchu Xu, "Mekong Hydropower Development", *Science*, Vol. 332, Iss. 6026, 2011, pp. 178–9.

22 William J. Schulte and Ashlee Stetser, "On the path to sustainable development: An assessment of Cambodia's Draft Environmental Impact Assessment Law", *Cambodia Law and Policy Journal*, Iss. 3, 2014, p. 103; Ly Kesa, "Hydropower development, economic growth and social equality: Mekong Region", *ASEAN-Canada Working Paper*, No. 5, 2014.

23 Alice D Ba, "Who's socializing whom? Complex engagement in Sino-ASEAN relations", *The Pacific Review*, Vol. 19, Iss. 2, 2006, pp. 160–2.

24 Apichai Sunchindah, "The Lancang-Mekong River Basin: Reflections on cooperation mechanisms pertaining to a shared watercourse", *NTS Policy Brief* (No. PO13–01), 2013, p. 7; Apichai Sunchindah et al., "Water diplomacy in the Lancang-Mekong River Basin: Prospects and challenges", paper presented at the Workshop on the Growing Integration of Greater Mekong Sub-regional ASEAN States in Asian Region, Yangon, Myanmar, 20–1 September 2005, p. 2.

25 Vannarith Chheang, "The Mekong Region: From a divided to a connected region", *KAS Discussion Paper*, Konrad-Adenauer-Stiftung, Cambodia, 23 February 2017, online at www.kas.de/wf/doc/kas_48018-1522-2-30.pdf?170223111209; N. Kittisenee, "Rethinking conceptions of borders in the Greater Mekong Subregion: An interview with Chayan Vaddhanabhuti (RCSD)", *Austrian Journal of South-East Asian Studies*, Vol. 4, No. 2, 2011, pp. 314–24.

26 Tim Oliver et al., *The Impact of the UK's Withdrawal on EU Integration*, Brussels: European Parliament, June 2018, pp. 6–7, online at www.europarl.europa.eu/RegData/etudes/STUD/2018/604973/IPOL_STU(2018)604973_EN.pdf.

2 Constructing a region (the Greater Mekong Subregion) out of a river

Nicholas Tarling

Introduction

The great rivers of the world can form the economic and geopolitical basis of major states and civilisations, attaining in the process a legendary, even mystical, character. The Euphrates and the Nile at once come to mind, the Mississippi, the Amazon, even the sweet and softly running Thames, and in East and Southeast Asia the Yangtse and the Red River. Yet the Mekong is different. It is indeed very long, but its character changes in the course of its length. It is supported by melting snow in its upper reaches, but monsoonal rains supply 80 per cent of the water in the lower reaches.[1] It is crossable, but not easily navigable. What can be done with it depends—as with other rivers—on technical capacity and political will, and they vary over time. In other words, it imposes challenging obstacles as well as offering particular advantages. It is thus not surprising that the Mekong has supported a variety of political entities along its course and that their interests and attitudes to it and to each other have differed. This chapter traces the history of these entities, interests, and attitudes, stopping at the recent historical period just before the present day.

The Mekong region as colonial spearhead

To refer to the "Mekong region" or "subregion" is bound to be rather a matter of construction than description. Even if modern technology can give it greater physical reality, that might risk undermining rather than enhancing political will and cultural support. To refer to the "Greater" Mekong Region or Subregion—a means of including China in the description—may expand the problem rather than the solution. Those outside—or largely outside—the region may have good reason to apply the label. Those inside the region may find it difficult to accept its implications. That does not necessarily mean that attempts have not or should not be made, or even that, over time, they will not enjoy increasing success. In a world that is constructing or has constructed regions as well as nations, it is not impossible to envisage the construction of subregions. But it is more likely to succeed—if it is to be done without violence—if it is approached as a long-term process and a collaborative one, based on confidence-building.

It is, of course, possible to find some cultural commonalities among the peoples who live along the Mekong. Bronze drums, for example, are part of the region's heritage and still in use.[2] Thousands of Buddhist pagodas and monasteries stretch from the Tibetan plateau to the Cochin-Chinese delta. "Buddhism has arguably exerted the strongest overarching influence over many centuries on the cultures of the peoples of the Mekong, regardless of whether they are Thai, Khmer, Lao, Vietnamese, Burmese or Chinese."[3] Nor have physical obstacles prevented petty trading in such goods as drugs, silk, and green tea, though, visiting Laos in 1641 on behalf of the United Dutch East India Company or Vereenigde Oost-Indische Compagnie (VOC), Van Wuysthoff was bewildered by the rapids. "It took the Dutch party a little over three months to reach Viang Chan by boat from Phnom Penh."[4]

Political fragmentation was, however, obvious even in the pre-colonial period. The political entities of that time did nevertheless accept and build upon the capacity of the river to provide a basis for unity by way of breadth rather than length: a section of the river could provide the centre for a kingdom or principality. That might be built round a trading town like Vientiane. Quite exceptionally, one was built around the Great Lake that the Mekong formed by reverse flow in what we know as Cambodia. It was only in the colonial period that—quite unrealistically—the Mekong River itself became a political frontier. But, of course, it was not alone in representing the way colonial powers drew frontiers for their own convenience rather than in respect of political or cultural continuity or even geographical reality.

In most cases the object was to avoid conflict between colonial powers. In this case the main concern of the French was to avoid a conflict with Siam, though they knew that the Thais looked to the British. The French had secured the protectorate of Cambodia in 1863. They sought in the 1880s and 1890s to take over the Laotian principalities over which the Thais had been asserting their claims. The climax to the conflict was the French bombardment of Paknam in 1893. The outcome was the division of the principalities largely along the Mekong River. That, as August Pavie insisted, was not "a rational frontier .... If we take over the rulers situated on our bank of the river, we would be giving the Siamese full possession of half of their territories."[5] As Soren Ivarsson has recently shown, the French sought thereafter to break the ties with the Thai kingdom across the river and with the Lao who live in "Isan", "to de-link 'French Laos' from a 'Greater Siam' in the making".[6] Vientiane, destroyed by the Siamese in 1827–8, was rebuilt as an administrative capital.[7]

A few years earlier the French had defined their empire in Southeast Asia as "French Indo-China", and Governor-General Doumer was to give it a new administrative reality in 1897. They had indeed an interest in China. That dated from the "opening" of China following the first Anglo-China war in 1840–2. France's involvement was not based on trade, even in potential. It had no interests to protect, but, as Louis Philippe's minister, Guizot, put it, France could not be absent from so great a part of the world when other European nations possessed establishments there.[8]

Napoleon III took up the general concept in the 1850s. The naval forces in the East, it was decided, would seize Danang in order to guarantee the execution of a treaty providing for the protection of missionaries in Vietnam and for commercial concessions. A joint Franco-Spanish expedition was authorised late in 1857. Danang was seized in 1858, but it proved impossible to attack Hué. Against the protests of the Spaniards and of the missionaries—whose interests focused on Tonkin – the French admiral moved south and captured Saigon early in 1859. The French were on the way to constructing the colony they were to call Cochin China. But its potential development they associated with China.

Saigon, Admiral La Grandière hoped, would become "the entrepot of western China".[9] The Doudart de Lagrée expedition of 1866–8, however, found the Mekong unsuitable for a commercial artery, its steamer stopped by the rapids that Van Wuysthoff had faced. Its second-in-command, Francis Garnier, concluded even so that France's position in Cochin China could be the base for a commercial and political influence in Indo-China and southern China with the potential to become "the exact counterweight to that of England in India".[10]

If the sense of rivalry with the British is apparent, the interest in China is also striking. If the Mekong was impracticable, the Red River might serve, as Jean Dupuis, trader and arms dealer, showed in 1871. Tonkin was, according to Paul Gaffarel, Professor of Geography at Dijon, the way to the "very heart" of China. "We have ... but ... to restore impetus and life to these intelligent Annamese and Chinese peoples, and, thanks to them, pacifically to invade interior China. These are our future Indias."[11]

Governor-General Doumer sought to make the Indo-Chinese Union the French created a reality by political and administrative reforms, and by constructing railways. But it was significant that among those railways the priority went not to constructing links with Cambodia and Laos, nor even to completing the Transindochinois – Saigon and Hanoi were not linked till 1936 – but to building the railway into Yunnan, which reached Kunming in 1910. It was designed to "open up" southwest China, and to stake a claim should China break up. China, however, did not break up. Indo-China remained the limit of the French empire in Asia, and it was somewhat exposed. Africa had taken priority.

The weakness of the French position was underlined by the Second World War. The Vichy regime came to terms with the Japanese, and was allowed to stay in power till March 1945. Through a conflict with the French, followed by a Japanese "mediation", the Thais regained some of the Laotian and Cambodian territory they had earlier lost, but the Decoux regime sought to build up a sense of identification both with the pays of Indo-China and with Indo-China itself. That was not, however, the same as building regionalism along the Mekong.

At the end of the war, the French sought to regain the territories the Thais had regained. Prime Minister Pridi [Luang Pradit] faced "intense public feeling on this question",[12] and brought the matter before the Security Council.[13] Following a US note, however, the French proposed that, after the territories had been returned, a "conciliation commission" should be appointed to examine the ethnic, geographic, and economic arguments. That was accepted in Bangkok after much debate only because, as Edgar Stanton reported, the US supported it, and because of a belief "that we will see to it that justice is done to Siam".[14] But the outcome was a rejection of the Thai claims.

The report of the Conciliation Commission did, however, recommend that the two governments should consider setting up an international advisory commission, probably in Bangkok, to consider technical matters of common interest. In July 1947 Georges-Picot, a French diplomat involved in the negotiations, discussed a "Mekong concept" with Pridi.[15]

Seven years later, in 1954, Georges-Picot – by now UN Secretary-General for Economic Affairs—raised the matter again. The context was different, and so was the purpose. Cambodia and Laos had secured independence, though still within the French Union. The French were, however, facing defeat at the hands of the Democratic Republic of Vietnam, and the US, as the Geneva Conference drew nearer, were anxious to boost their morale. Early in 1954 Bill Donovan, the US ambassador in Bangkok, argued for an initiative that would forestall a "sell-out", and he favoured the idea of a Mekong Valley Authority under UN guidance, underwritten by the US He saw it, however, only as a step towards military cooperation. "He talked in very large and woolly terms of the need to strengthen the 'flank' of Asia and of making Siam the 'fist'", as a British official put it.[16]

The British minister in Saigon, H. A. Graves, drew attention to "the preponderant importance of this river in the economy of the three Associate States", Cambodia, Laos, and Vietnam. It was "the economic life-line of Indo-China and the French very wisely regarded it as the main natural factor which bound together the diverse elements and races into a harmonious whole". A Mekong Valley Authority might provide "a means of welding the units together". If well-handled, the proposal could counteract "the short-sighted and dangerous tendency to separatism which the granting of independence to the three Associate States [replacing the former French Indochina] has provoked".

Graves thus thought the proposal had more advantages than those of being "simply a booster to French and Vietnamese morale before and during the Geneva Conference" that was about to meet. But he also saw it as important should Geneva lead, as the British Foreign Office (FO) was inclined to expect, to the partition of Vietnam. If the

> immense economic resources of the Tonkin Delta pass under Communist domination, the building of the national units to the South and West of this hostile enclave into a viable whole is of crucial moment. If we could turn the Mekong into the backbone, and not the western boundary, of a bloc solidly opposed to Communist encroachment some of the worst evils in partition might be exorcised.

Partition or not, it would be necessary to reckon with the "anxious interest" of the Chinese. If it came about, Ho Chi Minh would quickly be compelled to give them facilities at Haiphong by way of Lao Kay and the Yunnan railway. "In this case potential pressure on the new Mekong economic area would be present from the start." If Vietnam remained intact, on the other hand, "we should early need to decide our attitude towards Chinese participation in the traffic and commercial activities of her southern neighbours. Even in circumstances of restored peace in the Associate States, China would remain a neighbour heavy with menace".[17]

What did the State Department think of Donovan's proposal? Philip Bonsal told Michael Joy of the British Embassy that "everybody was in favour of any move to increase solidity in that area and the establishment of such an Authority could certainly do no harm". But the scope was small: the Mekong might be a great river, "but it was chopped up into separate reaches which were only independently navigable, and it was hardly practicable to consider the enormous development plans which would be required to change this state of affairs".[18] At the end of March 1954, indeed, Dulles and Eisenhower turned to an alternative strategy for backing up the French, the call for "united action". Behind that, of course, lay a concern about Thailand: the domino theory, enunciated by the President in April, was, among other things, a way of saying that it, too, might "fall" to the Communists unless backed by the West.

Such a concern had long been felt among the British, who, with the events of 1941–2 in mind, believed that the security of Malaya and Singapore, for which they were then responsible, was bound up with the fate of Thailand. In their preparations for the Geneva Conference, they, too, considered the future in both economic and political terms. The eastern border of Thailand was "not defensible", wrote B. R. Pearn of the Research Department.

> Much of it lies on the west bank of the Mekong River; but no river ever forms a good frontier. The true function of a frontier is to separate: a river tends to bring together. The terrain on either side of a river is usually much the same; peoples of the same types, speaking the same languages, pursuing the same ways of life, are found on either side; the river forms their common means of transport.

The frontier further south between Thailand and Cambodia, lying west of Mekong, was, however, equally unsatisfactory.

The natural line of defence was the Annamite mountain chain. It was also both "the ethnic frontier" and the economic one. The development of economic, political, and military cooperation would be a development "whose naturalness has so far been obscured by the artificial frontiers drawn as a result of the Western intrusion into the area". Economically some such development was "urgently needed", apart from any question of defence. "At the moment the existence of artificial frontiers is ruinous to the prosperity of the states of Laos and Cambodia." The breakdown of the Pau system which regulated the economic relations of the former Indochina Union obstructed trade even between the three Associated States. Yet they needed to cooperate among themselves and with Thailand.

"The economic development of the Mekong lands as a unit" was not impossible, Pearn argued, but it was a long-term policy. He focused on the need for military cooperation, since, with the approaching French withdrawal, some other agency would be needed to coordinate and support the local defence effort. The Western powers would need to back it, but the leading role would have to be played by the Thais. That would not be willingly accepted by the Laos or Cambodians.

> The cessions of territory made under duress in 1941, and the post-war encouragement given in Siam to rebel movements, are a sufficient reminder that Siam is no true friend. … Yet despite their natural fears, it remains true that neither country can stand alone, and responsible leaders in both states are not unaware of this unpalatable fact.

Participation in the Mekong system by the Western powers would, however, "suffice to deter the Siamese from taking undue advantage of their opportunities".[19]

Late in June Allan Dudley—of the office of the UK Commissioner-General for South-East Asia in Singapore—observed that Donovan's attention was now focused on military plans for the defence of Thailand rather on the Mekong project.

The march of events has overtaken this method of approach, and the Authority, if it came into being, would no doubt now be designed to bolster up whatever part of the Associated States remains free of communist domination at the close of the Geneva Conference.

Even if it turned out that Vietnam could not participate, it would still be useful. It could complement a defence organisation if one were set up. If such were "unnecessary or impossible", it would still be "feasible".

What could the Mekong Valley Authority do and how should it be constituted? Dudley was "not too happy about the name, though it has an attractive sound and might on this account be worth retaining if it seemed likely to encourage public support". It should, however, not lead to misleading comparisons with the Tennessee Valley Authority, the great enterprise of the Roosevelt New Deal in the 1930s.

> The Mekong and the economies of the riparian states do not lend themselves, so far as we can judge, to any integrated river basin development plan. It is true that any economic development programme for the region will include projects for the river (and the numerous minor waterways) but if the real purpose of the type of economic organization we are discussing is to forge stronger links between the riparian states we should merely tie our hands unnecessarily if we insisted on limiting its activities to the Mekong.

The first function would be to spend funds from outside the region – mainly the US – on economic development: food production, power, transport, the establishment of secondary industries. Second, it would foster "economic co-operation and treaty making between the countries of the region in such fields as trade, payments, inter-state transport (including river navigation, customs and frontier formalities, and the use of ports)". Such issues assumed greater importance now that the countries were no longer treated as a single unit, and should be handled so as to foster greater confidence among the governments concerned. Third, the organisation should be able "to assist the governments of the region directly in planning their own economic programmes and fiscal policy, though it would have to tread cautiously".

Indeed it would not be easy to persuade countries to agree to such a wide range of activities: "if they did so, it would presumably be largely because of the bait of economic aid, in much the same way as Marshall Aid created a favourable atmosphere for the broader activities of O.E.E.C." The first step should be an expert survey of the countries to be developed, in which "several sorts of engineers and agriculturalists would need to participate".[20]

The Geneva settlement in July 1954 produced a "temporary" partition of Vietnam. The subsequent Southeast Asia Treaty Organisation (SEATO) included Thailand, but not Laos or Cambodia or southern Vietnam, though a protocol covered them. Nothing was likely to come of the Mekong project, it seemed at the FO in London, but the United Nation's (UN's) Economic Commission for Asia and the Far East (ECAFE) might, it was thought, carry out the second and third of the functions Dudley had outlined.[21]

Dam it – for regional development

ECAFE had carried out a preliminary survey in 1952. P. T. Tan, the Chinese (ROC) member of the secretariat, had played a major role in bringing the concept to birth, and it had included the section of the river basin within Burma and China, not merely the "Lower Mekong Basin".[22] The preliminary report, a mere 18 pages, concluded only that feasibility and potential remained undemonstrated while the struggle in French Indo-China destabilised the region. But after the Geneva agreements were concluded, ECAFE again took the initiative, and the four riparian states, Thailand, Cambodia, Laos, and Vietnam, accepted its lead at its session in Tokyo in 1955.[23] A team from the US Bureau of Reclamation reported the following year: drawing on the experience of the Tennessee Valley Authority (TVA), it suggested a range of sites suitable for hydro-electric exploitation.[24] The US, however, put its emphasis on action by single countries rather than on cooperation, and its interests, moreover, were transparently strategic.[25] Indeed it was anxious to prevent ECAFE from "taking the running in something that the Americans increasingly saw in strategic as much as in economic and developmental terms".[26] Its aim was, as the National Security Council put it in 1956, to "deny the general area of the Mekong River Basin to Communist influence or domination".[27] Cambodia feared that its neutrality would be compromised, and the report was not well received.[28] The four states preferred the ECAFE approach.

"International river basin development will undoubtedly be one of the major means of accomplishing economic growth and social change in the next decades, especially in the developing countries", W. R. Sewell and Gilbert White were to write in 1966.[29] The ECAFE report of 1957, though drawn up without US participation, put an emphasis not on small-scale programmes, but on a large-scale vision of modernisation and industrialisation, flood control, and irrigation.[30] It envisaged in keeping the building of large dams, and called for "an integrated system". It identified for investigation five projects on the mainstream of the Mekong.[31] The largest dam would be at Pa Mong, upstream from Vientiane. Downstream there would be dams at the Khemerat Rapids, the Khone Falls, and the Sambor Rapids. A dam might also be built to regulate the flow in and out of the Great Lake.[32]

The British ambassador in Phnom Penh (H. N. Brain) found the Cambodians "very favourably disposed" towards the scheme, particularly the construction of a dam at Sambor. His "guess", however, was that they were "not so much fired by the ideal of developing the whole Mekong basin as by the notion that it would be useful to have well inside Cambodia a source of hydro-electric power and of irrigation control". Aside from the economic and humanitarian benefits that would result from the scheme, the "political benefits which could flow from the collaboration between the four riparian states in a scheme of this magnitude are great", Brain observed. But there were "certain political obstacles". Cambodia's approach was likely to be "almost wholly parochial. This reflects a lack of political solidarity with her neighbours. Her relations with South Vietnam are poor and there is not much warmth in her professed friendship for Thailand and Laos." A sufficient degree of collaboration, the Cambodians thought, could, however, be secured under an international umbrella. That was ECAFE. They hoped that American misgivings about it could be overcome by including "a substantial number of American experts in the group which comes out under the United Nations' auspices".[33]

The 13th ECAFE meeting, held at Bangkok in September 1957, set up a Committee for the Coordination of Investigations of the Lower Mekong Basin, focused on water resources development projects, adopting the basic principles of equitable utilisation and good neighbourliness, and, as a protection for sovereignty, requiring unanimity in decision-making.[34] The Committee comprised the four riparian states, but other states outside Southeast Asia were observers and supporters. The possibility of Burma's membership was left open. It did not include PRC. The focus was on the river south of its confluence with the Namruak in the Golden Triangle. Though there might be geographical reasons for distinguishing the upper and lower reaches, the main factors were political. The PRC was not then a member of the UN or ECAFE. Indeed the scheme was seen by many as a bulwark of development against the advance of communism.

At the request of the Mekong Committee a more detailed survey was carried out, and American experts were used. The survey was indeed led by a retired senior officer from the US Army Corps of Engineers, General Raymond A. Wheeler – he had organised the clearing of the Suez Canal[35] – and the US made the largest contribution to the Mekong Committee's costs. Published in February 1958, the Wheeler findings, like the earlier ECAFE report, supported dams at Pa Mong in Laos and at Sambor in Cambodia: they would improve navigation, generate electricity, and provide irrigation.

> Developed, this river could easily constitute one of the greatest national resources of each of the countries concerned. Wide conservation and utilization of its waters will contribute more towards improving human welfare in this area than any other single undertaking.

The immediate task, however, was data collection. The mission recommended a five-year programme of detailed investigation costing US$9.2 million.[36]

The investigations did not run smoothly. Denying the Mekong to the Communists had also led the US into backing the right-wing in Laos, and broken up Suvanna Phuma's attempts to create a neutral government. The Australian investigating team abandoned its camp at Pa Mong and the Harza Company and agencies of the Mekong Committee were bedevilled by terrorists in the Delta area.[37] The Laos Conference of 1961–2 did not raise the question of security for the investigations, though C. Hart Schaaf, the Committee's Executive Agent, suggested it should.[38] The agreement it reached failed, however, to provide for security more generally. That, indeed, it could hardly do, given the intensification of the struggle in neighbouring Vietnam. Yet the period of investigation was now complete, and the period of construction was at hand. Was it feasible?

By 1964, a number of projects were under way on tributary rivers, dams, hydroelectric schemes, irrigation works, agricultural schemes, and it was "widely held that the activities of the Mekong Committee have contributed to such political stability as exists in the area". Major mainstream projects, however, could hardly begin till the 1970s. "The investment will be formidable", the British Ministry of Overseas Development pointed out early in 1965, "and more stable political conditions are a sine qua non".[39] That view was underlined by the treatment of the Nam Ngum tributary project in Laos. The World Bank had declined to support it, "in spite of a virtual promise by the Thais to buy all the power produced, surplus to Laotian requirements". The main factor in its decision was "the unsatisfactory economic and security situation in Laos". It precipitated something of a crisis in the Committee.

> All three factions in Laos had approved of it and there were many who believed that construction could proceed in complete safety, and some who allowed themselves to think it would contribute to a political settlement. The rebuff was keenly felt by the Laotians and their friends alike, who had counted, against all likelihood, on a response that would be an "'act of faith".

In the Ministry of Overseas Development's view, the project could only be "safely and usefully" executed after a political settlement had been reached in Laos.

Behind all the proposals – alongside a recognition that a scheme would bring economic and social benefits – was the idea that they would bring political benefits, including cooperation among the states and their consolidation in face of the Communist threat. Economic development is dependent on political development, C. K. Jordan of the Ministry of Overseas Development observed, "not, as is sometimes argued, vice-versa".[40] The vice-versa argument indeed lay behind such projects as the Colombo Plan of 1950. Even if the Cambodians were not attracted by the cooperative aspect of the Mekong scheme, Brain had argued in 1957, "the experience of working with their neighbours may help to break up old prejudices and lead to collaboration in other fields". But the Colombo Plan was on a bilateral basis and had no precedent and the Cambodians had been more concerned with what was done in their part of the river than with what might be done in the basin as a whole. There was, however, something in what Brain said. Makim has certainly argued that the Mekong Committee kept channels open even amid antagonism.[41] The "Mekong spirit" it developed bears some resemblance to the "ASEAN" way.

Lyndon Johnson (LBJ) had visited Southeast Asia as vice-president in 1961. Before he left Arthur Goldschmidt, his old New Deal friend, now at the UN, had showed him plans for Mekong dams: it showed how four countries could work together despite "a lot of fussing". "It's a great thing when people of such different cultures can get together on power", LBJ commented. On his tour he met the ECAFE secretary-general, U Nyun. He said the project envisaged not only dams and conservation but highway construction, linking "old caravan routes and existing roads to provide an international highway that eventually will connect Asia and Europe". The Vice-President, his TVA experience in mind, interrupted: "I am a river man".[42]

As president he extended the US commitment to the Vietnam War, and after election in his own right, authorised the bombing of the north early in 1965. Senator George McGovern from S. Dakota, and with a PhD in History, had advocated ending the war, neutralising North and South Vietnam, and cooperative planning to develop the Mekong to benefit all Vietnamese. McGovern saw the President in vain in late March. "Goddam it, George, don't give me another history lesson".[43] But the idea found its way into his speech at Johns Hopkins on 7 April, when he offered the Democratic Republic of Vietnam (DRV) talks "without posing any preconditions", and, making a reference to the TVA, also held out a "billion-dollar carrot" in the form of an economic development programme for the Mekong in which North Vietnam might participate. An aide had found that the US contribution to the Mekong project so far had been US$5 million, less than four days' military aid. The State Department wanted the reference removed from the draft. After meeting Goldschmidt at Camp David – he had argued that the New Deal closed the gap between North and South in the US – the President put it back in. "Uncle Ho can't turn me down", he said.[44] He could.

The speech led the British Ministry of Overseas Development to prepare a brief for Prime Minister Harold Wilson's visit to Washington. The World Bank had not been encouraging about the Nam Ngum project, allegedly on technical grounds, "but probably really because of the economic and security situation in Laos". There were signs at the ECAFE meeting in Wellington, however, that it "might be disposed to change its tune". Investment could "lead to or help to prepare the way for a political settlement, or it could be regarded as a probable consequential effect of a political settlement". Britain had offered limited funds for the Mekong scheme, mainly for navigation improvement. "If the Americans turn on the heat the obvious move would be to show interest in the Nam Ngum project. We know that they are themselves ready to look at this again in conjunction with the World Bank." The project could make a contribution towards the absorption of labour from Laos and North Vietnam, "either as a prelude to or as a consequence of stability in the area". Britain considered that the project could only be "safely and usefully" carried after a settlement had been reached in Laos.[45] The Cabinet decided that it was desirable to offer a measure of support.[46]

At the British Embassy in Vientiane, J. B. Denson saw "no real economic justification" for the dam. One of the arguments advocating it was that it would supply extra electricity for the city, but the use would be almost wholly domestic, and he could not see that it would need so much power as the dam would produce in the foreseeable future. The surplus, it was argued, could be exported to Thailand. No doubt that would suit the Thais, who would make no financial contribution to the project.

But as the Mekong project was originally designed to benefit all four riparian countries equally, benefiting Thailand in this way would further increase the existing imbalance in her favour. This in turn might generate pressures for other dubious projects to restore the balance.

Security had indeed improved since the World Bank's report, but it could deteriorate, and it could never be guaranteed. Building the dam would, like maintaining the army, drain the countryside of labour, and generate purchasing power, inflation, and the need for more aid. If a settlement were reached, Denson agreed, the project would have merit. Otherwise Britain should contribute only if compelled to by political reasons and only in a limited way.[47]

Ambassador Warner commented on the political arguments. "To the Laotians this scheme has assumed the same psychological and emotional importance as the Aswan Dam to the Egyptians or the Volta River project to the Ghanaians". Laos had been independent for fifteen years, but there was "absolutely nothing to show for it except the half-finished Arc de Triomphe .... Concrete evidence of progress towards a modern economy is now badly needed by Prince Souvanna Phouma to boost the credit of his Government." It was perhaps a pity that Schaaf had "zoomed into the vacuum with his proposal for a somewhat over-ambitious dam. The inevitable result is that it has become the great national ambition." At least it was a basic utility, not, "as in the case of most countries, something totally unsuitable like a steel-mill or a motor car assembly plant". These attitudes had prompted re-thinking. The Thais were "persuaded" to accept electricity so that it would become a source of foreign exchange, and were also "seriously considering increasing their demands as a result of more ambitious schemes for the development of their North-East". The World Bank had now given "a belated blessing". The US had offered half the cost. The question now was what the Japanese would do. Half the remaining cost? Souvanna suggested. "It is very difficult for them to wriggle out of this since they originally thought up the scheme and it is a Japanese firm that has done the project study." Warner's own question was the involvement of the British. "Since for eleven years we have been cast to play the role of their second most influential friend [of Laos] I do not see how we can dodge out of all responsibility".[48]

Could it be, the British FO wondered, that there was some connection between the changed attitudes of the World Bank and of the Thais with President Johnson's appointment of Eugene Black, former President of the World Bank, to administer the billion-dollar programme for the Mekong Valley? At the F.O. in London James Cable suspected "that political pressures are moulding economic judgments .... Political factors are ... outweighing economic and practical considerations." A British contribution was desirable on political grounds, despite the uncertain political situation in Laos, and the fact that it already received more aid from Britain than any other non-Commonwealth country in Asia. "We have ... given our full and public support to President Johnson's proposals for aid to develop the Mekong", and – despite the pressure on Britain's balance of payments – it was desirable to give "some practical expression of this support". The navigational aid on the Lower Mekong was not really what was wanted when "national prides and imaginations" were engaged.[49] The UN Secretary-General (Thant) called a meeting at the end of July,[50] and a convention for the supply of power from Laos to Thailand was concluded at the 29th session of the Mekong Committee.[51] The scheme, "being steam rollered through due to political considerations", as C. K. Jordan put it, was to go ahead, the Committee decided, the Japanese offering US$4 million, though expecting to use their own contractors.[52]

The dam was built by a Japanese firm, and an agreement between the electricity authorities of the two states, concluded in June 1971, provided that Laos would sell its surplus power to Thailand in US dollars.[53] The Mekong Committee received the Ramon Magsaysay Award for international understanding in 1966.[54] But Nam Ngum, Joel Halpern complained, was "something being done to Laos by foreigners". Bureaucrats and engineers and international aid administrators, he believed, prioritised the power needs of "gaudy Bangkok" over the possibilities of raising the rural standard of living.[55]

Wars then progress then the PRC enters the picture

What was done in this period was limited and fragmented.[56] Political considerations weighed heavily, emphasising both the differences among the countries on the Mekong and the Cold War divisions among both the great powers and the regional states. They also helped to put emphasis on prestige projects, rather than agricultural development, though it was also true that economic analyses tended to emphasise the high economic returns of major infrastructural projects and play down the social returns of agricultural projects. The latter, Sir Arthur Gaitskell of the Committee's Advisory Board argued in 1971, should have priority, "given the precarious political situation in the region". Certainly the political disorder of the late 1960s and early 1970s stood in the way of the mainstream projects. It was impossible to carry out studies of the Stung Treng project, Sir Arthur said, and Viet Cong (VC) sabotage had caused expensive damage at Prek Thnot.[57] Indeed work on that dam – where the Snowy Mountains Engineering Corporation was active – was abandoned in 1973.[58] But, if there is something in Halpern's comments, perhaps delay was not altogether a disadvantage. It could permit reconsideration of large projects like Pamong.[59]

The activities of the Mekong Committee were interrupted after the end of the Second Indochina War in 1975.[60] The US withdrew all support after the Communist victories,[61] and the Khmer Rouge took over Cambodia. In 1978, however, Thailand joined Laos and Vietnam in setting up an Interim Mekong Committee. That suggested a wish to pursue development in the "Mekong spirit" despite political differences.[62] At the end of the year, however, Vietnam invaded Cambodia in order to displace the Khmer Rouget (KR). The subsequent non-recognition of the new Heng Samrin regime militated against the reconstitution of the full Mekong Committee, while Vietnam was at odds with Thailand, and indeed with much of the international community. The Interim Mekong Committee nevertheless sustained an element of neighbourliness,[63] and won support from middle powers like the Netherlands.[64] In 1987 it produced an Indicative Basic Plan, calling for smaller dams "with less harmful effects on the environment and reduced human dislocation".[65]

The resolution of the long Cambodian crisis led to the reinclusion of Cambodia, which Sihanouk had sought after the Supreme National Council met in Pattaya in 1991. But that took a long time, not because Cambodia was unwelcome, but because of the developments that had occurred since 1975. Thailand wanted all the basic documents of the Mekong Committee amended. In particular, in order to advance the vigorous programmes of development it had instituted, it sought the end of the unanimity rule in respect of projects on tributaries of the river. Vietnam was concerned lest the environmental problems of the Delta should be increased, and Thailand feared it would be in a minority of one on a committee of four. A compromise was reached only in 1994. An accord was signed in Chiang Rai on 5 April 1995.[66] The Mekong River Commission succeeded the Mekong Committee.

The schemes of the 1960s and 1970s were, of course, without the participation of the PRC, indeed in part directed against it. Yet it occupied the upper reaches of the river in Tibet and in the Sip Song Panna [Xishuangbanna] region of southern Yunnan. It was at Jinghong that Doudart de Lagrée had turned away from the river in 1867 and travelled north into China. The PRC saw it as a means of developing its southwestern provinces and of securing electric power, objectives extended by the Dengist reforms of the late 1970s and 1980s. A bridge had been built across the Mekong in 1960, and increasingly Jinghong had become a Han Chinese town.[67] In the 1980s the PRC began a long-term programme of dam-building along the river, starting at Manwan in 1984. Completed in 1993, it supplied power for industrial development round Kunming.[68] A second dam was started down-river at Daochaoshan in 1996, and others were to follow. What effects would they have down-river, economic, environmental, political? The Cold War had ended. But that revealed the disparity of power between China and all the other states of the Mekong, disparate as they had shown themselves to be. Would there be an extension of the "Mekong spirit"?

In October 1992, on the Asian Development Bank's (ADB's) initiative, a ministerial meeting of Mekong countries was convened in Manila and constituted the Greater Mekong Subregion (GMS), including China as well as Myanmar and Cambodia. China welcomed that.

> For China, the GMS programme offers a transport and trade link to Southeast Asia. The Chinese government seems to have overcome an initial fear that membership in such regional fora might weaken central government control in the peripheral provinces such as Yunnan. Further, by making the Mekong navigable for commercial ships from Yunnan, China also hopes to counter Japanese economic dominance in the region.[69]

Who, Philip Hirsch asked, controls the Mekong's development agenda?[70] Competing national interests mean that, even among Mekong River Commission (MRC) members, principles and mechanisms are not followed.[71] With what Osborne termed in 2000 its "almost infinite capacity to disregard external criticism", China seemed ready to pursue industrial development even at the cost of the interests of its much weaker neighbours,[72] though he has suggested more recently that its attitude to the Salween may imply a change in respect of both Southeast Asia and the environment.[73] That would be in line with the multilateral approach China's regional diplomacy has increasingly adopted. Like the US half a century before, China has a political agenda, though one designed in part to allay apprehension of its "rise".[74]

Nor can our focus be merely on governments and planners. "[N]atural resource policy", Simon Bush reminds us, "often emerges from long-established and ongoing interactions between various state and non-state organizations, which formulate and institute specific policy discourses ... without necessarily reflecting the interests of the people and the resources in question".[75] The perspective, as Diokno and Chinh argue, echoing Halpern, has to be

> not just of what the Mekong River obviously *presents* – a large body of water – but also what it *represents* to communities, foremost those who live alongside the river. ... Water worship and water processions are not a thing of the past; they hold meaning for residents of the Mekong. ... Planners tend to forget that these communities know the river best.[76]

If such comments arose in discussing the development of the river, they are surely even more relevant in discussing the development of the so-called subregion as it comes to encompass vast public/private infrastructural and other projects. Who indeed controls the agenda? The smaller states, the larger, the largest? The politicians, the planners, the people? And even if economic development is not, as in earlier decades, given a clear social and political purpose, it will have social and political effects. A subregional community will develop, if at all, only as a result of cooperation, based on the sovereignty of states, and their acceptance of obligations both to one another and to their citizens.

Conclusion

In 1992, the Asian Development Bank coined the term "Greater Mekong Subregion" and embarked on an extensive programme of development activities. In

1996 the ASEAN Mekong River Development Cooperation was formed, focused on infrastructural projects and cross-border activities. In December 2001 Cambodia opened its first bridge across the Mekong. The month before, Thailand, Laos, and Vietnam had agreed on a vast cross-river roading project.[77] The physical construction, particularly of infrastructure, continues to underpin the cultural and political construction of the subregion. As of this writing, it may well be that the mighty Mekong River will be tamed in the near future. Will this "river change" bring about a "sea change" in regional identity? Will those living inside the region accept the identity label of being part of the GMS? Thus far, collaboration has occurred rather than conflict. If this can continue, then possibly a region will be constructed out of a river during this century.

Notes

1 Abigail Gene Makim, "The politics of regional cooperation on the Mekong, 1957–1995", PhD thesis, School of Modern Asian Studies, Griffith University, 1998, p. 72n.
2 Maria Serena I. Diokno and Nguyen Van Chinh, "Introduction: Mother of Waters" in Maria Serena I. Diokno and Nguyen Van Chinh (eds.), *The Mekong Arranged and Rearranged*, Chiang Mai: Mekong Press, 2006, p. 5.
3 Ibid., p. 6.
4 Martin Stuart-Fox, *The Lao Kingdom of Lan Xang Rise and Decline*, Bangkok: White Lotus, 1998, p. 89.
5 Quoted in S. Sahai, *The Mekong River. Space and Social Theory*, Delhi: B.R. Publishing, 2005, p. 157.
6 Soren Ivarsson, *Creating Laos: The Making of a Lao Space between Indochina and Siam, 1860–1945*, Copenhagen: NIAS Press, 2008, p. 93.
7 M. Askew et al., *Vientiane: Transformations of a Lao landscape*, London and New York: Routledge, 2007, p. 78ff.
8 C. Lavollée, *France et Chine*, Paris: Plon-Nourrit, 1900, pp. 13–14.
9 Quoted in P. Tuck, *The French Wolf and the Siamese Lamb*, Bangkok: Cheney: White Lotus, 1995, p. 27.
10 Quoted in Mark W. McLeod, *The Vietnamese Response to French Intervention*, New York: Praeger, 1991, p. 99.
11 Quoted in Agnes Murphy, *The Ideology of French Imperialism, 1871–1881*, New York: Fertig, 1968 [reprint], pp. 205–6.
12 Yost/Acheson, Telegram, 10.4.46, 373. *Foreign Relations of the United States* [FRUS] 1946, Vol. VIII, p. 988.
13 Johnson/SofS, 16.7.46, 424. *Foreign Relations of the United States* [FRUS] 1946, Vol. VIII, pp. 1032–3.
14 Stanton/SofS, 17.10.46. *Foreign Relations of the United States* [FRUS] 1946, Vol. VIII, p. 1092.
15 Memorandum by Mackenzie, 12.3.54, in Gage/Tahourdin, 17.3.54. FO 371/112048 [DF 1071/77], National Archives, Kew.
16 Ibid.
17 Graves/Allen, 29.3.54. FO 371/112051 [DF 1071/187], National Archives, Kew.
18 Joy/Tahourdin, 20.3.54. FO 371/112048 [DF 1071/75], National Archives, Kew.
19 Memorandum, 22.3.54. FO 371/112113 [DF 1104/1], National Archives, Kew.
20 A. A. Dudley/R. L. Speaight, 23.6.54. FO 371/112113 [DF 1104/1], National Archives, Kew.
21 Minute by B. C. MacDermot, 30.8.54. FO 371/112113 [DF 1104/1], National Archives, Kew.

22 Whittington/Warner, 2.2.61. FO 371/159797 [DC 1421/10], National Archives, Kew.
23 Abigail Gene Makim, op cit., pp. 65, 69.
24 Milton Osborne, *The Mekong: Turbulent Past, Uncertain Future*, New York: Atlantic Monthly Press, 2000, p. 190.
25 Abigail Gene Makim, op cit., p. 70n.
26 Milton Osborne, 2000, op cit., pp. 190–1.
27 Quoted in ibid., p. 190; R. Fifield, *Americans in Southeast Asia: The Roots of Commitment*, New York: Crowell, 1973, p. 326.
28 Abigail Gene Makim, op cit., p. 70.
29 Quoted in J. Dosch, *The Changing Dynamics of Southeast Asian Politics*, Boulder, CO and London: Lynne Rienner, 2007, p. 118.
30 S. Sahai, op cit., p. 160.
31 Abigail Gene Makim, op cit., p. 71.
32 Milton Osborne, 2000, op cit., p. 191.
33 Brain/Lloyd, 23.10.57, despatch 65. FO 371/129684 [DU 1421/1], National Archives, Kew.
34 Abigail Gene Makim, op cit., pp. 75, 79, 82.
35 Ibid., p. 108n.
36 Milton Osborne, 2000, op cit., p. 192; S. Sahai, op cit., p. 161; IOC (FE) (61) 7, 2.61, draft. FO 371/159797 [CD 1421/11], National Archives, Kew.
37 Snellgrone/Petersen, 24.1.61. FO 371/159797 [DC 1421/7], National Archives, Kew.
38 Whittington/Warner, op cit.
39 Brief for 21st Session of ECAFE, 16–29.3.65 FO 371/183729 [USC 1422/8], National Archives, Kew.
40 Minute, 2.6.65. FO 371/183729 [USC 142/14], National Archives, Kew.
41 Abigail Gene Makim, op cit., p. 89.
42 Lloyd C. Gardner, *Pay Any Price: Lyndon Johnson and the Wars for Vietnam*, Chicago: Ivan R. Dee, 1995, pp. 52–3.
43 Thomas J. Knock, "George McGovern and Mr Johnson's War: A Liberal Democrat dissents" in Lloyd C. Gardner and Ted Gittinger (eds.), *The Search for Peace in Vietnam, 1964–1968*, College Station: Texas A and M University Press, 2004, pp. 103, 106.
44 Lloyd C. Gardner, op cit., pp. 191–2, 194, 197.
45 Brief in A. C. Maby/D.F. Murray, 9.4.65. FO 371/183729 [USC 1422/12], National Archives, Kew.
46 OPD (65) 22nd, 13.4.65, 2. CAB 148/18, National Archives, Kew.
47 Denson/Landymore, 19.5.65. FO 371/183729 [USC 1422/14], National Archives, Kew.
48 Warner/Cable, 21.6.65. FO 371/183729 [USC 1422/16], National Archives, Kew.
49 Cable/Maby, 5.7.65. FO 371/183729 [USC 1422/16], National Archives, Kew.
50 Jackling/Mson, 28.7.65. FO 371/183729 [USC 1422/29], National Archives, Kew.
51 Warner/Stewart, 12.8.65. FO 371/183729 [USC 1422/34], National Archives, Kew.
52 Warner/Stewart, 24.8.65, 31. FO 371/183730 [USC 1422/37], National Archives, Kew.
53 Abigail Gene Makim, op cit., p. 135.
54 S. Sahai, op cit., p. 161.
55 J. Halpern, *Mekong River Development Schemes for Laos and Thailand*, Brussels: Centre d'Étude du Sud-est Asiatique et de l'Extrême Orient, Université Libre, 1971, pp. 155, 144.
56 Abigail Gene Makim, op cit., p. 116.
57 Note of a meeting with Sir Arthur Gaitskell, 10.11.71. FCO 15/1428 [2], National Archives, Kew.
58 Milton Osborne, 2000, op cit., p. 247.
59 S. Sahai, op cit., p. 164.

60 Maria Serena I. Diokno and Nguyen Van Chinh, op cit., p. 9.
61 Abigail Gene Makim, op cit., p. 124.
62 Ibid., pp. 152, 154.
63 Ibid., p. 172.
64 Ibid., p. 158.
65 Maria Serena I. Diokno and Nguyen Van Chinh, op cit., p. 9.
66 Abigail Gene Makim, pp. 194, 197–8, 201, 218, 222.
67 Milton Osborne, 2000, op cit., p. 227–8.
68 Ibid., pp. 227–8.
69 Mak Sithirith, *Cooperation in the Mekong River Basin*, Chiang Mai: RCSD, Chiang Mai University, Working Paper No. 4, 2007, p. 30.
70 Milton Osborne, 2000, op cit., p. 261.
71 Maria Serena I. Diokno and Nguyen Van Chinh, op cit., p. 11.
72 Milton Osborne, 2000, op cit., pp. 228, 260.
73 Milton Osborne, *Paramount Power: China and the Countries of Southeast Asia*, Double Bay, Sydney: Lowy Institute, 2006, pp. 58–9.
74 M. Yahuda, "China's multilateral regional order" in Guoguang Wu and Helen Lansdowne (eds.), *China Turns to Multilateralism*, London and New York: Routledge, 2008, p. 87.
75 Simon R. Bush, "Contextualising fisheries policy in the Lower Mekong Basin", *Journal of Southeast Asian Studies*, Vol. 39, Iss. 3, 2008, pp. 329–30.
76 Maria Serena I. Diokno and Nguyen Van Chinh, op cit., pp. 12–13, emphasis in original.
77 J. Dosch, op cit., pp. 119, 127.

3 *100% Pure Mekong*

The key to identity, development, and tourism in the Greater Mekong Subregion?

Charles Samuel Johnston

Introduction

On 7 February 1992, the Maastricht Treaty was signed,[1] formalising decades of planning, and laying the final foundations for the European Union (EU). The euro was created as a currency, and the "pillar system" expanded economic relationships into foreign policy and justice areas. While falling short of creating a single European nation or a United States of Europe, the EU created a new, more formal form of regional identity for citizens of signatory nations. Subsequently, the study of European and EU identity has been a hot topic.[2]

In the same year, on the opposite side of the Eurasian Continent, a previously unnamed peninsula was designated the "Greater Mekong Subregion" (GMS) by the Asian Development Bank (ADB). The name created a functional identity for part or all of six countries: China (Yunnan Province); Myanmar, Lao PDR, Thailand, Cambodia, and Vietnam. The Bank's mission focused on its raison d'être – economic development and corresponding elimination of poverty. The rationale for the name was apparently that the Mekong River flowed through each of these countries. Malaysia, though also located on this peninsula, was excluded. Using the word "Greater" allowed China to be incorporated. Using the term "Subregion" highlighted that this was only one part of Southeast Asia, or of ASEAN. The term suggested the "view from Manila", the headquarters of ADB. Creating the GMS allowed the Bank to target a new region, one never previously having a specific identity. Since 1992, the ADB has been involved in many projects in a variety of areas. Collectively, these represent a comprehensive push towards development and poverty elimination. During the current century, the results of these efforts are likely to achieve significant results that will transform the included nations.

Yet one can wonder whether a decision by a development bank to give a set of countries a common name based on a shared river will be sufficient to create a true sense of regional *identity*. While the term "Greater Mekong Subregion" has proven quite useful in academia and at development project levels, it remains arguably the case that "people on the street" have mostly never heard of it. Average citizens mostly do not use the term as a source of personal identity. As a specific example, few Thais or Vietnamese think they have something in common because they are both living in the same region of the planet, based on the course of the Mekong River. Few individuals, if asked "where are you from?" would be likely to respond "I'm from the Greater Mekong Subregion". This suggests that, as a term, "GMS" has not yet, and likely will not, helped to create a regional sense of identity. If such an identity is not created, one can further question the extent to which the Bank's regional-scale development projects will succeed. Without a fully developed regional identity, one might argue, national interests may instead prevail. "Upstream" countries, acting in their own interests, have been in the process of developing the Mekong in ways that will severely impact "downstream" countries in the negative. This suggests, further, that success in regional development will be constrained because individuals of specific countries will be less likely to endorse regional goals. Without a fully formed regional identity, efforts to economically integrate the region could stand a greater chance of collapsing because of national-level political and/or economic conflicts.

This chapter focuses on the relationship between identity, development, and tourism in the GMS countries. It is conceptual in nature, rather than empirical, because it examines possibilities rather than realities. The goal is to assert a thesis that deliberate tourism marketing campaigns that are embraced by residents of the GMS countries as well as by tourists can be the key to enhancement of regional identity. The basis for this thesis is the "100% Pure" campaign that Tourism New Zealand[3] has used with extreme success for more than a decade. The chapter develops the thesis in the following sequence. The first section delves into identity issues, showing that a regional identity will be problematic. The second section illuminates how the nature of existing projects falls short of a comprehensive sustainable development and therefore could create conflict. The third section articulates ways that tourism can be the most appropriate sector to take up the challenge of identity relationships and development. The overall conclusion is that the tourism sector could hold the key to ensuring that the development of the GMS is comprehensively sustainable.

Identity

The Eurasian continent contains numerous peninsulas. For some, such as "Korea", the name of the land area exactly corresponds with the name of the nation, and the people. The Arabian Peninsula and Indian Subcontinent have also been named after the people who inhabit them. For these peninsulas, even though nation states and political boundaries may change over time, the names are evocative. Voicing the names of the peninsulas evokes stereotypes of the people who live there and the cultures that they have created.

Europe as an inspiration for an identity

Figure 3.1 indicates the importance of Europe. The landmass itself is called the Eurasian Continent even though Europe is only a large peninsula at the west end of Asia. It does not really have an independent standing from Asia on the basis of physical geography. This is a reminder that the term "Europe" is a cultural construction. As is widely known, the Greek god Zeus named the land area in honour

Figure 3.1 The Eurasian continent and its peninsulas
Source: https://commons.wikimedia.org/wiki/File:Eurasian_continent.jpg.

of his consort, the Phoenician noblewoman Europa. The geographic identity of the land is ancient yet, as a construction, both the boundaries and the substantive meaning of Europe continue to change.

In a study of European identity and the EU, Ifversen[4] has noted there are cultural practices that can be considered "essentialist" and also practices considered "constructivist". The former tend to create a conceptual entity that is relatively fixed and immutable, as the name of the region would be based on characteristics from the past. In this sense, "Europe" is conceived in terms of relatively fixed borders (extending inland to the Ural Mountains) and religion (initially just Western Christianity but more recently including Orthodox Christianity). The name is also attached to a "standard narrative"[5] based on Greek and Roman history. These histories in turn are the core for a contemporary philosophy, politics, and a set of customs for the region. Ifversen[6] has noted several features that constitute the European identity. First, Europe has a "historical current" and these "roots" give the region a "legacy" that is the basis for a region-wide "civilisation". Europe has "cultural markers" relating to customs and religion, though not language. Such cultural markers also create a set of values, a "soul", which leads to the existence of a European "philosophy" and "politics". Together, these synthesise into a set of "strategic" components – they carry European identity into the future.

By contrast, "constructivist" cultural practices do not rely on the past.[7] Rather, they utilise aspects of the present or hoped-for future to create names and identities. It appears obvious that future constructions of "Europe" will be different from the ones we have today. Ifversen notes that such identity creation "may be seen as a necessary attempt to further the development of the EU …."[8]

In contemporary usage it would seem the case that most regional identities include geographic and cultural attributes from both the past and the present. While certain discourses may be essentialist or constructivist to varying degrees, both exist simultaneously. Construction of a regional identity in an area that lacks it, however, involves finding identity attributes that are seen to be held in common by residents. At a conceptual level, Pace, in a book discussing construction of a regional "Mediterranean" identity, has noted that "social spatialisation" and "spatial socialisation" will be required.[9] Both of these, in their different emphases, involve constructing and accepting notions about the boundaries of held-in-common social practices; these help create the construction of an "us" who lives within and an "other" who lives outside the boundaries. In other words, it is necessary to find attributes that allow people to bond in a transnational setting – creating a sense that people from neighbouring countries share something significant.

Though the concept of Europe is often highly contested based on internal differences, there is no questioning that a European identity exists today and that the trend is for this to become more inclusive – to include ever-more nations and peoples rather than fewer. As a named-region, Europe can provide inspiration for the peninsula on the opposite side of the continent.

The GMS – no identity

It is clearly one of the great cartographic anomalies of the past few centuries that the very large peninsula on the southeastern side of the Eurasian continent, an area containing over 300 million inhabitants, has no name. It would appear that indigenous groups never gave the peninsula itself a name, based either on geography or culture. No Khmer or Chinese deity ever named the peninsula after a lover. Much more uncharacteristically, Western explorers and cartographers of the Exploration Age likewise failed to affix a name to the maps of this large peninsula. The Western powers who came to dominate much of the area through colonialism named their own territories but not the greater landmass.

Was the lack of a proper name the likely reason that the ADB created the term "Greater Mekong Subregion?" Did an ADB functionary coin the term given the spirit of Europeanisation of the 1990s? Krongkaew has noted that the origin cannot be pinpointed.[10] As a land area, the territory of the countries of the Mekong River obviously had potential for regional-scale, multinational development projects. Lacking a historical precedent, the flow of a river through all but one of the countries of this peninsula made "Mekong" an obvious choice of name in the absence of alternatives (in either English or regional languages). As a top-down choice, the importance of the ADB is such that it has been, and will continue to be, able to enforce the use of the name for its development projects. The use of the term has spread into academia; for example, Chiang Mai University in Thailand has created the "Greater Mekong Subregion Institute" as a way of delimiting the geographic scope of its academic research. Rajabhat

University, Chiang Rai, Thailand, puts out a quarterly newsletter, the *GMS News*, through its International College of Mekong Region. Yet the name does not appear to be in daily use by ordinary citizens, nor does there seem to be a sense of regional identity based on the River among residents of the Mekong countries. Rather, the people of each country seem to have their own cultural relationship to the Mekong River. It should be noted that, historically, the Mekong River has divided, not united, the peoples and cultures of this region. Even tourism websites[11] note this matter-of-factly. Geographic features such as Khon Phapheng Falls, Laos, have made navigation impossible. No single culture ever dominated in the way the Chinese empires dominated the Yangtse and Yellow Rivers. Use of the term "Mekong" therefore seems problematic as an identity-constructor. Effectively, there is only a river, not a culturally intact "subregion".[12]

In relation to Ifversen's work cited above, it is apparent that there is no basis for an identity based on essentialist features. These simply do not exist. This awareness forces the conclusion that a regional identity must be constructed. Possibly a "Mekong" identity can be constructed solely out of the development activity of the ADB. However, the "top down" projection of such a label would seem problematic as an identity-constructor for the average citizen. Will Pace's "social spatialisation" and "spatial socialisation" co-occur? In the near future, will the question "Where are you from?" generate an answer such as: "I'm from Greater Mekongia"? Will residents find essentialist features related to culture that can function as bonding glue for people from Vietnam to Myanmar? If they can, the Mekong River is perhaps the best choice for an "identity core" to bring residents together.

With most of the features required to essentialise a regional identity missing, it seems that a regional identity will need to be constructed. If this is the case then what values might be used to solidify people's thinking that "we" exist in relation to either a "you" or to something "we" hold in common? While there might be a number of values that can be chosen, one particular value focuses on the sustainable development of the Mekong River. It can be asserted that acceptance of the need to maintain and improve the environmental quality of the Mekong River is one thing that can be used to develop a Mekong regional identity. This is clearly not "us" versus the "other", but is an example of something "all of us share". Put another way, the Mekong River is a common pool resource and it is up to the Mekong nations to begin to identify with the River condition remaining "unspoiled" to the greatest possible extent. Those who deliberately pollute and degrade the River could then be identified as a sort of criminal "other", while villagers who degrade the River out of ignorance or poverty could be identified as "victims" in need of help. Development values thus take on something considerably larger than an economic concern, an identity politics based on improvement of River quality should in fact be constructed to bring the people of the region together socially, as well. Should this eventuate, the Mekong might take on a quasi-spiritual value that, in turn, would be a core component of a Mekong region cultural soul.

Who will create this identity? The thesis of this chapter is that the tourism sector is in the best position to do so. Through its activities outside the region, tourism marketing would create the "us-not-us" polarity that residents could identify with. The "Mekong" would be used as part of the brand name for tourism to the region, thus aspects of the river would need to be a central theme. This would involve creating experiences that in turn create memories; these experiences would undoubtedly be based on both existing environmental and socio-cultural resources. "Where did you go on vacation last year?" "I went to the Mekong" – the utterance of such a name needs to create the same level of awareness as "I went to Europe" currently does.

Development

There have been many definitions of "development" over the past several decades. However, no definition or concept could be found that also incorporated the idea that *regional identity* should become more highly developed. Hence it is not obvious that focus on development of any sort will produce a better identity for the six nations sharing the Mekong River. Lacking this, it is apparent that nations or citizens-within-nations will work for self-interest rather than shared regional interests. Therefore, bringing into existence a regional identity based around development of the Mekong River could be the key to ensuring successfully completed projects endorsed by the residents of the Mekong River nations. Such an identity would give individual residents of the GMS countries a salient stake in river development projects. The notion that "the" river is "our" river might be the aspect of identity that can guarantee that sustainable development is more than a normative ideal. A discourse, based on shared values, would emerge that unsustainable development projects, or contested ones, would not be good for the community-at-large. The reaction would be: "hurting our river hurts all of us". Conversely, projects agreed by all to produce sustainable development would create the opposite reaction: "helping our river helps all of us".

Lacking an identity-informed definition, this chapter relies on the more conventional notion that the core features of development are: (1) growth and (2) greater complexity. With respect to the development of nation states, definitional factors generally focus on economic growth and sometimes include improvement of social aspects such as education or health. Sustainable development has been emphasised since the 1980s. Many definitions also exist but the one put forward in the Brundtland Report, also entitled *Our Common Future*, is most commonly used: "Sustainable development is development that meets the needs of the present without compromising the ability of future generations to meet their own needs".[13]

Based on the work of Hunter,[14] Johnston[15] has noted that the concept of sustainability is relative. That is, people working in different sectors will have different ideas of what sustainable development means. For example, people working in the hydroelectric sector will have different ideas about sustainable development than will people working in the fishing, forestry, or tourism sectors. There will be some overlap but also some uniqueness. This can be modelled using Venn diagrams. Figure 3.2 models these relationships, indicating different levels of sustainability can be achieved.

The left-hand set of circles models a situation where four sectors are each in a situation of partial sustainability. That is, each sector has unsustainable aspects – those outside the centre circle. Each sector also has sustainable aspects – within the centre circle. Further, there is also overlap between one sector and others – the overlapping sections inside the centre circle. Twenty-five years of discussions about sustainability has shown that this initial level is very difficult to achieve.

The middle set of circles models a situation where sustainability can be said to exist based on standards internal to a specific sector. However, proponents advocating development of each single sector have some particular ideas about the nature of sustainability that clash with the ideas of people advocating development of the other sectors. A two-sector example would work like this: (1) people advocating hydroelectric development would claim that specific hydroelectric projects are sustainable; (2) people advocating fishing would claim existing fishing practices are sustainable. However, fishing advocates would contest that hydroelectric development is sustainable because it is negatively impacting fishing.

The right-hand set of circles models a situation where multi-sectoral sustainability exists. That is, people advocating sustainability from the perspective of one sector recognise that the development occurring in a different sector is sustainable by their own (external) standards. This is the most complete situation of sustainability because all parties agree that each other's development is sustainable. Using the previous example, people representing fishing development would agree that hydropower projects are sustainable because these projects are not creating negative impacts for fishing.

The examples thus far have focused on economic sectors but the model can be applied more generally – to national interests or to stakeholders. With respect to nations, the GMS represents a six-nation scenario. Each nation pursues national interests and so ADB development projects affect them in different ways. The

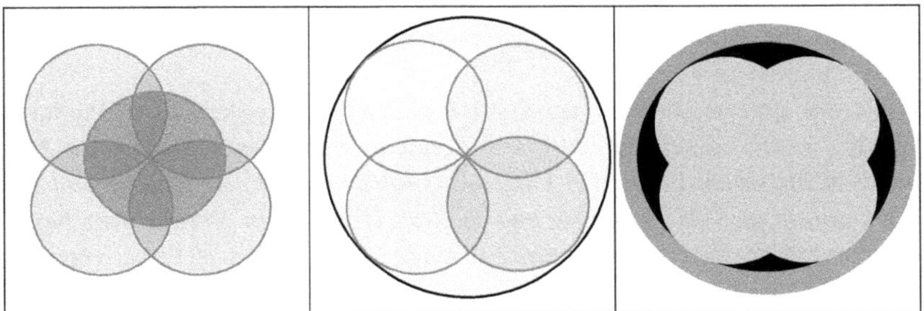

Each sector is partially sustainable by its own internal standards	Each sector is sustainable by its own internal standards	Each sector is sustainable by its own internal standards and the external standards of the other three sectors

Figure 3.2 Degrees of sustainability for a four-sector situation

right-hand situation would exist when all nations agreed that all development activity conducted by each nation was completely sustainable vis-à-vis the other nations. An obvious example would be that all six Mekong nations work to agree on development principles that would eliminate upstream-downstream impacts. In this scenario, a Chinese dam would be considered sustainable only when all five downstream nations perceived this from their own vantage points. Currently, this level of cooperation does not appear to exist.

The model can also be used to focus on stakeholders. In the GMS, there are many "players" focusing on both sustainability and development. In anticipation of the example to follow, ADB is one such player; the Bank advocates certain projects and discusses sustainable development in terms of those projects. Oxfam, a world-wide non-governmental organisation (NGO) that also focuses on poverty elimination, has a very different perspective on sustainable development. Currently, an analysis of recent documents shows that Oxfam contests some projects advocated by the ADB.[16] This represents a situation where the right-hand set of circles does not pertain. There is contestation between stakeholders, not agreement.

The ADB named the region the "GMS" and has, over the past 20 years, put considerable effort into the development of the six nations. Its *Strategic Framework 2012–2022* notes that, by 2011, 55 investment projects, costing US$14 billion, had been implemented.[17] As with all ADB projects, the vision is to eliminate poverty in the Asia and Pacific region and the mission is to help member counties reduce poverty and improve their citizens' quality of life.[18] The strategic framework notes[19] that, to date, "concrete results" have led to the "broader realization of a prosperous, integrated and harmonious GMS". These are qualified in terms of rise in national GDP, decline in poverty indices, and more open economies. Certain "strategic thrusts" such as "facilitating cross-border trade and investment", and the creation of "economic corridors" that cross national borders indicate that the ADB's development focus is regional in scale. In fact, "regional co-operation" is repeatedly stressed as an intended outcome of the Bank's activities.[20] Sustainability is likewise stressed repeatedly throughout the document, in a variety of contexts. The upshot is that, on the basis of this document, it can be interpreted that the ADB is working to reach the level of sustainability shown in the left-hand set of circles.

While this appears laudable, an NGO with reputable credentials – Oxfam Australia – has produced a document that is decidedly cautionary regarding the ADB's activities in the GMS. Entitled *A Citizen's Guide to the Greater Mekong Subregion: Understanding the GMS Program and the Role of the Asian Development Bank*, [21] this document stresses the importance of understanding that ADB activities focus on macro-economic growth (e.g. gross domestic product)[22] rather than helping "vulnerable communities".[23] The following quote from Oxfam reveals the nature of contestation between the two organisations:

> The ADB promotes a model of development which sees rapid economic growth as the best way for achieving poverty reduction, based largely on neo-

> liberal economics. Whether this model of development reduces or increases poverty has been the subject of hot debate for a couple of decades as neo-liberal approaches, such as increased privatisation of essential services and increased deregulation of markets, can result in vulnerable communities being worse off.[24]

The document goes as far as developing a "citizen's toolkit" entitled "Keeping the GMS Program Accountable". The mere existence of such a toolkit indicates there is severe contestation between the ADB and Oxfam over the proper approach to development – even though they are both organisations which have a mission to alleviate poverty. Clearly, the situation of sustainability portrayed by the middle set of circles has not yet been achieved.[25]

A third document – *Joint Initiative on Rapid Basin-wide Hydropower Sustainability Assessment Tool* – indicates the situation is even more complex. The multiple authors/contributors are the USAID, the ADB, the Mekong River Commission, and the World Wildlife Fund.[26] In this instance, four stakeholders having rather different perspectives towards development have worked together to produce a "tool" that will enable evaluation of the degree of sustainability of any particular hydropower project. Inspection of the particulars of the toolkit[27] indicates that any individual assessment of a project can begin from a variety of perspectives on the nature of sustainable development. Thus, the World Wildlife Fund might use the toolkit to assess the negative impact on endangered species such as the Mekong dolphin, while the Mekong River Commission might use the same toolkit to assess the downstream impact of a particular dam.

This document does not indicate that a state of sustainability exists anywhere yet. However, it does indicate that several major stakeholders have agreed on a method for evaluating the degree to which any particular hydropower project is sustainable from different perspectives. Such an evaluation would, normatively, allow for compromise in the nature of the activity so that all stakeholders could agree to allow a project to proceed, assured of the fact that there would not be excessive negative outcomes from any stakeholder's perspective. The existence of this toolkit suggests that the right-hand concept of sustainability has the potential to become reality.

Actualised development

The previous example indicates that cooperation between competing stakeholders is possible. NGOs with considerable power may be able to influence the behaviour of nation states regarding manipulation and modification of the Mekong River. However, this cooperation would result in response to contestation – one NGO accusing the other, or accusing a nation state, of unsustainable practices. The next section presents one possibility for reaching consensus based on a shared notion of a desirable future. This involves considering the relationship between the "ideal" form of development at the national level – sustainable development – and the "ideal" form of development at the level of the individual person – self-actualisation. The latter concept is part of a well-known construct – a needs hierarchy – created by Maslow[28] in the first half of the twentieth century. Combining the two concepts obviously begins by equating a development practice scale with Maslow's well-known need hierarchy.[29]

Development activity, in general, is a response to conditions where nations or regions live at the equivalent of Maslow's two lowest need levels: physiological and safety and security. The goal of development activity is essentially to lift people out of these levels. For the GMS, it is apparent that the ADB goal of eliminating poverty involves taking the GMS nations out of the physiological and safety and security levels to something higher. The various projects can be roughly related to a hierarchy equivalent to Maslow. Best practice development activity would actualise the result – sustainable development. This chapter suggests that the truest goal of developmental activity should strive to create conditions equivalent to self-actualisation. For the GMS, this goes well beyond the idea of joining the set of developed nations. The goal is for the entire region to have "actualised development". Tourism development projects evaluated roughly in terms of Maslow's need-hierarchy levels would produce the following relationships:

Worst. Would consist of GMS projects and economic activity with narrow goals that create negative impacts on the resource itself and create negative impacts of other types and/or in other places.

Poor. Would consist of GMS projects and economic activity with single-sector goals that partially maintain the resource base for that sector. This would be the equivalent to the left-hand set of circles in Figure 3.2.

Mediocre. Would consist of GMS tourism projects that were sustainable for tourism but unsustainable vis-à-vis other sectors. This would be equivalent to the middle set of circles in Figure 3.2.

Good. Would consist of GMS tourism projects that are sustainable for tourism as a sector and are partially sustainable with respect to other sectors.

Best. Would consist of GMS projects and policies that produce sustainable tourism *and* force/coerce/encourage other sectors to also be sustainable. This would be equivalent to the right-hand set of circles in Figure 3.2.

Table 3.1 Actualising development

	Maslow's need hierarchy levels	*Levels of development practice*
5	Self-actualisation (personal fulfilment)	Best
4	Esteem	Good
3	Love & belonging	Mediocre
2	Safety & security	Poor
1	Physiological	Worst

Source: Author's own

Applied to the GMS, the reality of development is that the Mekong River is currently used by several economic sectors. Therefore, the normative goal is to reach Level 5, where river development was "actualised" through each sector's developmental and economic activity being sustainable in terms of all other sectors, and where a consensus has been reached on this by all GMS nations and by all stakeholders such as Oxfam, the World Wildlife Foundation, and the ADB, as well as by GMS-nation citizens. However, though the Mekong River will be the subject of numerous development projects for the foreseeable future, it is apparent that many of these will be either unsustainable or contestably sustainable by proponents of other sectors/nations/stakeholders. The situation of actualised sustainability modelled by the right-hand set of circles in Figure 3.2 will likely not occur for most projects because no shared sense of development identity yet exists. The chapter will now turn to a particular development sector – tourism – which has at least the potential to create this sense of identity.

Tourism's role in creating actualised GMS development

The previous two sections have attempted to conceptualise the nature of a regional identity and the nature of sustainable development for the GMS. However, a gap between these two issues exists which could be bridged by creating a shared regional identity that will facilitate actualised development at large. This final section of the chapter looks at tourism's role in this identity construction. As with the previous sections, tourism's role in this is conceptual rather than based on GMS tourism projects. Specifically, the concept is based on a comparison with New Zealand and New Zealand's particular marketing slogan – "100% Pure New Zealand". Thus, the goal is to conceptualise a "100% Pure Mekong" tourism marketing strategy that encourages sustainable tourism (single sector), sustainable development (multiple sectors), and a sustainable regional identity.

100% Pure New Zealand

> Tourism New Zealand launched its "100% Pure New Zealand" campaign in 1999. A typical "100% Pure New Zealand" poster states these words and shows a distinct image.[30] While many of the images are environmental, others are cultural. The Tourism New Zealand webpage notes:
>
> When 100% Pure New Zealand launched in 1999, it was the first time New Zealand had one message in all of its tourism markets around the world. The campaign was developed to be clear and concise: to communicate a single message about New Zealand that captured the imagination of our target market.[31]

The success of the brand was immediate. By 2005, the company InterBrand found that the 100% Pure New Zealand brand had become worth about US$13.6 billion. This was good for a ranking of twenty-first in the world, one place ahead of Dell and one behind Samsung.[32] The *10 Years Young* website written by the Tourism New Zealand to celebrate the tenth anniversary of the slogan, noted that the goal was to create the impression that the image represented a 100% Pure New Zealand *experience* – this is what tourists could have when they visited the country. The slogan plus the image combined to form a holistic impression of the uniqueness of the country.[33] The same webpage further noted that the slogan had not been meant to send a message about the environmental *purity* of New Zealand.[34] Yet the slogan quickly played into the hands of critics who challenged New Zealand's environmental record, particularly outside the tourism sector.[35] Faced with criticism over the lack of environmental purity in the country, an awareness in the tourism industry emerged that the sector must live up to the implicit environmental assertion embedded in the slogan because tourists had come to expect it. Revisions of the New Zealand Tourism Strategy for 2007 and 2010, a combined effort of government and the private sector, thus set ideals related to the environmental sustainability of the sector.[36] Further efforts have included the national accreditation programme – Qualmark – adopting fully integrated environmental criteria across its assessments. The same webpage cites George Hickton, former head of Tourism New Zealand, as noting the brand has taken on an identity that is aspirational vis-à-vis the environment: "It's a promise, but it's a promise we believe the country can and should live up to, for New Zealanders and visitors alike".[37]

Analytically, it can be said that because of the 100% Pure New Zealand slogan the tourism sector has come closer to achieving the status shown in the left-hand diagram of Figure 3.2. The sector is not yet completely sustainable but great efforts are being made to achieve this. If that were the only impact of the brand this chapter could not have been written. What is more pertinent is the reality that this slogan has been widely influential *across* economic sectors. In other words, "purity" has become a bottom line not only for tourism but for other sectors such as agriculture. This is not by the choice of New Zealand's farmers, nor is it by coercion of the tourism sector. Rather, it is because the slogan is so successful that all sectors having a relationship with the natural environment are under pressure to conform. The slogan is functioning as an unintentional form of internal marketing.[38] Effectively, the outwardly aimed marketing slogan is back-spreading internally through the different sectors of New Zealand. This "spreading" situation has been modelled in Figure 3.3.

The upshot is that the slogan has not only been successful in attracting tourists, it has helped clean up the tourism industry. Even more importantly for this chapter, the slogan has back-spread to other New Zealand sectors and placed pressure on them to purify themselves. It is this back-spreading impact that makes the slogan relevant to the Mekong River and the GMS.

GMS tourism marketing

Within the larger ADB scheme for the GMS[39] tourism is one of ten economic sectors explicitly specified for development. According to ADB's *Tourism Sector Assessment, Strategy, and Road Map,*[40] the sector involves 13 spatial zones which include much of the total GMS area. Development is built on the sustainability principles of being

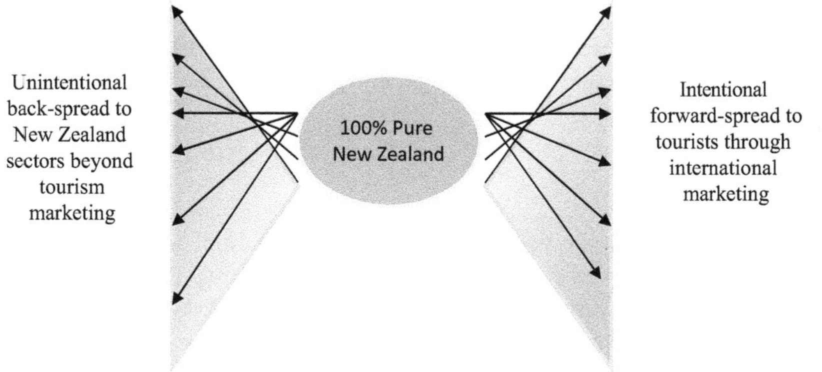

Figure 3.3 The forward-backward spreading impact of the 100% Pure New Zealand slogan
Source: Author's own

"economically viable, ecologically sound, and has minimal negative social impacts on the local community". This also includes a "vision" of a subregional tourism sector that serves a major engine for development and poverty reduction, with "particular focus on the protection of women and children, promoting the conservation of the natural and cultural heritage as well as peace and harmony in the GMS".

As a pair, these functions would seem to be just what is needed: the second creates a sense of identity that will help with the first – sustainable tourism sector development. However, examination of further published data indicates that adequate results, based on the sustainability concepts discussed above, have not yet been achieved. While numerous tourism projects have a cross-border component, and resolving poverty issues is important, the functioning of the Coordinating Office seems devolved to the national level;[41] member nations submit reports specifying the nature of tourism project activities within their own borders. There does not seem to be a focus on either the Mekong River as a transnational entity or on using tourism to create a regional identity. Effectively, the six national groups work together but do not try to integrate into a regional entity.

As a marketing strategy, selling the GMS as a single destination would seem to be a worthwhile endeavour with regard to a regional identity formation. Effectively, this could create a regional identity in the minds of international tourists that might eventually back-spread to GMS governments, developers, and residents. Arrived tourists thinking they were in the GMS would create a mindset that the locals were residents of "the GMS", not just their own country. To establish the GMS as a single region, however, requires a single visa for entry into any of the six GMS nations. The Mekong Tourism Coordinating Office and various GMS tourism working groups have been challenged to convince individual nations that a single-entry visa is viable. Of course, such a visa has existed in Europe for well over a decade. EU citizens can cross borders without passports. International tourists show their passports only when entering and departing the EU, not when crossing individual borders. However, at the time of writing no real progress has occurred to date with the GMS nations. Individual nations continue to want control over who crosses their borders. The GMS is far behind the EU on this issue and it is not apparent that a single entry visa could be used to establish a regional identity.

100% Pure Mekong

This final section takes the slogan "100% Pure New Zealand" and uses it with the points made previously to conceptualise a hypothetical "100% Pure Mekong". The goal will be for this concept to back-spread as widely as possible in order to help create a regional identity and to inform GMS development projects so that the normative multi-sectoral conceptualisation of sustainability is achieved. That is, a 100% Pure Mekong marketing campaign would go further than 100% Pure New Zealand has in the sense that back-spreading is an intentional function of the campaign. It is not just about luring tourists, it is about creating the identity that already exists in New Zealand.

The ADB has appropriated the name of the river – Mekong – as the central geographic concept bounding the scale of its work. Therefore, the river itself needs to become the core feature that residents and developers identify with. It was mentioned that, in the past, the nature of the river divided people, it did not unite them. To overcome this, the Mekong Tourism Co-ordinating Office must design a campaign that creates unity. The goal must be to construct a social "we people who share the Mekong" as well as an "other" who live outside the region. Using Ifversen's[42] and Pace's[43] concepts, the campaign must identify essentialist concepts and images that function as an existing identity core. This means features of a common past must likely be drawn upon. Hobsbawm and Ranger[44] have discussed examples of this in their book *The Invention of Traditon*. However, constructivist images and attributes might also imagine the future – 100% Pure Mekong would likely need to be about "becoming". The focus would be on what residents *will* share, not just the shared past but also the hoped-for future. The social spatialisation and spatial socialisation through marketing imagery and attribute construction could be about a developed future that does not yet exist.

The 100% Pure New Zealand campaign relies heavily upon scenery and nature and also culture. This suggests that 100% Pure Mekong would need to rely heavily on images of an unspoiled Mekong River. While the course of the river has not yet been heavily altered by dam construction or by blasting, fish stocks and the endangered Mekong River dolphin point to the reality that, in a biological sense, the river is no longer in its natural state. Hence, one angle to the campaign could be to promote endangered or declining species. For example, the images would not show giant catfishes being caught but swimming in their natural habitat, or could show the river being stocked with baby catfish by conservation officers. Just as Tourism New Zealand can replace "100% Pure New Zealand" with "100% Pure Middle Earth", the Mekong Tourism Coordinating Office could write "100% Sustainable Mekong" on a poster showing baby catfish being released into the river. Images of a sustained Mekong River dolphin population would likely cause a reaction of joy by both tourists and locals.

Using 100% Pure Mekong to create an identity that incorporates development becomes more complicated. At a basic level, tourism as a development sector must be at the forefront of the marketing. Thus the Mekong River must be marketed as a "pure" tourist attraction. This suggests that sites of unspoiled beauty along the river must be appropriated. However, sustainable features of existing river culture would also function to suggest an unspoiled quality. The tourist experience of the Mekong, in terms of existing essentialised images and constructed images would help create the common bond that could be used to induce back-spreading.

The multi-sectoral nature of development along the river provides potential for a 100% Pure Mekong marketing but any imagery must be used with great care. Images must be chosen for their potential to bind people and developers from different countries and sectors. Use of a photo of a dam would probably neutralise the potential for identity construction as all dams are perceived differently due to upstream-downstream impacts. In fact, the goal is to use imagery that would strengthen the resolve of citizens to prevent unsustainable and/or contestable projects from being pursued. The message must be to help, not hurt, the River. Projects must represent "actualised development".

Conclusion

This chapter has attempted to conceptualise how tourism might help create a regional identity for the GMS nations that enables sustainable development. There exists a large peninsula on the southeast side of the Asian continent that has no indigenous name, hence citizens of this region have no indigenous identity of themselves at this geographic scale. The "Greater Mekong Subregion" as a name is a creation of the Asian Development Bank. The name serves a useful purpose as a label that enables top-down cross-border development projects to be conducted. However, it is not clear that, as a label, this creates a sufficient sense of identity among the 300 million residents to avoid conflict based on national-scale identities. As long as residents see themselves as citizens of countries rather than a region, they will lack the sense of shared identity that would promote full cooperation.

The Asian Development Bank has the mission to reduce poverty hence its GMS projects attempt to develop the six nations. This is of course laudable. However, models developed for this chapter regarding the nature of sustainability indicate the GMS's situation is far from ideal at achieving sustainable development. Different governments, different NGOs, and different advocates of sectoral economic interests do not appear to have any common identity, thus differ in their vision of what sustainable development means and is. The interim conclusion is that, until a shared identity emerges, the normative situation of sustainability will not arise, or will be delayed by conflict/contestation. Thus, the creation of a shared regional identity would seem essential. Put concretely, citizens of GMS nations need to be able to call themselves something equivalent to "Europeans". To date, GMS tourism marketing activities do have the goal of creating a "single destination". However, it is not apparent that this has been successful. There has been no progress on agreement to have a single visa for entry into and travel between the six nations. Marketing activities stress attractions at the national level, not regional. Thus the tourism marketing is not being used to successfully create a regional identity that will back-spread into other development sectors or to local populations.

Tourism is one of the only sectors with the capability, through its marketing activities, to undertake to construct a regional identity which will, in turn, create an internally acceptable logic for making decisions about specific development projects. Because the Mekong River forms the core of the name chosen by the ADB, the River has an extremely strategic function in the marketing of the region. Promoting a "pure" river is likely the best way to begin to identify core identity features acceptable to all. With the belief in a pure river, development projects can be assessed in terms of whether they sustain or destroy the purity of the Mekong River. With the notion of purity established, an intentional goal to back-spread the message to citizens and developers will simultaneously sustain the Mekong and help the tourism sector to achieve something of a managerial capability to direct the course of development. The challenge will be for the tourism sector to rise to the occasion. If tourism does not do it, which sector will? If tourism does not do it, the chances of multi-sectoral sustainable development become much slimmer. As a development sector, tourism thus holds the key to actualised development in the GMS.

Notes

1 europa.eu. 1992. "Treaty of Maastricht on European Union", online at http://europa.eu/legislation_summaries/institutional_affairs/treaties/treaties_maastricht_en.htm.
2 See, for example, C. Radaelli, "Europeanization: Solution or problem?" in M. Cini and A. K. Bourne (eds.), *Palgrave Advances in European Union Studies*, Basingstoke, UK: Palgrave Macmillan, 2006, pp. 56–76; D. Fuchs and H.-D. Klingemann (eds.), *Cultural Diversity, European Identity and the Legitimacy of the EU*, Cheltenham, UK: Edward Elgar, 2011; D. Sanders et al. (eds.), *The Europeanization of National Polities? Citizenship and Support in a Post-Enlargement Union*, Oxford, UK: Oxford University Press, 2012.
3 Tourism New Zealand, "Campaign and activity", Wellington, NZ: Tourism New Zealand, 8 November 2017, online at https://www.tourismnewzealand.com/about/what-we-do/campaign-and-activity.
4 Jan Ifversen, "Europe and European culture – a conceptual analysis", *European Societies*, Vol. 4, Iss. 1, 2002, pp. 1–26.
5 Ibid., p. 8.
6 Ibid., p. 9.
7 Ibid., p. 13.
8 Ibid., p. 14.
9 Michelle Pace, *The Politics of Regional Identity: Meddling with the Mediterranean*, London: Routledge, 2006, p. 39.
10 Medhi Krongkaew, "The development of the Greater Mekong Subregion (GMS): Real promise or false hope?" *Journal of Asian Economics*, Vol. 5, Iss. 5, 2004, p. 979.
11 For example, "Viking River Cruises" website, www.vikingrivercruises.com.au/regions/asia/rivers/mekong/about.aspx.
12 The Both Ends.org, for example, notes ("The ADB-GMS support for hydropower dams and power grid", 2011, online at www.bibalex.org/Search4Dev/document/

378025): "The Asian Development Bank and the GMS are unknown among most citizens of the Mekong countries, in spite of the impact they create on many people's lives and on the natural resources that the people depend on". Andrew Walker ("Another Mekong Conference!" 2006, online at https://www.newmandala.org/another-mekong-conference), similarly, wonders whether "a hydrological entity is an any more legitimate basis for analysis than the now largely discredited nation state". Rasalia Sciortino ("Creating a Mekong Community", 2008, online at https://prachatai.com/english/node/564) further argues that the ADB's documents do not adequately discuss the process of how the Mekong community is to evolve. This is particularly important because recent conflict between nations has left "indelible marks" and new issues concerning resource conflicts make the "extent the peoples in the Mekong feel bonded to one another" quite questionable. Finally, Jakkrit Sangkhamanee ("Charting the Mekong: A configuration of the GMS 'geo-body' for development", paper presented at the RCSD International Conference, "Politics of the commons: Articulating development and strengthening local practice", Chiang Mai, Thailand, 11–14 July 2003) notes that the GMS is an "imagined community" because the Mekong River has never before been considered as a landmark so that its surrounding area is designated a "subregion".

13 World Commission on Environment and Development, *Our Common Future*, Oxford, UK and New York: Oxford University Press, 1987, p. 54.

14 C. J. Hunter, "On the need to re-conceptualise sustainable tourism development", *Journal of Sustainable Tourism*, Vol. 3, Iss. 3, 1995, pp. 155–65.

15 S. C. Johnston, "Towards a theory of sustainability, sustainable development and sustainable tourism: Beijing's hutong neighbourhoods and sustainable tourism", *Journal of Sustainable Tourism*, Vol. 22, Iss. 2, 2014, pp. 195–213.

16 Jessica Rosien and Reece Kinnane, "The role of the Asian Development Bank", 8 May 2013, online at https://www.oxfam.org.au/2013/05/the-role-of-the-asian-development-bank.

17 Asian Development Bank, *The Greater Mekong Subregion Economic Cooperation Program Strategic Framework 2012–2022*, Manila: Asian Development Bank, 2011, p. 1, online at https://www.adb.org/documents/greater-mekong-subregion-economic-cooperation-program-strategic-framework-2012-2022.

18 Ibid., back cover.

19 Ibid., p. 3.

20 Ibid., pp. 1–2.

21 Oxfam Australia, *A Citizen's Guide to the Greater Mekong Subregion: Understanding the GMS Program and the Role of the Asian Development Bank*, Melbourne: Oxfam Australia, 2008, online at https://www.oxfam.org.au/wp-content/uploads/2011/08/oaus-citizensguidemekong-11084.pdf.

22 Ibid., p. 17.

23 Ibid., p. 21.

24 Ibid.

25 As with identity, there is considerable academic contestation over the appropriateness of the ADB and other agency's roles in development. Jakkrit Sangkhamanee (see note 12 above) asserts that "not every actor involved is truly satisfied … with the agenda. A main concern for the opponents is that the growth-oriented plan for developing the subregion has often not been balanced by social and human aspects of development …" C. Sneddon and C. Fox ("Rethinking transboundary waters: A critical hydropolitics of the Mekong basin", *Political Geography*, Vol. 25, 2006, pp. 181–202) maintain that the goal to reinvent the basin as a development object obscures conflicts at the local and national scales.

26 See USAID et al., *Joint Initiative on Rapid Basin-wide Hydropower Sustainability Assessment Tool (RSAT)*, 2010, online at www.mrcmekong.org/assets/Publications/Reports/RSAT-Revision-3-for-printingOCT-3-2010-Corrected-FINAL.PDF.

27 Ibid., pp. 64–89.
28 A. H. Maslow, "A theory of human motivation", *Psychological Review*, Vol. 50, No. 4, 1943, pp. 370–96.
29 Although both concepts are widely used, little research appears to have combined Maslow's need hierarchy with sustainable development. For a quantitative analysis at the national scale, see V. E. Udo, Victor and P. M. Jansson, "Bridging the gaps for global sustainable development: A quantitative analysis", *Journal of Environmental Management*, Vol. 90, Iss. 12, 2009, pp. 3700–7.
30 See https://www.google.co.nz/search?q=100%25+Pure+New+Zealand+images&tbm=isch&source=univ&sa=X&ved=2ahUKEwiqtKb3gMfhAhUMW7wKHdmZD0cQsAR6BAgIEAE&biw=1200&bih=707 for examples.
31 Tourism New Zealand, 2017, op cit.
32 Tourism New Zealand, *Pure as: Celebrating 10 years of 100% Pure New Zealand*, Wellington, NZ: Tourism New Zealand, 2009, pp. 42–3, online at https://www.tourismnewzealand.com/media/1544/pure-as-celebrating-10-years-of-100-pure-new-zealand.pdf; N. Morgan et al., "Tourism places, brands, and reputation management" in N. Morgan et al. (eds.), *Destination Brands: Managing Place Reputation,* 3rd Edition, Oxford, UK: Butterworth-Heinemann, 2011, p. 9.
33 Tourism New Zealand, 2009, op cit., pp. 44–58.
34 Ibid., p. 54.
35 Agricultural practices by Fonterra, New Zealand's largest dairy cooperative, were a repeated concern in this regard. See for examples http://en.wikipedia.org/wiki/2008_Chinese_milk_scandal and www.stuff.co.nz/national/politics/opinion/9015873/Fonterra-reeling-from-intense-media-scrutiny.
36 D. G. Pearce and C. Schott, "Tourism and climate change: Public and private sector responses in New Zealand" in C Schott (ed.), *Tourism and the Implications of Climate Change: Issues and Actions*, Bradford, UK: Emerald Group Publishing Ltd, 2010, pp.173–5; Tourism New Zealand, 2009, op cit., p. 55.
37 Cited in Lyn McGaurr, *Environmental Communication and Travel Journalism: Consumerism, Conflict and Concern*, Abingdon, UK and New York: Routledge, 2015, p. 69.
38 See M. Rafiq and P. K. Ahmed, "Advances in the internal marketing concept: Definition, synthesis and extension", *Journal of Services Marketing*, Vol. 14, No. 6, 2000, pp. 449–62.
39 The Mekong Tourism Coordinating Office is the official arm of the ADB's GMS activities related to tourism (www.adb.org/countries/gms/sector-activities/tourism). This office has two main functions. A development function serves to "co-ordinate sustainable pro-poor tourism development projects in the Mekong in line with the United Nations Millennium Development Goals;" while a marketing function promotes the Mekong region "as a single travel and tourism destination" (http://mekongtourism.org/website/about-mtco/what-is-the-mtco).
40 Asian Development Bank, *Greater Mekong Subregion: Tourism Sector Assessment, Strategy, and Road Map*, Manila: Asian Development Bank, 2012, online at www.adb.org/countries/gms/sector-activities/tourism.
41 See GSM Tourism Working Group Meeting Minutes, online at https://greatermekong.org/search/node/MTCO.
42 Jan Ifversen, op cit.
43 Michelle Pace, op cit.
44 E. Hobsbawm and T. Ranger (eds.), *The Invention of Tradition*. Cambridge, UK: Cambridge University Press, 1983.

4 Developmental change in the Greater Mekong Subregion

Economic growth yes, community construction?

Kenneth Jackson

Introduction

In the last 20 years or so, global and regional economic liberalisation has produced many outcomes, positive and negative, for both communities and individuals in the several countries of the Greater Mekong Subregion (GMS). Vietnam, Lao PDR, Cambodia, Thailand, Myanmar, and part of China form the GMS. Notably, several of these countries have undergone a transition from centrally controlled economies to more open ones. Yet, many of the countries in the GMS continue to exhibit a major reliance upon the agricultural sector, as a source of livelihood and employment. Some farmers produce solely for themselves and their families. Some look to move into non-agricultural occupations, to supplement their agricultural activities, or to switch to cash production growing non-traditional crops. The central theme of the chapter is the presence of the Mekong River and its water. The GMS is, of course, named after the Mekong River, as if naming a region after a geographical feature could somehow unite disparate communities. Yet the chapter will try to show that the River does not consistently function this way. Rather, people continue to identify with their localities first, perhaps with a notion of national identity, but rarely with any trans-national concept of regional identity. Regional government cooperation is developing slowly and somewhat inconsistently over time. While economic growth produces rising incomes and reduces poverty, this benefit has not yet begun to construct a wider community identity.

This chapter discusses several economic development processes acting on the GMS, in relation to economic growth versus community construction. First, agriculture and food are discussed, focusing on rice. This is followed by an examination of Mekong River water issues. The third section focuses on globalisation and migration, addressing global causes of change applicable to the GMS. Subsequently, the causes of change internal to the GMS are considered. The final section examines some of the observed outcomes and responses to change, while the Conclusion ponders the relationship between prosperity and community.

Global food production, local rice production, and community change

Over the past few decades, global agricultural prices have followed general commodity prices by rising significantly at times, with some large short-run fluctuations and output responses. The Food Price Index (FPI) of the United Nations (UN) Food and Agriculture Organisation (FAO) reached 91.1 for the millennial year, 2000 (see Appendix 4.1). The peak value, 229.9, was reached in 2011. Thereafter, there was a drop to 161.5 in 2016 but this recovered into the 170s range in 2017, and has stayed in the high 160s ever since.[1]

The FAO price index for Cereals (see Appendix 4.1) has shown similar directional trends but with much larger year-to-year fluctuation. Rice is the dominant cereal crop for the countries through which the Mekong flows. Rice prices show some differences from the overall FPI and the Cereals commodity group. Global rice prices in 2016 were reported by FAO to have fallen somewhat over those of the previous twelve months with the dominant driver being falling Japonica quotations, which outweighed modest increases in the Indica and Aromatic rice segments. In general, there has not been a downward fluctuation in world rice prices since 2016.[2]

As with other general price information, these figures relate to internationally traded rice, rather than locally produced rice (for which good information is lacking). The broader price structure thus only partially reflects the experience of the Mekong region. GMS countries have experienced pricing changes somewhat different from the global averages. The years 2014 and 2015 in fact saw some rice price rises in the Mekong area because of drought conditions, reducing supply. Complicating matters, from place-to-place particular names are used for more than one variety and the same variety can be called by different names[3] leading to confusion in collection of reliable data. However, since both Japonica and Indica varieties are used throughout the Mekong region, some useful indications of price trends can be seen by starting with the composite indexes mentioned previously. But global figures are best used only as a first indicator of price movements for local farmers. Understanding the production situation requires local knowledge because the smaller farmers' outputs do not feature prominently in international trade. Those local small farmers producing cash crops sell to locally based markets and traders.

Acknowledging fluctuation, rice prices have generally risen over the past two decades. This may be classified as beneficial to market producers, neutral for subsistence producers, and detrimental for consumers. The price rise has been beneficial on a national basis for exporters, which in the GMS case is the five lower Mekong countries. China is the exception; the People's Republic of China (PRC) imports rice from other GMS countries, as well as other international suppliers. The six GMS members in total produce some 44 per cent of world rice output, all six figure in the top 20 producing countries, and all but China produce in excess of their own local consumption needs.

Southeast Asia accounts for more than 30 per cent of world rice output.[4] Within Southeast Asia the non-Chinese component of the GMS accounts for a notable, even significant, part of the total rice area under cultivation (Table 4.1). The area under irrigation is even more significant with only Vietnam demonstrating less than

Table 4.1 Area under rice cultivation in lowland Mekong sub region, minus China, 2012

Nation	*Direct rain water supply rice area in hectares*	*Irrigated water supply rice area in hectares*	*Total rice output area in hectares*
Cambodia	154,000	1,124,000	1,278,000
Lao PDR	40,000	319,000	359,000
Myanmar	1,124,000	4,166,000	5,290,000
Thailand	2,075,000	6,792,000	8,867,000
Vietnam	3,687,000	1,955,000	5,642,000

Source: An adaptation based on Suzanne K. Redfern et al. (2012, p. 295).

50 per cent of the total coming from irrigated land. Water from the Mekong is a dominant part of the water supply for the irrigation schemes in the GMS and for local small farm producers this is the cause of much dispute and concern as the high capital intensity of irrigated supply leads to the increasing domination of large scale farm operations (see next section).

Table 4.1 and the previous paragraphs establish that rice is an extremely important part of the GMS nations' economies. Yet, rice in these countries is much more than just a source of income. Rice remains the staple food source and has cultural significance extending beyond food production. The generally loose link between local rice of poorer quality and the traded rice and the different names from locality to locality both reflect how community identification is a stable cultural characteristic of the regions' residents. As Redfern et al.[5] eloquently put it: "rice is more than just food: it is the central subject of economic policy, a determinant of national objectives, and an important anchor in the maintenance of political stability". Rice production also plays a role in the way people identify with a locality. The customary and institutional arrangements affecting rice production and water supply become an important determinant of how people see themselves in terms of their identification with local communities, nations, and regions.

The decades-long rise in the FPI and the Cereals Price Index should mean good news for GMS rice farmers. However, the situation is complex and getting more so. With governments increasingly relying upon openness and market structures, relative price changes amongst agricultural products in the GMS have impacted on communities in two important ways. First, with irrigation schemes in place farmers switch their production from rice to non-rice cash crops. This switch impacts on rice prices and creates difficulties for those reliant upon market supplies for their food. Second, relative affluence can allow some family members to leave the farm. This occupational switch out of farming may include temporary migration, either internally or internationally, with remittance flows back to the home. There is certainly evidence of an increasing reliance on wages to secure food and other products rather than on the agricultural production traditionally used for securing food for own family consumption. Pure subsistence agriculture as a sole means of securing food is a conceptual ideal that is far from universally held, especially with the increasing intrusion of market mechanisms into the local economic system. Small-scale farmers can be adaptable and even entrepreneurial without a formalised market structure functioning as the dominant exchange mechanism. In recent decades, extra income often helps to pay for education fees, with the children looking to not follow their parents into small-scale farming. Agriculture is still a major source of livelihoods but not one which necessarily fits the ambition of either the current or the next generation.[6]

Better prices for food, and particularly rice, throughout the GMS generally have a positive impact. The consequent impact on community, however, is one of slow change. While not representing a socio-cultural upheaval, the change has not thus far indicated that a new GMS community is being constructed. Rather, increased openness has permitted capitalist agriculture to enter and grow, while also permitting individuals to move and/or leave. With respect to agriculture, economic growth does not enhance regional community construction.

Water, a unifying or a separating force?

Water is critical to the farmers in the GMS. In Southeast Asia as a whole some 45 per cent of rice production is irrigated. If the Mekong River is to be a geographical identifying factor – the source of a name for the region – this does not necessarily mean that it is a force for community unification. Water, and the right to use it, is the source of much disputation. China contributes some 18 per cent of the water that enters the river along its length, but by virtue of its location at the head of the river, China is seen by other GMS nations as responsible for many disputes – navigation, irrigation, electricity supply, fishing, and other uses to which the water can be put. The downstream countries often see China as a controlling and uncooperative actor in regional water issues and a major user of water in ways detrimental to the downstream recipients. Riparian co-presence is not sufficient to unify the GMS nations.

In 1995, Lao PDR, Cambodia, Thailand, and Vietnam engaged in talks on intergovernmental cooperation that resulted in agreement on the sustainable development of the Mekong River Basin through the establishment of the Mekong River Commission (MRC).[7] These talks formalised previous efforts at Lower Mekong Basin cooperation dating back to 1957, including the work of the Committee for the Coordination of Investigations of the Lower Mekong Basin, which was operated by these same four countries. The motive for this cooperation was the recognition by the four countries, along with the UN, that the Mekong River Basin and the related natural resources and environment represented natural assets of immense value, and thus should be used for the economic, social well-being, and improvement of the living standards of their peoples.[8] It was not until 2002 that China was fully included in such talks. Some antagonism and disputes had occurred in the intervening period, although Myanmar and China had dialogue status with the Commission. By 2016 there was a fuller level of agreement and cooperation, with the establishment of the Lancang-Mekong Cooperation (LMC). The first leaders' meeting, at the end of March 2016, saw recognition of the need for a more integrated and regional approach to solving disputes regarding water, irrigation, navigation, fishing, positioning of dams, and other matters related to the river.[9] Possibly the LMC will be able to resolve disputes at the national level.

Disputes, however, continue to occur at lower levels. If large projects were to go ahead and, due to the high cost of capital intensive irrigation works, there are charges and restrictions on water available for small farmers in an area where rainfall can be irregular or seasonal, this would lead to disputes. There is a clear demand for irrigation water in dry periods, especially when a production cycle of three rice harvests per annum is favoured. The capital intensive structures have favoured large-scale farming, with the ownership of corporates often located outside the country where production is located. This affects the degree of local identity and commitment to local communities and creates dramatic changes in the challenges faced by farmers. At the top, water is becoming perceived as a commodity rather than as a natural free good. At the bottom, in some localities, small farmers have broken into the distribution ditches and canals of irrigation schemes, in order to gain access to what they consider a long-established right – unfettered access to water for their crops. The long-established opinion remains that there are customary rights to water that come from tradition more than legal statute or current economic ideology. These disputes create an issue in terms of what community small farmers identify with. Regional cooperation and identification leading to community construction continues to be hampered significantly by the high level of contestation visible at all scales.

Globalisation and migration

The concept of economic openness has altered in meaning over time. Measurement definitions have changed. Edward Leamer[10] developed several measures of the phenomenon, but all of them were trade-related. Lant Pritchett[11] looked rather more carefully and explicitly at Least Developed Countries (LDCs) in his approach to policy stances, but his approach was still largely trade-related. Current approaches are somewhat broader and enhanced by consideration of technological change and innovation. The flow of ideas and finance is directly affected by changes in these factors.[12] It is possible to see, for example, that changes brought about by the US-Vietnam trade agreement go far beyond trade in their influence, as the importance of the US-Vietnam migration corridor emphasises.[13] Ideas concerning economic development have also continued to change and the GMS region has been remarkable for the degree to which economic liberalisation has been embraced. This embrace has almost certainly enabled avoidance of some of the worst negative community impacts of the "big bang" approach, although not all.

Recent international meetings (General Agreement on Tariffs and Trade (GATT), World Trade Organization (WTO), and the Doha trade negotiations) have seen trade in goods and services and investment issues side-lined into bilateral and regional agreements, with the consequent problems of higher transaction costs and partial geographical coverage becoming more visible. Migration, which had been a secondary issue under all of these agreements, has recently emerged by virtue of the determination of people to move at any cost. In the current world context, migration, with its corresponding flows of remittances, is seen as the most rapidly growing feature of liberalisation/openness. The global situation is officially summarised by the World Bank Migration and Remittances, *Factbook 2016*. The *Factbook* reports that worldwide remittance flows were in excess of US$601 billion for 2015,[14] with the major recipients being India, China, the Philippines, Mexico, and France. Within the GMS, Vietnam was in eleventh place with US$12.3 billion.[15] The *Factbook* also reveals that Vietnam, Thailand, Cambodia, and Myanmar are all in the top 10 East Asia and Pacific region figures for total remittances. Vietnam received an estimated 6.4 per cent of its gross domestic product (GDP) from this source, and Myanmar 4.8 per cent.[16]

These figures are likely to be under-estimates. Erin Deng's Auckland University Master's thesis suggests that in her sample of 100 Vietnamese construction workers in Kuala Lumpur, none used formal channels to repatriate their remittances.[17] A rough rule of thumb developed by examining a range of such surveys and responses suggests the official figures could be doubled as a general rule. Certainly, official figures are far less than the actual totals, for a variety of reasons that the World Bank sponsored working group, the Luxembourg Group,[18] have explored. Illegal immigration and informal remittance amounts must represent a significant if unknown addition to the official numbers.

Overall, the GMS region has shared developing countries' experience of benefitting from remittance flows as well as the upskilling of migrants and the technical transfer that occurs when they return. John Williamson has said: "People emigrate when they are allowed to and when their expected earnings in their alternative residence compensate for the costs and the deprivation (of family and familiar environment) of moving".[19] It is increasingly the case for a growing number of developing countries that the movement of people and subsequent remittances is likely to be a greater economic force than trade, aid, or foreign direct investment. The termination of aid from the former Soviet Union increased the importance of alternative fund sources for some of the GMS nations. Increasing openness has brought in ideas, including technological and social ones, which have impacted on many aspects of everyday life with multiple links to drivers of economic growth. An eternal search for betterment seems ongoing; the social ramifications include how people perceive themselves and their communities. It is thus not yet clear how globalisation will affect community identification and construction in the GMS.

Internal(?) causes of change

Causes of change internal to the GMS, and the consequences, include the geographical movement of labour and the functional movement of people between occupations. Internal geographical movement is normally within a country, but for current purposes is better conceived as occurring within the GMS at-large. The other five GMS countries are all principal sources of immigrants for Thailand, for example.[20]

Individual decisions to move in search of better opportunities, either within a country or within the region, can in extreme situations, create labour "supply shocks".

Yet, internal causes are often found to be underpinned by external or global factors. Recent Vietnamese policy measures, for example, have emerged from the need to respond to external factors arising from earlier liberalisation decisions. Land use change in Vietnam has responded to commercial opportunity. Rice growing techniques changed significantly in the 20 years prior to the mid-1990s.[21] Pro-market reforms have resulted in much change with some negative outcomes for certain groups.[22] The impact of external ideas and forces on local communities and individuals can be significant. Cropping choice changes as a response to international events can result. The move to cash crops such as coffee is an example. Ideas on management of crop production, people movement, etc. are thus connected to global factors, and, while the change will be regional or domestic, the source will have been a response to within-region interaction with the external world.

From a development perspective, community response is a key factor. The response may be more local in its effect than the original cause. Internal causes can in consequence be viewed as less important as sources of change but more important in terms of the impact and response. The consequential impact on Mekong water availability and the attempts to control this locally, nationally, and regionally is an example.

Regarding functional movement, the availability of non-farm employment opportunities seems to reduce short-term international migration. This is shown by, for example, the case of the rural dweller taking work in the construction or urban service sector during the agricultural slack time. Such an example does not affect the long-term propensity to shift for economic reasons, however.[23] Non-farm activity can assist productivity through increasing seed and livestock quantities, the variety of available services, as well as increasing the use of hired labour to replace the farmer's own.[24] The result is an expansion of employment and output in the farming sector, suggesting that any labour "supply shock" would not be a permanent result.

The question of impacts is significant because many of the internal processes are those of adaptation to the changes inherent in the transition to a more market-oriented economy, as Fforde describes so effectively in his study.[25] One positive impact has been that four of the six countries in the region have seen the poverty headcount significantly reduced in the last 20 years, with Myanmar and Lao PDR being the exceptions.[26] Similarly, the question of food security and crop production can be viewed in the context of adaptation to the world scene as it affects particular country cases. For several decades up to 1990, food output was consistently outstripping population growth. Since 1990 this has been less true, but the recent period of rapid food prices has again tilted the balance in favour of outputs. Increasing openness and ability to obtain food security through market and wage entitlement have led to significant increases in cash crop output and to using non-farm employment opportunities as both a buffer against hard times and a reliever of credit constraints.

More recently, the switch has been made to other crops more suited to giving high market returns, such as fruit or coffee, with generally beneficial results in terms of poverty alleviation. This will be described in the final discussion of the chapter; it is also suggested that adaptation has been beneficial from the economic perspective as shown by the appearance of multi-level governance structures focusing aspects such as the allocation of water.[27]

Outcomes and responses to change

Overall, income levels have risen rapidly in the last 20 years. At the same time, poverty rates have declined. Seasonal migration is claimed to have produced a 5 per cent growth in annualised expenditure during the 1990s, along with a 3 per cent reduction in the poverty headcount.[28] These outcomes of responses to change seem beneficial.

Generally, aggregate incomes have risen at a very fast rate, into double digit percentage terms, from the national-level shifts to a more open policy stance, with incorporation of the competition model and eventual privatisation being significant factors in efforts to reduce transaction costs.[29] The benefits accrue through growth in incomes leading to higher standards of living, better diets, and increasing demand for fresh fruit. All of this leads in turn to increasing opportunities for non-farm occupations as well as development of markets for farm produce. Vulnerability of farming families is reduced by the non-farm income available, particularly when migration with remittance income flow is added.[30] The potential for farmers to take greater risks in crop production is facilitated. All of these factors are drivers of growth – internally migrants move to faster growing areas and extra-regional migrants achieve raised income levels that then raises the sums they remit.

If the aggregate economic impacts are so positive, why should there be concern? Reduction in poverty rates would suggest a satisfactory outcome for many, if not most of the population. However, negative impacts on community development are sometimes seen as offsetting the benefits of growth. This can be shown through discussion of changes in the cropping pattern.

Vietnam has emerged as the world's second largest producer of coffee. The benefits of this are substantial but are not universal in their distribution. A study of Dak Lak Province in Vietnam's Central Highlands suggests that commercial transformation and the "competition for coffee space" has become problematic, revealing markedly different benefits between native and non-native ethnic groups, despite generally larger landholdings amongst the native group.[31]

Winkels' paper on Vietnam also suggests there are problems more directly related to the relationship of the internal to the external.[32] Her research shows that, as Vietnam strove for economic integration with the world economy, the coffee industry grew substantially due to internal migration to the Central Highlands region. While this provided opportunities for improved livelihood, the exposure to risk, and thus insecurity, also increased. Issues such as market fluctuation in coffee prices, decline in environmental quality, and social instability have increased the potential for negative impacts on migrants. Migrants can sometimes draw on their networks, family and social, to manage these challenges. However, reliance on safety nets can increase insecurity for an entire family network, not just an individual household. Crop cultivation shifts due to improved global market opportunities thus are not always straightforwardly beneficial.

Further, increasingly intensive cultivation that produces greater coffee output creates increasing demand for water supply and for improved water quality, thus increasing the number of domestic and regional disputes for the Mekong's waters. A regional approach to Mekong water has recently been developed (see above). Based on a liberalisation philosophy, the approach was intended to strengthen institutional capacity for improved governance. Such a focus accorded with the philosophy of both international finance organisations and many international donors. As Huyen Do[33] describes it: "Vietnam needs to move very, very quickly to get very good management practices in place because of the fact that it doesn't have enough water".[34] One of the institutional measures mobilises (*huy động*) water management market forces, with the government providing supportive legislation for water markets to perform and behave well.

The case of coffee growing in Vietnam illustrates that risks continue to occur alongside development opportunities. However, the severity of the social and environmental negative impacts seems dwarfed by the income benefits which have widely accrued, significantly reducing the poverty headcount ration for the overwhelming majority of people in the GMS. Yet, once again, improved standards of living at the individual, household, and family levels has not assured improved community construction.

Conclusions

Economic growth and openness/globalisation rarely have no effect on social cohesion, whether these impacts are positive or negative. Economic growth is seen here as good in many respects including poverty reduction in an income sense. Simultaneously it is seen as bad by negatively affecting the current distribution situation for some, as compared to the prior situation. The valence, positive or negative, depends on the nature and source of growth and how economic change effects social institutions. The distribution of rights and responsibilities can be altered significantly, affecting the possibilities for community construction.

Social change is a constant feature and looking back to the past as a "golden age" is not useful. We should rather think of the counterfactual and see if the current situation is preferable to the counterfactual, that is, what would the situation be if no change had occurred? With no *doi moi* (economic reforms) in Vietnam would life be better now? The answer is almost certainly not. The same could be said for the GMS in general. If no such opening to global forces had occurred, then any conceivable counterfactual situation would seem less preferable than the gains made from specialisation and exchange of trade, investment, and people that has occurred. The continuing high global levels of illegal migration would support such a conclusion, representing a desire to engage with the world and placing a high priority on personal or family economic advancement.

In this chapter the impacts on communities have been shown to be both positive and negative. The movement of people in search of work is an example; the implications for change for communities can be either good or bad. Similarly, the impact of external ideas and forces on local communities and individuals results in changes that can be beneficial or costly. Most of the time, change is both direct and indirect. Increased flexibility in crop choices (from rice to coffee production) directly creates impacts on Mekong water availability, which indirectly requires water use decisions; this is an example of the connectedness of issues. Economy, community, and government are rarely independent.

Issues such as management of crop production and migration have been discussed in global as well as regional terms. The response by communities has been shown to be adaptive rather than formative. The author's overall assessment is that the economic outcome to date has been positive in the aggregate (as judged best by reduction in poverty counts), although for some this has not been the result. Openness and liberalisation have been shown to impact on individuals, local groups such as small farmers, and communities. Again contemplating the aggregate, it has been difficult to show that community construction (local, national, regional) has been enhanced in

Appendix 4.1 Food Price Index and Cereals Price Index derived from FAO statistics

Year	*Index all food*	*Index all cereals*
2000	91.1	85.8
2001	94.6	86.8
2002	89.6	93.7
2003	97.7	99.2
2004	112.7	107.1
2005	118.0	101.3
2006	127.2	118.9
2007	161.4	163.4
2008	201.4	232.1
2009	160.3	170.2
2010	188.0	179.2
2011	229.9	240.9
2012	213.3	236.1
2013	209.8	219.3
2014	201.8	191.9
2015	164.0	162.4
2016 (April)	151.8	149.8

Food Price Index: Weighted average by trade share of major five food commodity groups: Meat, Dairy, Cereals, Vegetable Oils, and Sugar. Base prices taken from 2002–04 period.
Cereals Price Index: Combines 10 wheat price indices, 1 maize and 16 rice, all calculated to adjust to base period 2002–04. Rice figures are grouped into three main categories Indica, Japonica, and Aromatic varieties. Weighting related to trade levels, so may not reflect domestic market prices exactly.

Source: Derived from FAO Food Price Index (release date 5 May 2019)

any significant way. Whole-region identification, leading to community construction, to date appears limited in its extent. Continuity in rice production suggests the social status quo remains strong: national identities are often weaker than local ones for those living near borders, especially where traditional ethnic groupings cut across national boundaries and particularly where natural features such as the Mekong River create the political demarcation line between nations. Improvement in economic growth and increased consensus by the GMS nations regarding Mekong water rights and use may lead to prosperity but the transfer across to increased community construction cannot be shown to be an expected outcome.

Notes

1 FAO, *World Food Situation*. Rome, September 2019, online at www.fao.org/worldfoodsituation/foodpricesindex/en.
2 FAO, *FAO Rice Price Update.*. Rome, October 2019, online at www.fao.org/economic/est/publications/rice-publications/the-fao-rice-price-update/zh.
3 S. Appa Rao et al., "Naming of traditional rice varieties by farmers in the Lao PDR", *Genetic Resources and Crop Evolution*, Vol. 49, Iss. 1, 2002, pp. 83–8.
4 Suzanne K. Redfern et al., "Rice in Southeast Asia: Facing risks and vulnerabilities to respond to climate change" in Alexandre Meybeck et al. (eds.), *Building Resilience for Adaptation to Climate Change in the Agriculture Sector*, Rome: FAO, 2012, pp. 295–314.
5 Ibid., p. 296.
6 Akiko Horita, "Agrarian change in Vietnam's Northern Upland Region", *Journal of Contemporary Asia*, Vol. 33, No. 1, 2014, pp. 3–28.
7 MRC, "Agreement on the co-operation for the sustainable development of the Mekong River Basin", 1995, pp. 1–2, online at www.mrcmekong.org/assets/Publications/policies/agreement-Apr95.pdf.
8 Ibid.
9 MRC, "Lancang Mekong Cooperation, First Leaders' Meeting", 2016.
10 Edward E. Leamer, "Measures of openness" in Robert E. Baldwin (ed.), *Trade Policy Issues and Empirical Analysis*, Chicago: University of Chicago Press, 1988, pp. 145–204.
11 Lant Pritchett, "Measuring outward orientation in LDCs: Can it be done?" *Journal of Development Economics*, Vol. 49, Iss. 2, pp. 307–35.
12 Kenneth E. Jackson, "Diaspora and development: Technological change as a facilitating and enhancement tool", paper presented at Confronting the Challenge of Technology for Development: Experiences from the BRICS Conference, Oxford University, 29–30 May 2008.
13 World Bank, *Migration and Remittances Factbook 2016*, Washington DC The World Bank, 2016, p. 265.
14 Ibid., p. xii.
15 Ibid., p. 12.
16 Ibid., p. 26.
17 Erin Nguyen Thao Thi Dang, "A glimpse of hope: Migration a catalyst for socio-economic development in Vietnam?" MA thesis, University of Auckland, 2009.
18 World Bank, 2008, op cit., p. xii.
19 John Williamson, *The Open Economy and the World Economy*. New York: Basic Books, 1983, p. xiv footnote 1.
20 World Bank, 2008, op cit., p. 217.
21 K. Tanaka, "Transformation of rice based cropping patterns in the Mekong Delta: From intensification to diversification", *South East Asian Studies*, Vol. 33, No. 3, 1995, pp. 363–78.

22 B. Henin, "Agrarian change in Vietnam's northern upland region", *Journal of Contemporary Asia*, Vol. 33, Iss. 1, 2002, pp. 3–28.
23 N. T. Phuong et al., "Determinant and impacts of migration in Vietnam", DECOPEN *Working Papers Series*, No. 2008/01.
24 M. Stampini and B. Davis, "Does off farm labor relax credit constraints? Evidence from longitudinal data from Vietnam", *IZA Discussion Papers*, No. 3403, 2008.
25 Adam Fforde, *Vietnamese State Industry and the Political Economy of Commercial Renaissance: Dragon's Tooth or Curate's Egg*, Oxford, UK: Chandos, 2007.
26 Sergiy Zorya, "Five facts about poverty in the Greater Mekong Sub-region", *World Bank Blogs*, 15 December 2015, online http://blogs.worldbank.org/eastasiapacific/five-facts-about-rice-and-poverty-in-the-greater-mekong-sub-region.
27 L. Lebel and P. Garden, "Deliberation, negotiation and scale in the governance of water resources in the Mekong region" in C. Pah-Wostl, Pavel Kabat, and Jorn Moltgen (eds.), *Adaptive and Integrated Water Management: Coping with Complexity and Uncertainty*, Berlin; Heidelberg: Springer, 2008, pp. 205–225.
28 A. Brauw and T. Harigaya, "Seasonal migration and improving living standards in Vietnam", *American Agricultural Economics Association*, Vol. 89, Iss. 2, 2007, pp. 430–47.
29 Adam Fforde, op cit., p. 7.
30 X. T. Hoang et al., "Livelihood diversification and rural urban linkages in Vietnam's Red river delta", Food Consumption and Nutrition Division Discussion Paper No. 193, 2005, IFPRI-Washington, DC.
31 S. Doutriaux et al., "Competing for coffee space: Development-induced displacement in the Central Highlands of Vietnam", *Rural Sociology*, Vol. 73, No. 4, 2008, pp. 528–54.
32 A. Winkels, "Rural in-migration and global trade: Managing the risks of coffee farming in the Central Highlands of Vietnam", *Mountain Research and Development*, Vol. 28, No. 1, 2008, pp. 32–40.
33 Huyen Thi Than Do, "When global water policy goes local: Mainstream versus everyday water governance in Vietnam", MA thesis, University of Auckland, 2007.
34 Quoted from an interview done by Huyen Do in Hanoi on 5 December 2007 for the above MA thesis.

5 The Sino-US strategic rivalry in the development of the Mekong

Dinar Swastiningtyas Theosa

Introduction

Since 1992, China has been continuously engaged with the Mekong Subregion through its cross-border infrastructure investment under the Greater Mekong Subregion (GMS) umbrella. Moreover, Beijing's involvement in GMS has been rapidly growing into development partnership schemes, including the ASEAN (Association of Southeast Asian Nations) Mekong Basin Development Cooperation (AMBDC) in 1996 and the China-initiated framework of Lancang-Mekong Cooperation (LMC) in 2014. Alongside China's ever more intensive infrastructure investment in the region is its increasing power presence in the Mekong countries. A case in point is Cambodia, where China's pragmatic policy on regional infrastructure investments adopted in the 1990s has reportedly evolved into its dominant influence on the former's foreign policy preferences within ASEAN.

Meanwhile, Washington's involvement in the Subregional development practices during the Cold War era was largely exemplified by the hydroelectric infrastructure project under the Mekong River Basin Proposal, or Tennessee Valley Authority (TVA) for Southeast Asia. Initiated by the Lyndon Johnson administration in 1965, the TVA model was designed to eradicate poverty and deter Communist influence in the Mekong riparian countries through water resources management in the Mekong Basin.[1] After the loss of the Vietnam War in the late 1970s, however, Washington made few significant efforts to become actively involved in the Mekong Subregion until 2009, when the Obama administration announced its "rebalance to Asia". In accordance with the policy, the US launched the Lower Mekong Initiative (LMI) on 23 July 2009 to re-establish its active presence in the Subregion and its development efforts. Washington's comeback should be seen as a strategic move in the context of power constellation in the region.

This chapter examines how the US and China have characterised their strategic power rivalry in the development of the Mekong and their methods of attaining strategic objectives in the Subregion. The author argues that Beijing has two objectives: accelerating its national economic growth by increasing cross-border infrastructure links and raising its aggressive power status in the Subregion. To a certain extent, Cambodia's continued effort to water down ASEAN's joint position statements on the South China Sea dispute indicates that Beijing has already achieved some degree of success in pursuing its objectives. Washington, on the other hand, engages with the Mekong Subregion to maintain its status quo power and guard against rising power challengers, such as the Soviet Union during the Cold War and China at the present time. To attain its strategic objectives, the US tries to maintain existing norms and institutional linkages with ASEAN and Japan. Geopolitical competition between the two great powers is thus all but inevitable.

In exploring the US-China strategic rivalry in the Mekong Subregion, the chapter first presents the conceptual framework upon which this study is grounded. It then examines the key strategic and institutional measures adopted by Washington and Beijing to achieve their respective goals in the Mekong Subregion. The following section discusses the commitments made by China and the US to accelerate economic development across the Mekong Subregion. The chapter then explores the strategic objectives underlying the commitments and the facilitating roles of ASEAN and Japan.

The Sino-US strategic power rivalry in the Mekong Subregion

Neo-realism assumes that international anarchy shapes world affairs. It thus follows that state to state cooperation should be aimed, first and foremost, at ensuring one's own survival and security. Along this line of reasoning, argues Mearsheimer,[2] "the stronger a state is relative to its potential rivals, the less likely it is that any of those rivals will attack it and threaten its survival". In this regard, a widely adopted indicator of a state's strength is its ability to exert leverage over its potential rivals and to offset their influence. Viewed through the neo-realist lens, strategic competition between great powers like the US and China is both logical and necessary. That nation states strive to keep or gain strategic advantage in and from their interactions, in turn, leads to more strategic rivalries, particularly among great powers.[3]

Wallerstein[4] points out more explicitly that strategic rivalry is part of the inter-state system, which happen recurrently between hegemonic powers or between them and de facto dissatisfied client states. Chan[5] further notes that strategic rivalry is a typical process in which states rise and fall in their international status. It is thus normal for a "rising dissatisfied challenger" to compete with a status quo or declining hegemonic power. Cheng[6] echoes this argument, stressing that status quo and ascending powers likely engage themselves in strategic rivalries because they can afford to do so.

As for what makes a status quo or ascending power, Cheng[7] categorises the former as a first-rank state and the latter as a second-rank country. Similarly, Organski and Kugler[8] define a status quo power as a dominant nation in the world, which is in a superior position to influence the behaviour of other states and shape the world order to its own advantage. Also, a status quo power only wants to share a small portion of its geopolitical opportunities in the existing world order with "newcomers", or ascending power countries. An ascending power, on the other hand, is a status quo challenger. While still less powerful than a dominant country, it ventures to accumulate resources for the day when it can take over its target status quo power. A rising power is generally incentivised to take this path by the belief that a dominant position in world affairs brings unlimited benefits and privileges.

To sum up, a vital national interest for a sovereign country in the international anarchy system guarantees its survival in competitions and contentions among states. A commonly accepted security assurance mechanism in this regard is to build a stronger leverage than potential rivals. Yet in a self-help international system, only status quo states and rising powers can afford to be involved in strategic rivalries for greater influence on the "rules of the game". In the power competition, the status quo power tries to prevent the power transition process from taking place, while the ascending power endeavours to set in motion the process and build its momentum. This is what is going on, particularly in the Mekong Subregion, between the US, the current status quo power, and China, likely its successor.

In fact, the Mekong Subregion has, since the dawn of the Cold War, always been a geopolitical battlefield where great powers tussle for political proxies. While the balance of power seldom remains constant, the current power constellation in the region is subject more to Beijing's influence than that of Washington. This suggests the decline of the US hegemony in Asia and the weakening of US capabilities to counter the rise of China's power and influence in the Subregion.[9]

In responding to China's salient ascent to Subregional leadership, the US tries to maintain its primacy through a rebalance-to-Asia strategy, but at the same time to reduce the risk of open wars that have occurred repeatedly in history between ruling and rising powers.[10] Translating its vision into action, Washington pushes to widen its influence and sustain the established "rules of the game" by "encircling" areas heavily influenced by China.[11] The US counterbalance effort in the Subregion is partially exemplified by the Lower Mekong Initiative launched on 23 July 2009. The objective of this programme is for the US to offset China's economic reach and infrastructure spree in the Mekong region.

China, by contrast, has been seeking the status of an international power since the mid-1990s when it achieved and sustained a near-miraculous growth rate. Not surprisingly, the greater its economic wealth, the more influential China is in the region.[12] Specifically, China tends to use its economic diplomacy to gain greater leverage over others in the region. China's objective is to encourage its neighbours to act in favour of Beijing's rather than Washington's interests in the region.[13] Yet Beijing does not want to engage in a direct confrontation with Washington in the existing US-led-liberal international order. China thus keeps a low profile in its efforts to exert greater regional influence and assume a greater global leadership role, all of which is meant to eventually change the "western-dominated world order".[14] In other words, China's active involvement in regional institutions, such as GMS, AMBDC, and LMC, may serve as a showcase for its important place in regional governance, and in turn provide a sound basis for its major power role on an international scale in the future.[15]

Institutional norms and linkages as strategic means

Finnemore[16] argues that state interests and behaviours are deeply influenced by the socialisation of norms, rules, and political ideas at the international level. Following this logic, it seems only natural that major power states like the US and China try to socialise their own norms as a strategic means to gain greater influence over other states. Once other countries' behaviours are in line with the norms introduced by one or more powerful states, the latter's dominant position is at least indirectly legitimised. Thus, if a state wants to be branded as a dominant power, it needs to be able to establish a set of norms that other states would voluntarily internalise to guide them to behave in a manner that favours its policies and interests.[17]

While their competition for regional and global influence bears out this neo-realist premise, the US and China push for different types of norms as their means to strengthen and sustain their power status. The US, for example, is well-known for its liberal ideals, values, and standards, which inform its perceptions of national interests and decisions on foreign policy. The liberal norms that the US tries to uphold in the international system enshrine the principles of democracy, including the rule of law, self-determination, human rights, open markets, and multi-lateralism.[18] In the context of economic development, Washington supports the promotion and maintenance of the (neo-)liberal global economic order, and at the same time cherishes the concept of sustainability and shares international environmental concerns.[19]

In contrast, China adopts a flexible and pragmatic approach towards many internationally established norms. Westwood and Lok[20] reason that by using this tactic as its state policy, China can readily make a case for why its decisions and actions have to accommodate specific circumstances and expectations for gaining material rewards. In other words, China's flexible pragmatism is intended to be an excusable pursuit of its state goals particularly when its actions fall short of its promises to comply with internationally recognised values and standards. Yoshimatsu[21] points out that, instructed by its pragmatic ethics, China's international commitments are often loaded with concrete calculations of self-benefitting/profiting results and of feasible measures to circumvent inconvenient restrictions.

Besides competing to influence the socio-political norms, standards, and values of the Mekong countries, Washington and Beijing also endeavour to build institutional linkages with organisations and other nations that are heavily involved in Subregional development. As may be expected, the most important partnerships in this regard are those with ASEAN and Japan. One obvious purpose for the US and China to participate in regional initiatives is to reduce the potential for direct conflict. At a more fundamental level, however, they wrestle with each other to incentivise more countries and institutions to internalise their respective prescribed standards and act them out in their decisions. Furthermore, regional cooperation necessitates and hence generates principles, norms, and rules. The contention between Washington and Beijing in the Mekong Subregion is thus also aimed at swaying the development of these "soft laws" so that they may eventually discourage state and institutional players to take unpreferred actions.[22]

Additionally, institutional linkages may serve as a "soft balancing" means for the US and China to reduce the cost of competition and confrontation in their power politics.[23] Kai He[24] further describes building institutional linkages as a "balancing strategy" which is vital in today's world as great powers are, on the one hand, highly interdependent in their economic activities, but, on the other, viciously competing for regional and global influence. The potential for dominance in existing multilateral institutions and the probability of initiating and setting up new ones may thus construct a political space for allied as well as major powers to fight for national competitive advantages at both regional and international levels.

In their application of the institution-linkage tool, the US and China both try to engage with Japan and ASEAN for strategic partnership in their Subregional rivalry and competition. Japan and ASEAN have first and foremost helped China to become an economic superpower. In the case of ASEAN, China became its dialogue partner in 1991, and has since actively worked with the Association to push forward economic integration in Asia, especially regional schemes and arrangements that exclude the US.[25] Sino-Japanese bilateral relations have, on the other hand, been burdened with political ups and downs, the uncertainty of which is often triggered by lingering misconceptions and historical animosity. Despite persistent diplomatic turmoil and tensions, however, Japan remains a crucial strategic partner of China. Beijing has never stopped putting efforts into maintaining effective channels for engagement and negotiations with Tokyo, especially when it comes to launching and aligning regional economic integration initiatives.[26]

By contrast, the U.S.-Japan relations are commonly viewed as being supported by their shared vital interests and democratic values. Washington also attaches particular importance to its bilateral partnership with Tokyo because of the latter's prominent role in the US-Pacific Alliances Network, which always supports and facilitates the US presence in the regions of Asia. It is therefore crucial for the US to be able to count on Japan's full support for its continued standing as a status quo power in the region so as to deter China's increasingly aggressive influence.[27] Besides Japan, Washington has also been proactively strengthening its relations with ASEAN to counterbalance Beijing's growing clout in Southeast Asia.[28] In 2009, for example, the US decided to accede to the ASEAN Treaty of Amity and Cooperation (TAC) as its first institutional linkage with ASEAN.[29]

China's involvement in the development of the Mekong

Deng Xiaoping's "Southern Tour" of China in 1992 reportedly triggered the Chinese action plans for expanding the rapid economic growth from coastal regions to inland and border provinces.[30] This economic adjustment has since seen China becoming ever more committed to connecting its southern border districts with the Mekong Subregion. Its first move was in 1992, when Yunnan Province joined the other five countries in setting up the GMS Economic Cooperation Program under the supervision of the Asian Development Bank (ADB). In 2004, Beijing successfully managed to get its Guangxi Zhuang Autonomous Region, another rural province in South China, included in the GMS framework.

Through Yunnan and Guangxi, China could directly interact with Cambodia, Lao PDR, Myanmar, Thailand, and Vietnam on various cross-border infrastructure projects under the GMS framework.

Not coincidently, a central focus of the GMS framework has been the construction of cross-border transportation networks in the region. Some of the key projects in this regard include the North-South Economic Corridor (NSEC), the East-West Economic Corridor (EWEC), and the Southern Economic Corridor (SEC).[31] Among those completed is the Phnom Penh-Ho Chi Minh City Highway Project approved in 1998 and finished in 2006. This project was largely financed by the ADB which granted Cambodia a low-interest loan of US$40 million and Vietnam one of US$100 million.[32]

In addition to the GMS, China also tries to implement its Mekong strategy through linking up with the AMBDC. Established in 1996, the AMBDC cooperation scheme is also aimed at promoting economic growth by strengthening physical connections within and between the countries involved. Accordingly, the cornerstone of the AMBDC infrastructure project is the Singapore-Kunming Rail Link (SKRL), which also plays a crucially supportive role in the GMS "North-South Economic Corridor" (NSEC). Furthermore, since the AMBDC is composed of 11 member states, 10 ASEAN countries plus China, its cooperation framework has been aimed at attracting continued comprehensive Chinese support for greater integration of physical infrastructure and human capital in the region. The GMS and the AMBDC thus share a common objective of promoting closer interconnections for greater economic growth in their member states.

China of course has its own priorities on its engagement with the GMS and the ASEAN. One of them is to help some of its still underdeveloped rural provinces get out of poverty through tapping their renewable energy sources, and in turn satisfying the country's ever-growing energy demands. Driven by this pragmatic consideration, in 2004 China established the Regional Power Trade Coordination Committee (RPTCC) in Guangxi Autonomous Region, which is under the administration of the GMS Intergovernmental Agreement on Regional Power Trade (IGA) signed in 2002. Beijing meanwhile designated the state-owned China Southern Power Grid Co. (CSG) to participate in the planning and implementation of regionally proposed power trade projects.[33] China's intention was further complemented by the agreement reached at the 5th Meeting of the Planning Working Group (PWG-5) of RPTCC in 2008, which commissioned CSG to take charge of some hydroelectric projects across the Mekong region. These included the Nam Ou Hydropower Station in Laos, the Sambor and Stung Chay Areng Hydropower Projects in Cambodia, and the Ta Sang Hydro-Electric Plant on the Thalwan River in Myanmar.[34]

From a broader prospective, CSG's direct involvement in hydropower projects overseen by the RPTCC provides Beijing with a channel to perform economic diplomacy towards the Mekong countries, which often features the participation of state-owned/backed enterprises and the offering of low-interest loans. These measures facilitate direct economic linkages between recipient states and China, which in return better serve its own domestic development needs.[35] Specifically, to help CSG and other similar companies expand their business in the Mekong Subregion, China has developed the "Build-Own-Operate-Transfer" scheme (BOOT).[36] Participating companies are typically offered financial assistance with the initial development costs of their contracted hydropower projects. A commonly cited reason for this generous offer is that the BOOT scheme requires participating companies to hand over the ownership of what they build to the host countries in 25 years. During the allowed time, however, these Chinese state-backed companies not only operate and maintain hydropower facilities, but also strongly influence regional electricity trade. Carrying such a great clout, they can surely make China a major export destination of hydroelectric energy, which is expected by Beijing in the first place. The Mekong countries for their part seem to welcome this arrangement, primarily because the "generous" scheme makes their own hydro development affordable and therefore achievable. As a result, few in the region are raising the alarm about the potential of becoming overly dependent on China for economic growth. [37]

China's "generous" assistance to the Mekong Subregion, as mentioned earlier, has not been confined to hydro development. Determined to close its rural-urban economic gaps, China has also invested heavily in building an infrastructure network to better connect its border provinces with the Subregion countries and other ASEAN member states.[38] A good case in point is the SKRL Project, which the AMBDC announced in 1995 and has been continuing to highlight since its 7th Ministerial Meeting in 2005.[39] As suggested by its increasingly popular byname, the Pan Asian Railway Network, the SKRL will connect China, Singapore, and all the countries of mainland Southeast Asia. Yet given that the costs have to be shouldered nationally, and given that technological systems vary across the region, the SKRL Project has been progressing slowly. It has also had to battle, virtually from day one, with the near-constant doubt and scepticism about its eventual profitability. Yet China ploughs on. Not only does its investment in the SKRL network across the region continue to grow, but it has finished the construction of the Yuxi-Mengzi segment on its side of the border.[40] Since coming into operation in late 2012, this 141-kilometre train route , has made it much easier and faster to travel between Kunming, the capital city of Yunnan, and the town of Hekou on China's border with Vietnam.

More importantly, Beijing expects that the Kunming to Hekou rail line will help accelerate the development progress of other sections of the SKRL. China's keenness may be explained by the fact that when completed, the rail network will have the northern terminus of all its three main routes in Kunming.[41] Needless to say, the SKRL will allow for freer and greater cross-border movement of people and goods, likely accompanied with growing demand for complementary businesses and services.[42] To a great extent, this is already happening, and China has also begun to reap the rewards of its linkages with ASEAN through the AMBDC.

To maximise its benefits from the Subregion economic integration and infrastructure connectivity, and to minimise uncertainty, Beijing has placed considerable emphasis on the Japan-China Policy Dialogue on the Mekong Region since its first session in 2008. The two leading Asian powers established the platform to discuss their respective concerns on trade, investment, and development in the

Mekong Subregion.[43] The Dialogue, however, has yet to achieve any meaningful collaborative result. In other words, constant diplomatic frictions between the two countries across Asia have rendered it practically impossible for China to score, through the Dialogue, bilateral endorsement of its strategic objectives in the development of the Mekong. Amid the Dialogue, for example, Japan categorised China as a threat in its 2011 Defense White Paper. Then, in 2012, the Tokyo Governor proposed that his prefecture "buy" the Senkaku/Diaoyu Islands. China meanwhile self-announced its establishment of the East China Sea Air Defense Identification Zone (ADIZ) in 2013.[44]

Further complicating the situation, the US launched its Lower Mekong Initiative in July 2009. Whether or not it is meant to balance China's rapidly ascending influence in the development of the Subregion, the Initiative expresses the US's intention to be also involved in infrastructure projects in the Mekong countries. The LMI also envisions a partnership with the region to overcome challenges faced by locals but unattended by Beijing, such as strengthening public health, environmental protection, sustainable energy technologies, implementing good governance, and community building. Yet a more fundamental motivation behind the US "Pivot to Asia" project is to rebalance China's growing leverage in shaping the geopolitical and geoeconomic landscape of Asia.[45]

Not surprisingly, China has not taken the strategic challenge as a stop sign, but strived to meet it with determined but not confrontational responses.[46] Since a key premise of the US "pivot" to the Mekong Subregion is that China's contributions and commitments remain insufficient, China intensified its engagement with ASEAN by creating the Lancang-Mekong Cooperation mechanism in 2015.[47] Under this regional framework, Chinese leaders host regular meetings with their counterparts in the Mekong countries about China's pledged support for and participation in ever more projects in the areas of water resource research/management, physical connectivity, industrial capacity, border trade, agriculture, and poverty alleviation.[48] Since five of its six participating states are also members of ASEAN, the LMC may be viewed as a regional cooperation pillar in parallel with the Southeast Asian Association. Yet, since one of its primary purposes is infrastructure development in the Subregion, the LMC does not hesitate to subscribe to the Master Plan on ASEAN Connectivity (MPAC). China supports the Master Plan particularly because it embraces not only the ASEAN Highway Network, but also the SKRL network as two flagship infrastructure projects. Another pragmatic calculation behind Beijing's approval of the MPAC is that it allows China to carry forward its earlier commitment under the GMS and AMBDC frameworks. Finally, linking up the LMC scheme with the ASEAN Connectivity endeavour may empower the China-sponsored Asian Infrastructure Investment Bank (AIIB) to redraw the regional and global financial maps.

China's objectives and strategies for the development of the Mekong

Between the late 1990s and early 2000s, China began to get seriously involved in the development of transportation infrastructure and trade routes in the Mekong Subregion. Beijing's main purpose then was, as mentioned, to help boost economic growth in its still poverty-stricken Yunnan and Guangxi Provinces by connecting them with the Mekong and other ASEAN countries. Through its involvement in the GMS and AMBDC, China further anticipated Yunnan becoming an economic hub for multilateral trade in goods and services between China and Southeast Asia.[49]

Whether or not China has achieved its goal, its continued massive investment in the Mekong infrastructure connectivity and electrical grid network has surely enabled Beijing to gradually accumulate its influence over the Subregion. A good example in this regard is China's growing economic and political leverage over Cambodia. Beijing began to buy its way in this Mekong country in the mid-1990s when it inked millions of dollars in support of the latter's development. By 2008, US$5.7 billion worth of investment and foreign aid had been channelled from China to Cambodia. In 2008 alone, Beijing's donation to Phnom Penh totalled US$257 million, while the US commitment was US$57 million.[50] The difference in amount resulted in China becoming Cambodia's largest foreign partner particularly in the development of its hydro dams and transportation networks.[51] Among the immediate beneficiaries of Beijing's ascending power were two Chinese government-backed private firms that were contracted in 2013 to kick-start a US$11.2 billion mega-project, consisting of a 400-kilometre rail line, a seaport, and an iron/steel plant.[52] When finished, the rail line will connect the steel facility in the Preah-Vihear Province on Cambodia's northern border to the seaport in the southernmost province, Koh Kong. The improved connectivity will make it much easier to export steel made by Chinese investors in Cambodia back to China and other countries.[53]

China's cooperation with Cambodia in the latter's infrastructure development is, however, aimed not merely to accelerate its own economic growth. Its strategic target is to gradually take control of Cambodia's foreign policy preference so that the latter will not challenge China's position in the South China Sea dispute in regional forums. This indeed happened at the ASEAN Summit and ASEAN Foreign Ministers' Meeting in 2012; Cambodia insisted that the issue of China and the South China Sea dispute should not be discussed in the Association's official assemblies, but addressed at the bilateral level. Cambodia's stance left ASEAN in disarray, as the Philippines and Vietnam, two key territorial claimants in the South China Sea dispute, strongly objected to the Cambodia initiative, and insisted on relevant ASEAN multilateral forums addressing maritime issues in the Asian waters.[54]

ASEAN descended into a similar disarray during the ASEAN-China Foreign Ministers' Meeting in Yunnan in June 2016. Once again, ASEAN countries failed to reach a consensus on the South China Sea territorial dispute.[55] In that episode, Malaysia released a draft ASEAN joint statement immediately after the summit, which stated resolutely that ASEAN "cannot ignore what is happening in the South China Sea". Within a few hours, however, the ASEAN Secretariat issued a recall of that document. It turned out that Cambodia and Laos had withdrawn their endorsement of the joint statement, allegedly under pressure from Beijing.[56]

China's growing influence in Southeast Asia and the resultant disruption of its regional cohesion has prompted the US to take action against Beijing's aggressiveness. First, Washington criticised Beijing's assertive policy in the South China Sea dispute and demanded Beijing abide by the existing Code of Conduct between ASEAN and China.[57] Secondly, the US has, as discussed earlier, launched the LMI which primarily emphasises sustainable development values to undermine Beijing's dealings in the Subregion, especially the Mekong River management. Through initiating the LMI, the US expressed its explicit concerns over China's forceful push for large hydro schemes in Cambodia, with their social, economic, and environmental impacts. There are indeed increasing reports that the hydro dams Chinese companies propose to build will adversely affect the fishing sector and the flood control in Cambodia and across the region.[58]

To help counter the pressure from the US and ease the criticisms of hydro development projects, China has persuaded the Mekong countries to form the LMC and partnered it with ASEAN. Given China's unfavourable position as a rising power in existing multilateral banks led by status quo power alliances, and given that the latter may not be able to address the Subregional infrastructure deficit in the first place, Beijing has also encouraged 60 plus countries to join the AIIB, and has committed the new development bank to finance LMC projects.[59] Through these two mechanisms, China has become an alternative and deep-pocket source of funding and other resources for smaller developing economies in the Mekong region. Yet the more dependent the LMC members become on China's goodwill and generosity for their development, the greater sway Beijing has over their policy decisions, which in turn means a better prospect for China to reap its expected economic and strategic benefits from the many LMC, GMS, and AMBDC hydro and infrastructure projects.

On the operation side, China's pragmatic and flexible approach to the development of the Mekong and cooperation has not only enabled it to leverage its growing economic clout in furthering its objectives, but also suited the economic interests of the riparian states in the region. In other words, so long as a partnership is beneficial to China, Beijing does not have any real problem with, or take objection to the political systems, state ideologies, or domestic decisions made or adopted by the partners involved, be they GMS or AMBDC members. China meanwhile acknowledges that the Mekong countries are at different stages of development, some of which are still in the least developed category. To demonstrate its awareness of the regional development gaps, China has been agreeable and accommodating to the varied levels of readiness of the Mekong countries for GMS projects. This easy-going, but goal-driven position towards partnership and joint ventures in the Subregion surely aligns with the proposal of the 2005 Kunming Declaration.[60]

Consensus-building in decision-making has been instrumental in enhancing solidarity in the Subregion. Coupled with flexibility on, inter alia, timing and participation, this approach, to the largest possible extent, accommodates the different needs and concerns of different members while reflecting the common interests of all. We have managed to build broad-based support for our common development agenda, and above all, for advancing our process at the project-level by conducting thorough consultations and pooling our comparative advantages and strengths.

Beijing follows the same flexible and pragmatic norms in its engagement with ASEAN and Japan on issues related to the development of the Mekong. Its collaboration with ASEAN in the Subregion has been fostered and carried out under the AMBDC mechanism. Put differently, Beijing's rapidly expanding bilateral economic ties with the Mekong states have not only helped China achieve its pragmatic agenda for greater trade and connectivity on mainland Southeast Asia, but have also significantly substantiated its relationship with ASEAN. Beijing's strong institutional linkage with the ASEAN members in the Mekong Subregion is, however, posing a serious threat to the still evolving unity of the Association. As shown in the Cambodia case above, the "ASEAN way", or ASEAN norm of decisions by consensus also works to China's advantage as Beijing can attempt to prevent the organisation from taking collective action against its policy by chipping away at the regional bloc.

In contrast to the China-ASEAN institutional connection, the Beijing-Tokyo linkage remains stuck in the "exploration stage". In other words, China and Japan continue to "dialogue" on the development of the Mekong, and there does not seem to be any concrete action plan in sight. Yet Beijing's pragmatism leads it to continue engaging with Japan in the Mekong Subregion not only because the latter is an important power in Asia, but also because it has a broad knowledge of and rich experiences in the mainland Southeast Asia.[61]

US involvement in the development of the Mekong

US involvement in the development of the Mekong dates back to the years immediately after World War II. Convinced of the close relationship between hydroelectrical development and economic prosperity in the region, Washington openly and loudly voiced its support for the Committee for Coordination of Investigations of the Lower Mekong Basin when it was created in 1957.[62] The US Bureau of Reclamation (USBR) also began a feasibility study of constructing a major hydro dam in Pa Mong on the Thai-Lao border.[63] The research lasted for 12 years at a cost of US$10 million, but the proposed Mekong mainstream hydropower project never proceeded beyond the planning stages.[64]

The uneffectuated Pa Mong project, however, did not deter Washington from its commitment to the development of the Mekong. With the support of President Lyndon Johnson, the USBR proposed in 1965 another and more ambitious project for the lower Mekong region, a Basin-wide network of dams. The Bureau of Reclamation expressly modelled the integrative development scheme on the Tennessee Valley Authority programme and offered about US$2 billion to "transform" the Basin into a "TVA on the Mekong".[65] However, this grand plan did not materialise either, due to its "intractability" both at home and abroad.[66] Among the almost unwieldy challenges for the envisioned "Mekong Valley Authority" was surely the intensification of armed conflicts and political instability across the region.[67] Ultimately, the 1965–73 war in Vietnam dulled, if not altogether wiped out, the US fascination with hydro development programmes in the Mekong region at both bilateral and multilateral levels.[68]

The absence of the US from the Subregion lasted until the mid-1990s when Washington began to re-energise its bilateral relationships with the Mekong countries. It first restored the ambassadorial-level relations with Lao PDR in 1992. It focused the US re-engagement effort primarily on building this small and poor agrarian country's technical and institutional capacity to implement trade agreements, modernising its legal and regulatory framework, advancing its rule of law and civil liberties, and ending its human rights abuses against former US-backed ethnic Hmong insurgents and their families.[69] The post-diplomatic-normalisation decades have seen steady broadening of the bilateral relations between the two countries from accounting for missing US personnel and clearing unexploded ordnance (UXO) in Laos, to cooperation in areas of health, child nutrition, education, English language training, law enforcement and counter-narcotics, environmental protection, and trade liberalisation.[70] The total trade between the US and Laos in 2018 was valued at US$157 million, 23 times higher than the US$6.6 million in 1992.[71] On top of that, the US government has contributed hundreds of millions of dollars to support Laos' UXO clearance, poverty alleviation, and economic development programmes.[72]

A more significant bilateral event for Washington in the Mekong region was perhaps the re-establishment of its formal diplomatic relations with Hanoi in 1995. The two governments signed a sweeping Bilateral Trade Agreement in 2000.[73] Their bilateral trade has grown from US$451 million in 1995 to US$58 billion in 2018.[74] Furthermore, the US and Vietnam formed a Comprehensive Partnership in 2013, which "underscores the enduring U.S. commitment to the Asia-Pacific and provides a mechanism to facilitate" all-round cooperation between the two.[75] The upgrade in bilateral ties has also seen more foreign aid being channelled from Washington to Hanoi, the cumulative total of which since 2001 has amounted to US$1.4 billion.[76]

Yet in maintaining its bilateral relations with the Mekong countries, the US has not only given aid, but also imposed bans, sanctions, and restrictions, often for the stated purpose of advancing human rights and democratic governance in the region. An often-cited example in the latter category is Cambodia. As part of its efforts to push Phnom Penh into restoring democratic institutions and norms, pursuing the rule of law, and increasing civic participation in government decision-making, Washington began instituting in 1998 a recurrent ban on official aid to the government of Cambodia. The sanction remained in effect until 2007 when Washington was convinced that Phnom Penh had begun to make progress on the road to democracy.[77]

A similar story may be told about the evolution of the US-Myanmar bilateral relations. For 25 years after Burma's military leaders refused to recognise the landslide victory of Aung San Suu Kyi's National League for Democracy (NLD) in the 1990 election, US policy towards Myanmar was overshadowed by the reported arrest, detention, prosecution, and imprisonment of political prisoners in that country.[78] Successive administrations in Washington continued taking a hard line against the Burmese government, restricting high-level contacts and refusing to resume any bilateral assistance.[79] The long-standing ban was ended in 2016 when the NLD became the governing party following its triumph in the national election the year before, and Aung San Suu Kyi became the de facto head of the Myanmar state.[80] Yet as suggested by US direct and indirect criticism of the Aung San Suu Kyi government's handling of the 2017 Muslim Rohingya crisis in Myanmar, human rights violation remains a central issue in the relations between the two countries.[81]

While working hard on bilateral relations in the Mekong region between the mid-1990s and the mid-2000s, however, Washington did not commit to multilateral engagement with ASEAN. It was not until the Obama government acceded to the ASEAN Treaty of Amity and Cooperation (TAC) in July 2009 and launched the Lower Mekong Initiative in the same month that the US began to seriously partner up with the Association on regional development. Under the two frameworks, the US has since been supporting the Southeast Asian Association in its effort to narrow the development gaps between ASEAN's six founding members and the four new members in the Mekong region.[82] Washington obviously also hopes that by involving the Mekong and other ASEAN countries, the LMI programme will in return help the US realise its strategic objectives in the Subregion, an important one of which is to balance China's fast-expanding assistance and associated influence.[83]

The focuses of the Washington-led LMI projects and approaches taken are indeed different from those of the Chinese endeavours. While China's multilateral commitments by and large centre on self-serving infrastructure connectivity, the US, the essential status quo power in the world, "hears" the primary concerns of the Mekong countries, which include not only connectivity, but more importantly sustainable water resource management, food and energy security, environment and health, accessibility in education, and gender equality.[84] Thus at the very first LMI Ministerial Meeting in 2009, the US pledged US$147 million to the Subregion's health improvement effort, US$16 million to its educational support, and US$7 million to its sustainable environmental programmes.[85] By 2015, Washington had provided over US$100 million for LMI programmes and projects.[86] Adding to the LMI's environment programmes, the US government facilitated the establishment of a sister river partnership between the Mississippi River Commission and the Mekong River Commission (MRC) in May 2010. The two organisations have since been actively cooperating on strengthening sustainable development and management of the Mekong River.[87]

In responding to the resurgence of Chinese power in the Mekong Subregion, Washington has also been trying to build alternatives to China's ambitious infrastructure development plans.[88] Besides promoting the still "nebulous" "Free and Open Indo-Pacific Strategy",[89] the US also competes with China over involvement in ASEAN's Master Plan on Connectivity. Yet unlike China, its assistance is delivered mainly in the form of technical support, capacity building help, infrastructure improvement for everyday life, and people-to-people connectivity. By doing so, the

US aspires to highlight the LMI's pillar concept, "Smart Infrastructure for Mekong", so as to effectively line up LMI projects with the MPAC connectivity agenda.[90]

To achieve the LMI's mission and vision, the US has set up a mechanism under the Initiative, Friends of the Lower Mekong (FLM), to help coordinate donor contributions and programme development assistance.[91] The key Friends thus far are Australia, South Korea, Japan, New Zealand, the European Union, the ADB, and the World Bank. All these donor Friends share Washington's opinion that the development of the Mekong Subregion should rely on the sustainable management of water and related resources. They applaud the FLM for bringing them together with the five Lower Mekong countries and the Mekong River Commission in 2015 to make their collective commitment to Mekong resilience and sustainability.[92] This pledge is of particular strategic significance because China's dam construction projects have stirred wide regional and international concerns about their impact on the environment and people's livelihoods.

US objectives and strategies for the development of the Mekong

The US involvement in the Mekong Subregion has mostly been driven by its intention to reduce the potential of geopolitical and/or macroeconomic instability arising from ascending powers rivalling ruling powers. This was first shown during the Cold War era, when Washington actively participated in hydro development initiatives in the Mekong River Basin. The US placed great priority on economic and technical assistance to the "backward" countries on the Southeast Asian mainland so as to render them less susceptible to Communist influence.[93] In other words, the US government deemed the prevailing poverty as a principal driver of Communist movements in the region, and hence joined forces with the Mekong Committee to tap water resources for growth and development.[94]

In executing its geopolitical objective of getting involved in the Mekong development efforts, Washington has always stood firm on following the core values of liberal democracy and human rights. To highlight the importance of public participation in decision-making for governance and development of the Mekong River, the US introduced the TVA model in the 1960s. The message coming through was clear: the intended outcomes of the US economic and technical assistance to the riparian countries in the region were multifaceted, impacting their hydropower development, economic growth, social well-being, policy choices, and political orientation. All of that was expected to ultimately help deter the spread of Communism in mainland Southeast Asia that had picked up speed at the end of World War II and the beginning of the Cold War.[95]

Similarly, the US's recent return to the Subregion has been energised by and targeted at the potentially disruptive effects of a rapidly ascending China. Put another way, Washington is becoming progressively more uneasy about the fact that China is not only rapidly filling the vacuum in Southeast Asia left by the US since the ill-fated Vietnam War, but also eroding the leverage commanded by the US, the established global power, over policy choices/decisions of the countries in that region, in particular the poor Mekong riparian nations.[96] Most worrying for the US is that the rapid rise of China may upset the existing balance of power and hence stability of the region.[97] To counter Beijing's growing power, the US has been trying to shift the focus of its attention back towards Asia. In this endeavour, the Mekong Subregion has been chosen as a testing ground for Washington's re-engagement policy,[98] and the LMI initiative has become a key strategic vehicle for opposing China's increasingly assertive economic influence in mainland Southeast Asian countries.[99]

When embarking on the implementation journey, the US strove to confront China's flexible pragmatism with the same democratic values and good governance standards that it previously had pushed to popularise in the region. Washington thus insisted on Myanmar venturing into a democratic transition before it could be welcomed into the LMI. As for Mekong regional development, in 2012 the US announced its Asia-Pacific Strategic Engagement Initiative and "LMI 2020" plan, where it pledged financial support for the Subregional connectivity efforts.[100] Yet it has always attached greater importance to the concept that only sustainable economic growth can effect poverty reduction without compromising the ability of future generations to meet their needs.[101] Putting belief into action, it promotes the Mississippi-Mekong Sister Partnership and speaks up for sustainable water development and management programmes under the framework.[102]

To advance democratic norms and sustainability standards in the Subregion, and to counteract the growing power of China's money in the development of the Mekong, the US vigorously seeks alliance with Japan and ASEAN at large. It sponsors multilateral platforms like the FLM for it to work with Japan and the ADB on building a strong financial reservoir to support LMI programmes and projects. By building institutional linkages with ASEAN, Washington demonstrates its willingness to help restore the unity and cohesion among the Southeast Asian countries. As a ruling status quo nation in the world today, the US does indeed have the responsibility and capability to curtail China's charming but aggressive diplomatic and economic posturing in the Subregion, which has been disrupting the unity of ASEAN, and challenging the sustainability of the development of the Mekong.

Conclusion

Through its active presence in development of the Mekong, China is not only enhancing the potential to boost the economic growth of its lagging border provinces, but also gaining a major power's weight in Subregional affairs.[103] China's rapid ascent in Southeast Asia has prompted the US to re-engage with the region, after more than a two-decade absence, so as to uphold its regional leadership and preserve its strategic standing over the rising dragon.[104] In their growing strategic rivalry, China and the US both endeavour to tilt the balance in their own favour through building up institutional connectivity with established regional organisations, financial joint agencies, and multilateral forums in mainland Southeast Asia, including ASEAN, the MRC, the AMBDC, and the ADB. To ensure against the other assuming a dominant role in the Mekong Subregion and beyond, both countries also seek to team up with another major power in the region, Japan.

China and the US, however, differ considerably in their focuses on, approaches to, objectives of, and core values underlying the development of the Mekong. Another marked, perhaps even greater, difference lies in the fact that China is accelerating its involvement by putting the Lancang-Mekong Cooperation scheme and projects on the fast track portal of the Belt and Road Initiative and the AIIB. Yet if the US "rebalance to Asia" strategy was criticised in the Obama administration's final year for lacking "a clear, coherent, and consistent" narrative about its implementation and purpose,[105] its orientation, and for that matter continuity, seems more unpredictable under the Trump government.[106]

Predictably, the unclear direction of "rebalance" and the "America First" doctrine have generated a great deal of "anxiety" about Washington's "missing Asia strategy" and subsequent diminishing of its "capacity, competence and resolve to retain its position of leadership in the region".[107] Worse yet, there are grave concerns that the "more muscular" and "greater burden-sharing" security policy adopted by the Trump administration in the Asia-Pacific may make its relations with US allies and partners in the region "more volatile".[108] There are particular worries that the "pragmatic" drift in US policy towards Southeast Asia will put the region on "shaky ground" since ASEAN's internal "cleavages" and "limited institutional capacity" make it "unprepared for addressing major shocks or crises". In other words, any "effective regional cooperation" in Southeast Asia "may be difficult to achieve and sustain without consistent American support".[109]

There is certainly hopeful anticipation, however, that President Trump will "end up being more effective" for US-Southeast Asia relations, and hence "mak[e] more inroads" for the US into the region.[110] There are other expectations that he will rebalance more towards "trade, investment and economic relations" with Asia.[111] Some "brave analysts" have further discerned "a grand design" in the Trump government's Indo-Pacific strategy for "greater cooperation between America and Southeast Asian countries, which lies at the 'strategic crossroads'" linking the two regions and connecting the US with Japan, Australia, and India.[112] Yet while the "Indo-Pacific dream" is admittedly positioned as a challenge to the "China dream" in Asia, it has not evolved from a "rhetorical swipe" to explicit policy propositions. Whether this means China is "winning" in Southeast Asia remains an open question, but the answer largely lies with the countries of the region in their struggle to "assert" their own visions of the future.[113]

Notes

1 M. Nakayama, "International collaboration on water systems in Asia and the Pacific: A case of transition", *International Review for Environmental Strategies*, Vol. 3, No. 2, 2002, p. 276.

2 J. Mearsheimer, "Anarchy and the struggle for power" in J. Mearsheimer (ed.), *The Tragedy of Great Power Politics*, New York and London: W.W. Norton & Company, 2001, p. 33.

3 J. Mearsheimer, "Structural realism" in T. Dunne et al., (eds.) *International Relations Theories: Discipline and Diversity*, 3rd Edition, Oxford, UK: Oxford University Press, 2013, pp. 77–9.
4 I. Wallerstein, "Three instances of hegemony in the history of the capitalist world-economy", *International Journal of Comparative Sociology*, Vol. 24, Iss. 1–2, 1983, pp. 100–08.
5 S. Chan, *China, the US and the Power-Transition Theory: A Critique*, New York: Routledge, 2008.
6 J. Y. Cheng, *China's Foreign Policy: Challenges and Prospects*, Singapore: World Scientific Publishing, 2016.
7 Ibid.
8 A. F. K. Organski and Jacek Kugler, *The War Ledger*, Chicago: University of Chicago Press, 1980, pp. 13–24.
9 S. Reich and R. Lebow, *Good-Bye Hegemony!: Power and Influence in the Global System*, Princeton, NJ: Princeton University Press, 2014, p. 3; K. Campbell and B. Andrews, "Explaining the US 'pivot' to Asia", *Americas 2013/01*, London: Chatham House, 2013, p. 2; C. Freise, "By invitation, mostly: The international politics of the US security presence, China, and the South China Sea", *RSIS Working Paper*, No. 247, 2012, p. 3, online at https://www.files.ethz.ch/isn/153028/WP247.pdf; W. Overholt, *Asia, America, and the Transformation of Geopolitics*, Cambridge, UK: Cambridge University Press, 2008, p. 243; T. J. Christensen, "Fostering stability or creating a monster? The rise of China and U.S. policy toward East Asia", *International Security*, Vol. 31, No. 1, 2006, p. 105.
10 H. Meijer, "The reconfiguration of American primacy in world politics: Prospects and challenges for the US rebalance toward Asia" in H. Meijer (ed.), *Origins and Evolution of the US Rebalance toward Asia: Diplomatic, Military, and Economic Dimensions*, New York: Palgrave Macmillan, 2015, p. 7.
11 Z. Xu, "US Policy towards China: Recent trends?" in M. Ghosh et al., (eds.), *US Policy Towards China, India and Japan New Challenges and Prospects*, New Delhi: Atlantic Publishers and Distributors, 2013, pp.: 111–12; A. I. Johnston, "Is China a status quo power?" *International Security*, Vol. 27, No. 4, 2003, p. 9; A. F. K. Organski and Jacek Kugler, op cit., pp. 19–21.
12 J. Y. Cheng, 2016, op cit., pp. 139, 156, 184.
13 A. L. Friedberg, *A Contest for Supremacy: China, America, and the Struggle for Mastery in Asia*, New York and London: W.W. Norton & Company, 2011, p. 200.
14 Y. Deng, *China's Struggle for Status: The Realignment of International Relations*, Cambridge, UK and New York: Cambridge University Press, 2008, p. 54.
15 J. Y. Cheng, 2016, op cit., pp. 14, 35, 187.
16 M. Finnemore, "Norms, culture, and world politics: Insights from sociology's institutionalism", *International Organization*, Vol. 50, No. 2, 1996, pp. 325–47.
17 G. John Ikenberry and Charles A. Kupchan. "Socialization and hegemonic power", *International Organization*, Vol. 44, No. 3, 1990, p. 283.
18 G. John Ikenberry, "Culture and foreign policy: The American liberal tradition and global order building" in Jing Huang (ed.), *The Impact of National Cultures on Foreign Policy Making in a Multipolar World* (forthcoming), pp. 1, 6, 7, 9, online at https://scholar.princeton.edu/sites/default/files/gji3/files/ikenberry-berlin-paper-culture-foreign-policy-oct-2014-2.pdf.
19 S. Bernstein, "Liberal environmentalism and global environmental governance", *Global Environmental Politics*, Vol. 2, No. 3, 2002, p. 1; Timothy Doyle, "Sustainable development and Agenda 21: The secular bible of global free markets and pluralist democracy", *Third World Quarterly*, Vol. 19, Iss. 4, 1998, p. 771.
20 R. Westwood and P. Lok, "The meaning of work in Chinese contexts: A comparative study", *International Journal of Cross Cultural Management*, Vol. 3, Iss. 2, 2003, pp. 139–65.

21 H. Yoshimatsu, "The United States, China, and geopolitics in the Mekong Region", *Asian Affairs: An American Review*, Vol. 42, Iss. 4, 2015, p. 180.
22 R. O. Keohane, "Twenty years of institutional liberalism", *International Relations*, Vol. 26, Iss. 2, 2012, p. 128; R. O. Keohane, "Cooperation and international regimes" in R. Keohane (ed.), *After Hegemony: Cooperation and Discord in the World Political Economy*, Princeton, NJ: Princeton University Press, 1984, p. 59.
23 J. D. Ciorciari, "The balance of great-power influence in contemporary Southeast Asia", *International Relations of the Asia-Pacific*, Vol. 9, No. 1, 2009, pp. 157–96.
24 Kai He, "Contested Multilateralism 2.0 and regional order transition: Causes and implications", *The Pacific Review*, 2018, online at https://www.tandfonline.com/doi/full/10.1080/09512748.2018.1465455.
25 J. Y. Cheng, 2016, op cit., pp. 110, 124.
26 Ibid., pp. 302–3.
27 P. D. Miller, *American Power & Liberal Order: Conservative Internationalist Grand Strategy*, Washington, DC: Georgetown University Press, 2016, pp. 170–1.
28 C. C. Kuik et al., "The China factor in the U.S. 'Reengagement' with Southeast Asia: Drivers and limits of converged hedging", *Asian Politics & Policy*, Vol. 4, Iss. 3, 2012, p. 322; M. Manyin et al., "U.S. accession to the Association of Southeast Asian Nations' Treaty of Amity and Cooperation (TAC)", *CRS Report for Congress*, 13 July 2009, p. 4, online at https://fas.org/sgp/crs/row/R40583.pdf.
29 M. Manyin et al., op cit. p. 2.
30 S. Ho, "River politics: China's policies in the Mekong and the Brahmaputra in comparative perspective", *Journal of Contemporary China*, Vol. 23, Iss. 85, 2014, pp. 16–7.
31 T. Ogasawara, "Emergence of Greater Mekong Subregion: Its impact on ASEAN regional integration", 山梨学院大学法学論集 [Yamanashi Gakuin University Law Review], Vol. 68, 2011, p. 454, online at file:///C:/Users/xche011/AppData/Local/Packages/Microsoft.MicrosoftEdge_8wekyb3d8bbwe/TempState/Downloads/KJ00007324719%20(1).pdf.
32 M. Vachon, "Phnom Penh-Ho Chi Minh City Highway Project gets VIP visit", *Cambodia Daily*, 31 July 2001, online at https://www.cambodiadaily.com/archives/phnom-penh-ho-chi-minh-city-highway-project-gets-vip%E2%80%88visit-24773.
33 Asian Development Bank, *Greater Mekong Subregion First Meeting of the Regional Power Trade Coordination Committee (RPTCC-1): Summary of Proceedings*, July 2004, online at https://www.adb.org/sites/default/files/publication/29597/gms-rptcc1.pdf.
34 Asian Development Bank, *Summary of Discussions Fifth Meeting of the Planning Working Group (PWG-5) of the Regional Power Trade Coordination Committee (RPTCC)*, June 2008, pp. Appendix 4, online at https://www.adb.org/sites/default/files/publication/29596/gms-pwg5.pdf.
35 T. Lum, "China's assistance and government-sponsored investment activities in Africa, Latin America, and Southeast Asia", *CRS Report for Congress*, 25 November 2009, pp. 1–3, online at https://fas.org/sgp/crs/row/R40940.pdf.
36 The BOOT model refers to business contracts between private entities and government agencies to build up public infrastructure assets. Following this model, private entities may own and operate the assets that they are contracted to construct for a defined period of time. They will then transfer the assets to the entitled government agencies. For details of BOOT, see Brian Donaghue, "Statistical treatment of 'Build-Own-Operate-Transfer' Schemes", *IMF Working Paper* WP02/167, October 2002, pp. 1–2, online at https://www.imf.org/en/Publications/WP/Issues/2016/12/30/Statistical-Treatment-of-Build-Own-Operate-TransferL2306-Schemes-16067.
37 R. P. Cronin, "China's activities in Southeast Asia and the implications for U.S. interests", Testimony before the US-China Economic and Security Review Commission, 4 February, 2010, on line at https://www.stimson.org/sites/default/files/file-attachments/USCC_Hearing_statement_Cronin_2_03_2010_FINAL.pdf.

38 *People's Daily*, "The 10th Five-Year Plan", n.d., online at http://en.people.cn/data/China_in_brief/Economy/The%2010th%20Five-Year%20Plan.html.

39 Association of Southeast Asian Nations, *ASEAN Annual Report 2007–2008: One Vision, One Identity, One Community*, Jakarta: ASEAN Secretariat, 2008, p. 21, online at www.iri.edu.ar/publicaciones_iri/anuario/Anuario%202009/Asia/documentos/Association%20of%20Southeast%20Asian%20Nation%20-%20%20Annual%20Report%202007-2008.pdf.

40 N. Kurian, *India-China Borderlands: Conversations beyond the Centre*, New Delhi: SAGE Publications India Pvt Ltd, 2014, pp. 68–70.

41 C. Horton, "Yuxi-Mengzi railroad to be operational this year", *GoKunming: A New Perspective*, 30 January 2012, online at https://www.gokunming.com/en/blog/item/2567/yuxi_mengzi_railroad_to_be_operational_this_year; Asian Development Bank, *Technical Assistance to the People's Republic of China for Preparing the Railway Development Project*, 2005, online at https://www.adb.org/sites/default/files/project-document/69089/tar-prc-39153.pdf, p. 3.

42 Asian Development Bank, 2005, op cit., p. 6.

43 Ministry of Foreign Affairs of Japan, "The first Japan-China Policy Dialogue on the Mekong Region", 22 April 2008, online at www.mofa.go.jp/announce/event/2008/4/1179410_932.html.

44 Ministry of Foreign Affairs of Japan, "Statement by the Minister for Foreign Affairs on the announcement on the 'East China Sea Air Defense Identification Zone' by the Ministry of National Defense of the People's Republic of China", 24 November 2013, online at www.mofa.go.jp/press/release/press4e_000098.html.

45 K. Campbell and B. Andrews, op cit., p. 2; C. Freise, op cit., p. 3; T. J. Christensen, op cit., p. 105.

46 F. Zhang, "Challenge accepted: China's response to the US rebalance to the Asia-Pacific", *Security Challenges*, Vol. 12, No. 3, 2016, p. 45.

47 Ministry of Foreign Affairs of the People's Republic of China, "Sanya Declaration of the First Lancang-Mekong Cooperation (LMC) Leaders' Meeting: For a community of shared future of peace and prosperity among Lancang-Mekong Countries", 23 March 2016, online at www.fmprc.gov.cn/mfa_eng/wjdt_665385/2649_665393/t1350039.shtml.

48 L. Zhou, "Five things to know about the Lancang-Mekong Cooperation summit", *South China Morning Post*, 9 January 2018, online at www.scmp.com/news/china/diplomacy-defence/article/2127387/five-things-know-about-lancang-mekong-cooperation.

49 S. Ho, op cit., pp. 16–7.

50 T. Bradley, "China's Cambodian hegemony", *The Diplomat*, 7 May 2009, online at http://thediplomat.com/2009/05/chinas-cambodian-hegemony.

51 H. S. Toh, "Controversial Chinese projects in Cambodia bow to public pressure", *South China Morning Post*, 3 September 2011, online at www.scmp.com/article/977985/controversial-chinese-projects-cambodia-bow-public-pressure.

52 C. T. Prak, "Chinese firm plans $11 bln rail, port, steel projects in Cambodia", *Reuters*, 2 January 2013, online at www.reuters.com/article/cambodia-china-investment-idUSL4N0A71JL20130102.

53 Reuters, "Chinese companies to invest billions on Cambodia projects", *The New York Times*, 3 January 2013, online at www.nytimes.com/2013/01/04/business/global/chinese-companies-to-invest-billions-on-cambodia-projects.htm.

54 C. A. Thayer, "ASEAN, China and the Code of Conduct in the South China Sea", *SAIS Review of International Affairs*, Vol. 33, No. 2, 2013, p. 78.

55 P. Wen, "South China Sea: ASEAN ministers retract joint statement on dispute – but why remains mystery", *The Sydney Morning Herald*, 15 June 2016, online at https://www.smh.com.au/world/south-china-sea-asean-ministers-retract-joint-statement-on-dispute–but-why-remains-mystery-20160615-gpje10.html.

56 Kyodo Staff Report, "China's insistence on bilateral territorial talks behind ASEAN roadblock", *The Japan Times*, 19 June 2016, online at www.japantimes.co.jp/news/2016/06/19/asia-pacific/chinas-insistence-bilateral-territorial-talks-behind-asean-roadblock-sources-say/#.WSbSuLSXwlJ.

57 M. Taylor Fravel, "U.S. policy towards the disputes in the South China Sea since 1995", *Policy Report*. Singapore: S. Rajaratnam School of International Studies, 2014, pp. 1–2, online at https://www.rsis.edu.sg/wp-content/uploads/2014/11/PR140330_US_Policy_Towards_Disputes.pdf.

58 H. S. Toh, op cit; International Rivers, "Lancang River dams: Threatening the flow of the Lower Mekong". *International Rivers*, August 2013, online at https://www.internationalrivers.org/sites/default/files/attached-files/ir_lacang_dams_2013_5.pdf.

59 H. K. Park, "AIIB can fill infrastructure gap", *The Korean Times*, 12 June 2017, online at www.koreatimes.co.kr/www/biz/2017/06/488_231036.html.

60 Ministry of Foreign Affairs of the People's Republic of China, "Kunming Declaration: A stronger GMS partnership for common prosperity", 5 July 2005, online at www.fmprc.gov.cn/mfa_eng/topics_665678/dmghcqydecldrhi_665836/t202381.shtml.

61 Phuong Nguyen, "Washington needs a new approach to the Lower Mekong – 'the Next South China Sea'", *Southeast Asia from Scott Circle Newsletter*, Vol. 5, Iss. 8, 17 April 2014, p. 3, online at https://csis-prod.s3.amazonaws.com/s3fs-public/legacy_files/files/publication/140417_SoutheastAsia_Vol_5_Issue_8.pdf.

62 B. Over, "The true intentions behind the Lower Mekong Initiative: American involvement in the field of water management in Southeast Asia placed in historical perspective". MA thesis, Universiteit Utrecht, The Netherlands, 24 January 2017, pp. 10–12, online at https://dspace.library.uu.nl/bitstream/handle/1874/347610/The%20true%20intentions%20behind%20the%20Lower%20Mekong%20Initiative.pdf?sequence=2.

63 F. K. Chang, "The Lower Mekong Initiative & U.S. foreign policy in Southeast Asia: Energy, environment & power", *Orbis*, Vol. 57, No. 2, 2013, p. 291.

64 C. Sneddon and C. Fox, "Water, geopolitics, and economic development in the conceptualization of a region", *Eurasian Geography and Economics*, Vol. 53, Iss. 1, 2012, p. 148.

65 P. O. Cohrs, "Towards a new deal for the world? Lyndon Johnson's aspirations to review the twentieth century's Pax Americana" in F. J. Gravin and M. A. Lawrence (eds.), *Beyond the Cold War: Lyndon Johnson and the New Global Challenges of the 1960s*, Oxford, UK: Oxford University Press, 2014, pp. 58–61; D. Ekbladh, "'Mr. TVA': Grass-roots development, David Lilienthal, and the rise and fall of the Tennessee Valley Authority as a symbol for U.S. overseas development, 1933–1973", *Diplomatic History*, Vol. 26, Iss. 3, 2002, p. 363.

66 C. Sneddon and C. Fox, op cit. p. 148; D. Ekbladh, op cit., p. 337.

67 J. W. Jacobs, "The Mekong River Commission: Transboundary water resources planning and regional security", *The Geographical Journal*, Vol. 168, Iss. 4, 2002, p. 358; M. Schaller, "TVA on the Mekong: LBJ, the New Deal, and the tragedy of Vietnam" (book review), *Reviews in American History*, Vol. 24, No. 4, 1996, p. 692.

68 F. K. Chang, op cit., p. 291.

69 T. Lum, "Laos: Background and U.S. relations", *CRS Report for Congress*, Washington, DC: Congressional Research Service, 2010, online at https://fas.org/sgp/crs/row/RL34320.pdf.

70 US Department of State, "U.S. relations with Laos", *Bureau of East Asian and Pacific Affairs Fact Sheet* (website), Washington, DC: US Department of State, 13 December 2016, online at https://www.state.gov/r/pa/ei/bgn/2770.htm.2016.

71 US Census Bureau, "Trade in goods with Laos", *Foreign Trade* (website), Washington, DC: US Census Bureau, 2018, online at https://www.census.gov/foreign-trade/balance/c5530.html.

72 USAID, "White House Fact Sheet: U.S.-Laos relations", *News and Information* (website), Washington, DC: USAID, 2017, online at https://www.usaid.gov/laos/fact-sheets/sep-2016-white-house-fact-sheet-us-laos-relations.
73 M. Manyin, "U.S. assistance to Vietnam", *CRS Report for Congress*, Washington, DC: Congressional Research Service, 2005, p. 1.
74 US Census Bureau, "Trade in goods with Vietnam", *Foreign Trade* (website), Washington, DC: US Census Bureau, 2018, online at https://www.census.gov/foreign-trade/balance/c5520.html.
75 US Department of State, "U.S. relations with Vietnam", *Bureau of East Asian and Pacific Affairs Fact Sheet* (website), Washington, DC: US Department of State, 11 December 2017, online at https://www.state.gov/r/pa/ei/bgn/4130.htm.
76 USAID, "U.S. foreign aid by country – Vietnam", Washington, DC: USAID, 2018, online at https://explorer.usaid.gov/cd/VNM?fiscal_year=2018&measure=Obligations.
77 T. Lum, "Cambodia: Background and U.S. relations in brief", *CRS Report for Congress*, Washington, DC.: Congressional Research Service, 14 December 2018, online at https://fas.org/sgp/crs/row/R44037.pdf.
78 M. F. Martin, "Burma's political prisoners and U.S. policy: In brief", *CRS Report for Congress*, Washington, DC: Congressional Research Service, 24 September 2018, online at https://fas.org/sgp/crs/row/R44804.pdf.
79 B. Xu and E. Albert, "Understanding Myanmar", *CFR Backgrounder* (website), New York: Council on Foreign Relations, 25 March 2016, online at https://www.cfr.org/backgrounder/understanding-myanmar; L. Niksch, "Burma-U.S. relations", *CRS Report for Congress*, Washington, DC: Congressional Research Service, 4 October 2007, pp. 3–4.
80 G. Harris, "Obama lifts some sanctions against Myanmar", *The New York Times*, 3 December 2016, p A8.
81 Z. Barany, "Where Myanmar went wrong: From democratic awakening to ethnic cleansing", *Foreign Affairs*, May/June 2018, online at https://www.foreignaffairs.com/articles/burma-myanmar/2018-04-16/where-myanmar-went-wrong.
82 White House, "Joint Statement on the ASEAN-U.S. Strategic Partnership 2015", *Statements and Releases* (website), Washington, DC: White House, 21 November 2015, online at https://obamawhitehouse.archives.gov/the-press-office/2015/11/21/joint-statement-asean-us-strategic-partnership.
83 E. Z. Bower, "U.S. moves to strengthen ASEAN by boosting the Lower Mekong Initiative", CSIS *Commentary* (website), Washington, DC: Center for Strategic and International Studies, 24 July 2012, online at https://www.csis.org/analysis/us-moves-strengthen-asean-boosting-lower-mekong-initiative.
84 S. Charles, "Mekong states to close the development gap", *Khmer Times*, 20 October 2016, online at https://www.khmertimeskh.com/news/31043/mekong-states-to-close-the-development-gap.
85 V. Chheang, "Environmental and economic cooperation in the Mekong region", *Asia-Europe Journal*, Vol. 8, No. 3, 2010, p. 363.
86 US Department of State, "Lower Mekong Initiative FAQs", Washington, DC: US Department of State, 2015, online at https://2009-2017.state.gov/p/eap/mekong/faq/index.htm.
87 Mekong River Commission, "Mekong and Mississippi River Commissions strengthen its partnership", *MRC News* (website), Vientiane: Mekong River Commission, 16 January 2017, online at www.mrcmekong.org/news-and-events/news/mekong-and-mississippi-river-commissions-strengthen-its-partnership.
88 T. Pongsudhirak, "Where ASEAN meets Southeast Asia: Policy implications for post-Obama America" in Asia Foundation (ed.), *Asian Views on America's Role in Asia: The Future of the Rebalance*, San Francisco, CA: Asia Foundation, 2016, pp. 13–24.

89 M. J. Valencia, "What does a 'free and open Indo-Pacific' actually mean?" *The Diplomat*, 30 March 2018, online at https://thediplomat.com/2018/03/what-does-a-free-and-open-indo-pacific-actually-mean.

90 USAID, "Smart infrastructure for the Mekong", USAID *Fact Sheets* (website), Washington, DC: USAID, August 2014, online at https://www.usaid.gov/sites/default/files/documents/1861/Smart_Infrastructure_for_the_Mekong.pdf; US Department of State, "Sixth Ministerial Meeting of the Lower Mekong Initiative Joint Ministerial Statement", Office of the Spokesperson *Media Note* (website), Washington, DC: US Department of State, 1 July 2013, online at https://2009-2017.state.gov/r/pa/prs/ps/2013/07/211394.htm.

91 USAID, "Lower Mekong Initiative: Friends of the Lower Mekong", USAID *Friends of the Lower Mekong Factsheet* (website), Washington, DC: USAID, June 2013, online at https://www.usaid.gov/sites/default/files/documents/1861/FLM%20Factsheet%20June%202013.pdf.

92 Lower Mekong Initiative, "Extraordinary friends of the Lower Mekong: Conference on Mekong Sustainability, Summary of Joint Discussion", 3 February 2015, online at https://www.lowermekong.org/news/extraordinary-friends-lower-mekong-conference-mekong-sustainability-summary-joint-discussion.

93 C. Sneddon, "The 'sinew of development': Cold War geopolitics technical expertise, and water resource development in Southeast Asia, 1954–1975", *Social Studies of Science*, Vol. 42, Iss. 4, 2012, pp. 571–9.

94 M. Nakayama, op cit., p. 276.

95 D. Ekbladh, op cit., pp. 336–7.

96 R. Mishra, "The US rebalancing strategy: Responses from Southeast Asia" in S. D. Muni and V. Shadha (eds.), *Asian Strategic Review*, New Delhi: Pantagon Press, 2014, p. 149; C. C. Kuik et al., op cit., pp. 322–3.

97 Ely Ratner, "Rebalancing to Asia with an insecure China", *The Washington Quarterly*, Vol. 36, Iss. 2, 2013, pp. 21, 34; M. Manyin et al., op cit., p. 8.

98 R. P. Cronin and T. Hamlin, *Mekong Turning Point: Shared River for a Shared Future*. Washington, DC: The Henry L. Stimson Center, 2012, p. 49.

99 H. Yoshimatsu, op cit., pp. 181–5; F. K. Chang, op cit., pp. 295–6; R. P. Cronin and T. Hamlin, op cit., p. 151; US-China Economic and Security Review Commission, *Hearing: China's Activities in Southeast Asia and the Implication for U.S. Interests*, Washington, DC: US -China Economic and Security Review Commission, 2010, pp. 140–7, online at https://www.uscc.gov/sites/default/files/transcripts/2.4.10HearingTranscript.pdf.

100 US Department of State, "Asia-Pacific Strategic Engagement Initiative", Office of the Spokesperson *Media Note* (website), Washington, D.C.: US Department of State, 13 July 2012, online at https://2009-2017.state.gov/r/pa/prs/ps/2012/07/194960.htm.

101 J. F. Kerry, "From a swift boat to a sustainable Mekong", *Foreign Policy*, 2 February 2015, online at http://foreignpolicy.com/2015/02/02/from-a-swift-boat-to-a-sustainable-mekong.

102 T. L. Cosslett and P. D. Cosslett, *Sustainable Development of Rice and Water Resources in Mainland Southeast Asia and Mekong River Basin*, Singapore: Springer, 2017, p. 134.

103 J. Y. S. Cheng, "China-ASEAN economic co-operation and the role of provinces", *Journal of Contemporary Asia*, Vol. 43, Iss. 2, 2013, pp. 317–26.

104 M. Lumbers, "Whither the pivot? Alternative U.S. strategies for responding to China's rise", *Comparative Strategy*, Vol. 34, No. 4, 2015, p. 312.

105 M. J. Green and K. H. Hicks, "Revving up the rebalance to Asia", CSIS *Commentary* (website), Washington, DC: Center for Strategic and International Studies, 26 January 2016, online at https://www.csis.org/analysis/revving-rebalance-asia; G. Webster, "Asia pivot: Does the US need to 'rebalance harder'?" *The Diplomat*, 29 January 2016,

online at https://thediplomat.com/2016/01/asia-pivot-does-the-us-need-to-balance-harder.

106 P. Cullen, "The rebalance to Asia under Trump: What comes next?" *The RUSI Journal*, Vol. 162, Iss. 2, 2017, p. 8.

107 T. Huxley and B. Schreer, "Trump's missing Asia strategy", *Survival*, Vol. 59, Iss. 3, 2017, pp. 81–4.

108 MAREX, "More volatility expected between U.S. and Asia", *The Maritime Executive*, 15 March 2017, online at https://www.maritime-executive.com/editorials/more-volatility-expected-between-us-and-asia#gs.6PokROE.

109 J. I. Chong, "Deconstructing order in Southeast Asia in the age of Trump", *Contemporary Southeast Asia*, Vol. 39, No. 1, 2017, pp. 29–31; R. Sutter, "Trump and China: Implications for Southeast Asia", *East Asia Forum*, 3 July 2017, online at www.eastasiaforum.org/2017/07/03/trump-and-china-implications-for-southeast-asia.

110 T. Pongsudhirak, "Trump's pragmatic pivot back to Asia", *The Straits Times*, 6 June 2017, online at https://www.straitstimes.com/opinion/trumps-pragmatic-pivot-back-to-asia.

111 S. Limaye, "Trump in Asia: A 'rebalance' toward trade", *NPR News*, 13 November 2017, online at https://www.npr.org/sections/parallels/2017/11/13/563722510/trump-in-asia-a-rebalance-toward-trade.

112 B. Garekar, "One year of Trump: Trepidation, then relief for Asia", *The Straits Times*, 21 January 2018, online at https://www.straitstimes.com/world/united-states/one-year-of-trump-trepidation-then-relief-for-asia; B. Kausikan, "Dodging and hedging in Southeast Asia", *The American Interest*, Vol. 12, No. 5, 2017, p. 2.

113 R. Doshi, "Trump's 'Indo-Pacific dream' stumbles – but China alone won't fill the void", *War on the Rocks*, 15 November 2017, online at https://warontherocks.com/2017/11/trumps-indo-pacific-dream-stumbles-china-alone-wont-fill-void.

6 Regional cooperation through the Greater Mekong Subregion programme

Focus on hydropower development and the Mekong power grid

Nayeon Shin, Seungho Lee and Ilpyo Hong

Introduction

According to a report jointly done by a consortium of institutions led by the United Nations (UN) Environment Programme (UNEP) and the DHI Centre for Water and Environment in 2016, the world, as of today, has 286 transboundary river basins that span over 151 countries.[1] To address cross-border water issues and to improve the governance of integrated water resources, the UN member countries signed, as far back as 1997, the Convention on the Law of the Non-Navigational Uses of International Watercourses.[2] In 2015, the UN further specified the Sustainable Development Goal No. 6.5 to guide cross-border water management and cooperation.[3] It was against this backdrop that, in 1992, the Asian Development Bank (ADB) launched the Greater Mekong Subregion (GMS) programme, which was followed by the establishment of the Mekong River Commission (MRC) in 1995. The MRC has since served as a vehicle for the six Subregional states to cooperate in growing their economies and reducing their poverty rates. Yet the MRC has also shown its limitations in tackling conflicting interests, and even in securing full participation of all its member countries. The engagement and cohesion deficit has seriously curtailed the mandate of the MRC as a regional organisation in mediating potential conflicts in the Mekong River Basin.

Nevertheless, the GMS programme has been regarded as successful in terms of getting all the Subregional countries on board. The GMS programme has also been commended for its resolution to embrace a poverty-reduction agenda and for its attempt to improve socio-economic development in sectors closely related to growth and well-being. In this regard, the GMS programme is applauded for having contributed to and facilitated investments in region-wide hydropower development and transportation improvement. The construction of the Mekong Power Grid is considered of particular importance as it enables cross-border energy trade, which helps to significantly ease the pressure of the soaring demands of electrification in the Subregion. Meanwhile, hydroelectricity trade brings multifaceted benefits to all the Mekong riparian countries.

The purpose of this chapter is to investigate the extent to which the GMS programme has enabled China, Myanmar, Lao PDR, Thailand, Cambodia, and Vietnam to secure the envisioned socio-economic benefits from their cooperation. Special attention will be devoted to hydropower development in the Subregion and the growth of the Mekong Power Grid. The development evaluation and outcome assessment included in this chapter will be founded on the theoretical framework of benefit sharing. Structure-wise, the chapter consists of six sections. Following the introduction is a brief review of academic research on the Mekong River Basin, with a focus on the benefit-sharing concept and approach. The third section will provide an overview of the Mekong River Basin, in particular issues related to Subregional politics, socio-economic development, and environmental sustainability. Section four will elaborate on the GMS programme and hydropower development in the Subregion and the function of Mekong Power Grid. Section five will examine the overall achievements and challenges in the operation of the GMS programme.

Transboundary waters and benefit sharing

Issues and studies

According to the UN's Environment Freshwater Strategy 2017–21, increasing efforts will be made and more measures rolled out to address the ever more pressing challenges facing the management of transboundary river basins.[4] Meanwhile, the Global Environment Facility (GEF) and the UNEP step up their support for the Transboundary Waters Assessment Programme in the latter's effort to provide a regular "baseline assessment of all the planet's transboundary water resources".[5] The indicator-based assessment, in general, not only identifies and evaluates at-risk water bodies, but, more importantly, signifies the integrated nature of risk and hence the need for joint and coordinated governance in order to effectively sustain ecosystem health and human well-being.[6]

Meanwhile, the complexity of human and natural impacts on transboundary rivers and lakes and the intricacy of shared resource conflicts and management have also attracted considerable scholarly and policy attention. Concerned academics and experts have been studying virtually all the critical issues related to transboundary water security, sustainable socio-economic development, equitable access to safe drinking water, and adequate sanitation facilities. Reflecting the complicated nature of shared use, governance, and protection of cross-border waters, their analytical approaches vary, drawing from such disciplines as environmental science, economics, politics, and security studies. Yet they all reference relevant UN resolutions to substantiate their arguments and justify their proposed policy choices and action plans. Moreover, they all echo the UN's consistent message that security, safety, and sustainability of shared water resources are matters of human rights. They further subscribe to the UN's persuasion that regional cooperation is essential for creating trust and collective visions among relevant riparian countries on allocation, exploitation, conservation, and management of their shared water resources.[7] Not surprisingly, one often cited case in these studies is the Mekong River, in the process of which the Subregion has also been scrutinised on every key issue and challenge arising from transboundary waters.

Han Li,[8] for example, identifies and examines major geographical, sociographical, and physical factors of urban expansions in the Mekong River Basin and their impact on changes and development of political, economic, and social systems in the countries of the region. Susanne Schmeier[9] discusses potential cooperation in the Subregion for resource dispute mitigation and sustainable development by assessing the institutional evolution and polycentric politics of the MRC and the GMS. Choi and Lee[10] investigate whether China's hydro-hegemony approach to the Mekong River Basin and increasing investment into other riparian countries will not only result in more hydropower dams, but also help promote economic cooperation in the region.

Comparatively, and understandably, there are more studies and findings on overall impacts on China's section of the Mekong River Basin than those of its neighbours. Zhenming Zhu[11] illustrates that by directly and actively engaging with the GMS programme, China's Yunnan Province has seen its international profile rapidly rising and its role in Subregional economic cooperation and growth growing. Evelyn Goh[12] details economic, environmental, and security implications of China-built/supported hydro dams on the Mekong River and the countries on its banks. Tubilewicz and Jayasuriya[13] cast doubt on China's argument that its water resource development on the upper Mekong within its territory should be able to lend the Subregion a hand with its economic growth agenda. To a certain extent, as Urban et al. stress,[14] China's continuous economic growth and escalating investment in GMS-led hydropower projects seem to have been contributing to the economic growth of the GMS countries.

Turning to the Lower Mekong Basin (LMB), Hiroshi Hori[15] outlines current social, economic, and political situations in the countries of the region. Focusing particularly on the dam-building boom and its environmental consequences, the author highlights the urgency for the MRC to address public concerns about the Mekong River more proactively. Kummu and Varis[16] further gauge the impacts of hydropower development in the Upper Mekong Basin (UMB) on the Lower Basin. Their study underscores the importance of concerted efforts and data sharing in minimising consequential effects of dams and reservoirs on the Mekong River's natural flow and sediment regimes. Subregional cooperative endeavours are especially imperative for lowering the risk of massive socio-economic disruptions stemming from dam/reservoir-induced hydrological and climatic changes. Invoking published Chinese reports that annual incomes of its relocated communities have on average decreased by 62 per cent, Zhang et al.[17] call for greater attention to resettlement packages, income restoration/improvement programmes, responsibilities and effective ways forward, and implementation outcome measures. Piseth and Sophearin[18] further emphasise the compelling need for the GMS program to work harder on mitigating negative social, economic, environmental and financial impacts of hydro development on local communities. Studies by Weatherby and Eyler[19] and by Shrestha and Chongvilaivan[20] meanwhile suggest that energy trade among the GMS member states may help increase their economic growth, which should in turn better enable the Subregion to achieve sustainable and shared prosperity.

The GMS programme, on the whole, positions development as its core objective and advocates open economies supported by market mechanisms.[21] Not unexpectedly, many studies have been devoted to assessing both payoffs and issues related to economic corridors, cross-border movements of products and people, and transport agreements and management in the Mekong River Basin.[22] With China's dominant role in the region, its economic interactions with other GMS countries and its profit-sharing performance have naturally also been attracting scrutiny.[23] While China is commonly believed to have benefited substantially from the GMS-led energy grid and trade, studies have also found that the Lower Mekong Basin countries respond positively towards Beijing's participation in emerging Subregional cooperation and benefit-sharing frameworks. Moreover, the evolving cooperation among the GMS members has already begun to generate constructive impacts on sustainable hydro development along the Mekong River. Yet along with reports of heartening progress are constant reminders of the reality that the varied levels of economic development across the region and lingering political uncertainty in some Mekong member states may undermine the economic benefits of the GMS programme.[24]

Benefit-sharing approach

The benefit-sharing approach is generally defined as "any action designed to change the allocation of costs and benefits associated with cooperation".[25] Recognising the potential of cooperation for sustainability and productivity growth, riparian countries on international rivers typically opt for cooperation. Yet few expect the equal-share-rule presumption to be automatically applied in transboundary water development. There are thus continuous interest in and efforts to achieve the optimisation of equal resource/gain allocation and unified governance of cross-border rivers and lakes.[26] In this sense, access and benefit-sharing principles provide an analytical framework for appraising the extent to which transboundary cooperation among the Mekong River Basin countries has been achieved.

While the notion of benefit is defined differently by different parties, Sadoff and Grey[27] have distinguished four general types of benefits from cooperation on international rivers development and conservation. These are benefits: (1) to; (2) from; (3) because of; and (4) beyond the river. Specifically, benefits "to" the river centre on collaborative ecosystem management, including conserving watersheds and riverine biodiversity, avoiding water pollutants, managing rain flows, and enhancing water quality. The notion of benefit in this regard is built on the recognition that transboundary rivers are especially vulnerable to water quality degradation caused by upstream discharges. Given that secured supply of safe water is essential for sustaining livelihoods, environmental management is high on virtually all riparian countries' development and cooperation agendas.

Benefits "from" cross-border waters refer to economic gains from cooperative management and development, including increased food productivity and energy generation. Benefits "because of" cooperation implies reduction of costs incurred from tensions and conflicts among riparian states. Such contentions discourage regional trade and other exchanges, animate protectionism, and hence hinder riparian states' domestic economic growth. Finally, benefits "beyond" the shared waters stem from the combined effects of economic benefits of Type 2 and political benefits of Type 3.[28] Benefit-sharing efforts in this category may culminate in greater economic integration and better political understanding among riparian countries, which in turn may help boost their respective political commitment and collective institutional capacities towards a globalising world.

In the Mekong Subregion, the GMS programme plays a significant role as a catalyst for cooperation and benefit sharing. It champions both direct (Type 2) and indirect (Type 4) economic cooperation in regional hydropower development. It also takes a Type 4 benefit-sharing approach to facilitating regional economic integration in non-water sectors, such as transportation, human resource development, and tourism. Positive results of its efforts have in return motivated the Mekong riparian countries to further their involvement in cooperative activities that it promotes for their economic growth.

The Mekong River Basin

From the Tibetan Plateau, the Mekong River flows through six countries before emptying into the South China Sea. The Mekong River Basin (MRB) consists of two regions, the Upper Mekong Basin located in China and Myanmar, and the Lower Mekong Basin shared by Lao PDR, Thailand, Cambodia, and Vietnam.[29] The significance of the MRB lies in the fact that it is presently home to about 67 million people, the number of which is projected to reach 90 million by 2025.[30]

Economy

The GMS countries cover an area of 2.6 million square kilometres with a combined population of 339 million.[31] In 2014, their total GDP based on purchasing power parity (PPP) was recorded at US$2,734 billion, and GDP per capita at US $22,166 billion. Thailand accounted for the largest shares, 39 per cent of the former and 26.8 per cent of the latter. The rest were made up by Vietnam, China's Guangxi and Yunnan Provinces, Myanmar, Lao PDR, and Cambodia.[32] The country breakdowns of these economic indicators are displayed in Table 6.1.

Table 6.2 further shows that while the majority of GMS economies remain heavily reliant on agricultural production and exports, this sector went through major structural changes between 1993 and 2015. As a result, its contribution to gross domestic product (GDP) shrank by half between 1993 and 2015 in all GMS countries, except for Thailand, which experienced a similar, proportionate decline in its agriculture sector a decade earlier, during the ten-year period of extraordinarily high economic growth in 1986–96.[33] As in the case of Thailand, the

Table 6.1 Economic indicators of the GMS countries in 2014

	Area (km²)	*Population (million)*	*GDP at PPP* (billion US$)*	*GDP per capita (billion US$)*
Yunnan	394,139 (15.3)	47 (14.2)	364 (13.3)	4,425 (19.9)
Guangxi	248,390 (9.6)	48 (14.6)	446 (16.3)	5,367 (24.2)
Myanmar	676,577 (26.2)	53 (16.1)	255 (9.3)	1,263 (5.7)
Lao PDR	236,800 (1.8)	7 (2.1)	35 (1.3)	2,018 (9.1)
Thailand	513,120 (19.9)	68 (20.7)	1,070 (39.1)	5,942 (26.8)
Cambodia	181,035 (7.0)	15 (4.6)	51 (1.9)	1,099 (5)
Vietnam	331,212 (12.8)	91 (27.7)	513 (18.8)	2,052 (9.3)
Total	2,581,272.4 (100.0)	329 (100.0)	2,734 (100.0)	22,166 (100.0)

Source: The authors' adaptation from data presented in ADB (2016/June), and T. Kudo and M. Ishida (2013).[34]

GDP and employment gaps left by the shrinking agriculture sector in the other GMS countries are quickly filled by rapidly growing industrial and service sectors. As indicated in Table 6.2, for example, the 2015 services share in GDP rose to 50.2 per cent in China, 38.5 per cent in Myanmar, and 49.4 per cent in Lao PDR.[35]

Environment

The flows in the Mekong River are related to the variation in monsoon rainfall. The mean annual precipitation in the LMB ranges from 1,000 mm on the Khorat Plateau in Thailand to more than 2,500 mm on the highlands of Laos,[36] while the mean annual rainfall in the UMB varies from 300 mm at its source on the Tibetan Plateau to 1,600 mm before it enters the Golden Triangle.[37] Similarly, whereas the UMB in the Himalayas provides 15 per cent of the River's discharge, monsoon rainfalls across the rest of the basin supply about 75 per cent of the total runoff, which causes annual flooding in the lowlands of Cambodia and Vietnam.[38]

In general, the water quality of both the Upper and Lower Mekong Basin is acceptable. Yet there are increasing concerns about the growing problems of sedimentation, saline intrusion, and eutrophication. Given the productive value of the Mekong ecosystems, the conservation of their biodiversity is becoming imperative for the livelihoods of both the rural and urban populations in the UMB and LMB.[39] The following sections will explore how the GMS programme functions as a regional cooperation scheme in developing the Mekong Power Grid and safeguarding the region's lifeline, the Mekong River.

The GMS Programme at a glance

Initiated in 1992 by the ADB, the GMS programme is expected to bolster socio-economic cooperation among the six member states and achieve enhanced

Table 6.2 Agricultural and service values of the GMS countries between 1993 and 2015

Variables	*China*		*Myanmar*		*Lao PDR*		*Thailand*		*Cambodia*		*Vietnam*	
	1993	*2015*	*1993*	*2015*	*1993*	*2015*	*1993*	*2015*	*1993*	*2015*	*1993*	*2015*
Agricultural value added (% of GDP)	19.7	8.8	63	26.7	57.5	19.7	10.3	8.7	46.5	28.6	29.9	18.9
Service value added (% of GDP)	33.7	50.2	28.1	38.5	24.7	49.4	50.9	54.9	40.5	41.5	41.2	44.2

Source: The authors' adaptation from data presented on the World Bank Databank website.[40]

connectivity, increased *competitiveness*, and a great sense of *community*. Of the three-pronged/three-Cs strategy, connectivity is arguably central to the programme, as it involves transforming major transport corridors into transnational economic corridors, working towards a Subregional power network and market, improving the core/backbone telecommunications structure, and lowering barriers to cross-border flows of goods and people. Connecting the Subregion through these infrastructure networks is perceived as instrumental in making its member countries more attractive as both markets and centres for production. In this sense, physical and non-physical integration processes are essential for the Subregion and its affiliates to enhance their competitiveness. Meanwhile, it is widely accepted that sustaining competitiveness requires long-term national and Subregional efforts in identifying and exploiting technological innovations, investing in human and institutional capital, and building policy and regulatory frameworks.[41]

Underpinned by the three-Cs mission and strategy, the GMS-led projects are by and large intended to enable its members to trade efficiently not only among themselves, but also in wider, regional, and international economic communities. Furthermore, GMS projects are generally aspired to contribute to the Subregion's shared objectives, which are developing sustainable economies, improving living standards, and eradicating poverty in all the member states. Over the past 20 years, the GMS countries have indeed recorded an average annual GDP growth of 6.5 per cent. Rapid economic development and steady expansion of Mekong-wide transport routes, production networks, and trade connections have, in turn, significantly improved the livelihoods and socio-economic conditions of people living in the GMS.[42]

Since launching its Strategic Framework 2012–22, the GMS programme has been striving to further accelerate the development of the economic corridors and has promoted multi-sectoral cooperation through investment facilitation and project initiatives.[43] Among the priority sectors is, perhaps not surprisingly, the energy sector in which the Strategic Framework has also identified four key areas of attention. They are: environmentally sustainable power development and trade, energy efficiency and conservation, renewable energy resources and clean fuels, and national policies and mechanisms to accomplish the other three.[44] The GMS programme makes it clear that by emphasising energy trade, the Strategic Framework is tasked to tackle one of the fundamental challenges, unequal distribution of energy resources in the Subregion. Specifically, energy trade is projected to help ensure all member countries an affordable and reliable supply of electricity, and in the process to balance energy supply/demand with environmental protection. Earnings from the energy trade should at the same time help boost the growth of the sector, other related industries, and ultimately the scale of the economy. All this may result in greater financial capabilities and market demands for clean/renewable energy across the Mekong region.[45] Table 6.3 provides a snapshot of the evolving GMS energy market in the first 20 years after the six Subregional countries came together in 1992.[46] Table 6.4 spells out actions to be taken by the GMS for enhancing energy cooperation in the Subregion.

Table 6.3 Key milestones in GMS regional power trade and cooperation

Year	*Activities*
1992	GMS Economic Cooperation initiated.
1994	The Subregional Energy Sector Study completed and published in the subsequent year.
	Eight hydro and transmission line projects, two oil and natural gas projects, and one institutional project, all recommended by the Subregional Energy Sector Study endorsed at third and fourth Ministerial Meetings in Ha Noi and Chiang Mai.
1995	Subregional Electric Power Forum (EPF) launched.
1998	Experts Group on Power Interconnection and Trade (EGP) established by the EPF.
1999	Policy Statement on Regional Power Trade in GMS adopted by the EPF.
2000	Policy Statement on Regional Power Trade in the GMS endorsed at GMS Ministers Meeting.
2002	Regional Indicative Master Plan on Power Interconnection completed and approved.
	Intergovernmental Agreement (IGA) on regional power trade in GMS signed at the First GMS Summit.
	Regional Power Trade Coordination Committee (RPTCC) set up to coordinate implementation of regional power trade pursuant to IGA.
2004	IGA on regional power trade ratified by all GMS Basin countries.
	Guidelines for the RPTCC issued.
2005	Memorandum of Understanding on Guidelines for Stage 1 Implementation of Regional Power Trade Operating Agreement (MOU-1) signed.
	Regional Master Plan on Power Interconnection updated.
2009	Study on building a sustainable energy future in GMS was published [RETA 6301].
2010	Second update of Regional Master Plan completed by RTE International [RETA 6440].
2011	Discussions on establishment of Regional Power Coordination Centre (RPCC) and dedicated coordination centre for regional power trade commenced.
2012	Two working groups began working on: (1) performance standards and grid code, and (2) regulatory issues.
	Intergovernmental MOU initiated by all GMS Basin countries.

Source: ADB (September 2012: 28–9).[47]

By concentrating on cross-border electricity trade, the GMS programme pushes for the interconnection of transmission networks between districts of abundant energy resources and centres of high economic growth and hence high energy consumption. The GMS countries certainly understand the importance of reliable access to affordable energy to economic growth, human well-being, and social

Table 6.4 GMS roadmap for expanding energy cooperation

Stages	*Activities*
Stage 1	Building bilateral cross-border connections through power purchase agreements.
Stage 2	Pressing forward grid-to-grid power trading between any pair of GMS countries to eventually utilize transmission facilities of a third regional country.
Stage 3	Developing of transmission links dedicated to cross-border trading.
Stage 4	Moving to multiple sellers-buyers regulatory frameworks, to allow a competitive regional electricity market to be developed.

Source: The authors' adaptation from data presented in ADB (2013: 47).[48]

Table 6.5 Hydropower capacity in GMS countries

The GMS countries	*Hydropower installed (MW)*	*Hydropower potential (MW)*
Yunnan and Guangxi Provinces of China	20,000	122,000
Myanmar	3,100	100,000
Lao PDR	4,100	18,000
Thailand	4,500	4,600
Cambodia	1,300	10,000
Vietnam	15,800	35,000
Total	48,800	289,600

Source: The authors' adaptation from data presented in Weatherby and Eyler (2017), ADB (2016/June), Intelligent Energy Systems (2016), and World Energy Council (2016: 38–47).[49]

development. Banking on the potential of reaping sustained economic gains from Subregional energy cooperation, they have demonstrated no hesitation in signing up to the GMS effort to establish an interconnected regional energy market by 2025 and hence complete the Roadmap Stage 4.[50]

Yet there has also been an ever clearer recognition throughout the Mekong River Basin that a regional grid infrastructure alone is not sufficient to ensure energy security and reliability. The GMS programme has thus been placing increasing emphasis on development of sustainable/clean/renewable energy. Whether it is schemes for poverty reduction, or initiatives for expanding regional grid infrastructure, or plans for cross-border economic corridors, the GMS cooperation and integration framework encourages public-private partnerships in establishing and maintaining a sustainable and competitive energy supply system in the Subregion. Through providing policy, financial, and technical assistance, it also helps the member countries to be proactively innovative and cost-efficient when participating in its effort to grow the renewable energy make-up of the Sub-regional power grid. Equally important, the GMS programme has begun addressing, in both institutional and public spheres, issues related to fair and equitable sharing of the benefits arising from the utilisation and management of the Mekong's water resources.[51]

Hydropower development on the Mekong River

It has been widely acknowledged that while the Mekong River Basin is well endowed with hydropower and fossil fuel resources, most of its exploitable natural energy endowments are unevenly distributed across the Subregion. Among the natural deposits, the hydropower resources are abundant in Lao PDR, Myanmar, and China's Yunnan Province, and their hydroelectric potential is expected to exceed their own demands for the foreseeable future.[52] The GMS programme has thus been promoting and facilitating not only hydropower development, but also region-wide cooperation in the construction and governance of a high-voltage transmission network to more effectively connect rapidly growing electricity supply and demand.

Table 6.5 displays the GMS member states' respective installed hydropower capacity and potential. The two pie charts of Figure 6.1 further illustrate the country-specific percentage of Mekong River flow and hydropower capacity. Both data sets help quantify the different development stages that the Mekong countries are at and their domestic actual/potential electricity supply-demand gaps. The data also make clear that a Mekong country's hydropower capacity may not be related to its contributing percentage of the River's average flow. An immediately obvious conclusion is that effective energy trade and interconnection is essential for GMS countries.

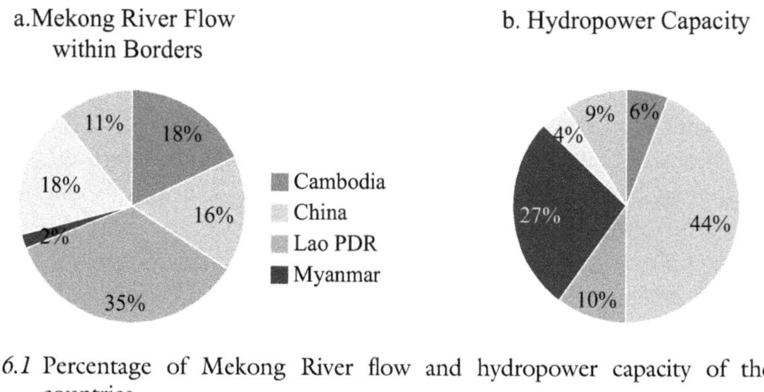

Figure 6.1 Percentage of Mekong River flow and hydropower capacity of the GMS countries

Source: Roland-Holst and Heft-Neal (2012: 487).[53]

Taking up 44 per cent of the total hydropower capacity in the GMS, China is the region's and the world's largest builder and financier of mega-dams.[54] Given that China accounts for 23 per cent of the world's primary energy demand, and given the mounting public outrage over the worsening environmental degradation and pollution originating from China's domestic energy production, the Chinese government invested more than US$100 billion into the renewable energy sector including large hydropower dams between 2014 and 2016.[55] According to a 2017 Mekong River Commission's report, China has already built nine major hydropower dams on the upper reaches of the Lancang River.[56] Yet China remains the only Mekong riparian country to have completed hydro projects on the River's mainstream.[57] Moreover, even the oversupply-induced-curtailed hydropower capacity of the Yunnan Province is greater than the total installed capacity of mainland Southeast Asia. China, however, does not seem ready to slow down, but is planning to construct 13 more large-scale dams in the Mekong River Basin.[58]

On the other end of the spectrum is Myanmar, whose energy system is commonly considered as being the least developed among the GMS member countries. Yet even there, the installed hydropower capacity is already accounting for around 65 per cent of the country's total electricity-generating capacity.[59] Moreover, this share is expected to grow still larger by 2030 when 36 more hydro projects are planned to be completed.[60] Upgrading the power sector of a country like Myanmar, however, does not involve issues related to only hydroelectric generating capacity. Equally challenging, if not more so, is that to see a "brighter" future, Myanmar will also need to modernise its aging and already strained transmission network so that the installed hydropower will be fully available, rather than only partially as of now. With most of the dams built in disadvantaged areas, greater and speedy rural electrification may prove an effective means of building public support for a more inclusive Myanmar.[61]

Like Myanmar, both Lao PDR and Cambodia are endowed with abundant energy resources, including considerable hydropower potential. Yet both are also characterised by low household electrification rates. Furthermore, the upsurge of hydropower development and ready-but-yet-to-take-off economic growth results in both countries' domestic electricity consumption lagging behind their national energy generation.[62] Nevertheless, public access to electricity remains inadequate, particularly in rural areas.[63] Viewing low power availability as a major cause of the country's poverty, the Lao government has been striving to raise the electrification rate to 90 per cent in 2020. Laos is also banking on increased electricity exports to shore up its economy. More than 50 hydropower plants are thus being installed or planned to meet the 2020 target of exporting 7,000 MW to Thailand and 5,000 MW to Vietnam.[64] Similarly, to meet its basic electricity needs and improve its national energy security, Cambodia plans to have nine more hydropower plants running by 2020. Even with the additional megawatts, however, Cambodia may still have to import 30 per cent of its electricity from Lao PDR, Thailand, and Vietnam. Also, while increased hydropower will likely help speed up the electrification pace in rural areas, coal, oil, and gas may remain among the primary energy sources in cities.[65]

In contrast, Thailand has already substantially developed its hydro energy potential in the Lower Mekong River Basin. Large-scale hydropower dams are today regarded as unsustainable and harmful options across the social spectrum in Thailand. The Thai government has thus been forced to be the main sponsor of small hydropower projects with a total capacity of 102 MW. There have certainly been discussions and plans to increase the capacity to 1,608 MW by 2021. Yet the latest Alternative Energy Development Plan, AEDP2015, has set the target at 376 MW for 2036, which may not significantly impact the current 10 per cent hydro share of Thailand's total system capacity.[66]

Vietnam, on the other hand, not only encompasses high potential for hydropower, but the electricity produced from this renewable source already accounted for 47.5 per cent of the country's total installed generating capacity in 2013. In this regard, Vietnam is perhaps in a more favourable position than its neighbours as it can reap the benefits of diversity in hydrological conditions across different river systems with different flow patterns across its north, central, and south regions. Yet Vietnam is believed to have basically exploited all the large-scale hydro resources that are considered economically feasible. Further development on that front may prove unproductive or even harmful. The Vietnamese government therefore gives greater attention to the potential to build small, mini, micro, and pumped storage hydro plants.[67]

The Mekong Power Grid

The Mekong Power Grid is one of the major initiatives undertaken by the GMS programme. The objective of the Grid is to promote a commercial energy system that supplies electricity to the entire Mekong River Basin. The network involves installing transmission lines across the region, constructing 12 hydropower projects in Thailand and Vietnam, and enabling trade of electricity among China's Yunnan Province, Lao PDR, Myanmar, and Cambodia.[68]

Hydropower development across the Subregion is by and large associated with the evolving Mekong Power Grid. In other words, the Grid has helped build a platform for regional power trade and for private companies to join the World Bank, the Japan Bank for International Cooperation, and ASEAN in investing in the Subregion's extended power sector. When completed, the transmission lines of the Grid are designated, for example, to link Thailand with the Jinghong and Nuozhadu Dams in China, the Salween River Dams in Myanmar, and the Nam Theun 2 Dam in Laos. Cambodia may more cost-effectively import hydroelectricity from Thailand and Vietnam. Meanwhile, Myanmar may attract more funding and technical assistance for its planned dams from countries and institutions within the Subregion.[69]

Table 6.6 shows the already established hydropower plants and cross-border transmission connections across the GMS. The data also epitomise the consolidation of the integrated energy market in the Subregion and the aspiration of the

GMS countries for better inclusion and fully-fledged participation in transnational electricity trading. There is indeed a myriad of commercial dealings between national power grids that have been going on for decades in the Mekong region. According to the ADB's records,[70] Thailand has been importing hydropower from Laos since 1971. On its side, Laos has also been importing electricity from Thailand since the late 1990s and from China's Yunnan Province since 2009. Vietnam has meanwhile been importing electricity from Yunnan since 2004, the Chinese province of which has itself been importing hydropower from Myanmar since 2008. Similarly, Cambodia has been importing electricity from Vietnam since 2008, from Thailand since 2009, and from Laos since 2010.

However, the recent hydropower boom in most GMS member countries has further increased the urgency of establishing a smart, reliable, all-encompassing regional power network in the Mekong region to effectively deal with grid congestion and inter-state/locality competition problems. A well-developed regional power grid, in other words, may help more effectively alleviate the coexisting problem of continuously insufficient public access to electricity and the growing underutilisation of installed hydro capacity in many parts of the region. That may in turn enable emerging GMS countries to better implement their strategy of bringing about national development through the sale of hydroelectricity. Just as importantly, regional coordination in hydro development may be an immediate and sincere response to growing criticism from civil society groups and international observers of the social and environmental consequences brought about by dam constructions.[71]

Given that the bilateral power trading is not only already in existence, but thriving in the Mekong River Basin, the GMS program and the ADB logically focus their effort for greater connectivity in this sector first and foremost on expanding cross-border transmission links to interconnected, cross-regional

Table 6.6 Exiting regional power interconnections between the GMS countries (220 Kv and above)

Positions of transmission plants in the GMS countries		*Voltage*
China (Yunnan): Xinquao to	Vietnam: Lao Cai	220 kV
China (Yunnan): Malutang to	Vietnam: Ha Giang	220 kV
Myanmar: Shewli I HPP to	China (Yunnan): Dehong	220 kV
Vietnam: Chau Doc to	Cambodia: Takeo	220 kV
Laos: Nam Theun 2 HPP to	Thailand: Roi Et 2	500 kV
Laos: Nam Theun 2 HPP to	Thailand: Ou done 3	500 kV
Laos: Houayho HPP to	Thailand: Ubon 2	230 kV
Laos: Theun Hinboun HPP to	Thailand: Sakhonnakhon	230 kV
Laos: Sekaman 3 to	Vietnam: Thanh My	220 kV
Laos: Moung Kua to	Vietnam: Dian Bian	220 kV
Laos: Ban Hat to	Cambodia: Chiang Teng	220 KVdouble circuit

Source: The authors' adaptation from data presented in ADB (2016/June: 9).[72]

networks. There is, however, also a widely shared understanding that the energy sectors of the six GMS countries are at varying development levels, and the national physical networks, institutional capacities, and regulatory management exhibit different degrees of sophistication. That perhaps helps explain why the ADB estimates that the GMS power grid plan may be of only medium-term relevance to some member countries because of the fragmented nature of their electric power sectors.[73]

It takes little guesswork to figure out that Laos, Myanmar, and Cambodia fall in this category. Yet whether encouraged or compelled by the ADB's assessment, these countries all continue accelerating and gaining momentum in building, linking, upgrading, and expanding their still scattered, and often underdeveloped electrical grids. They also actively carry on with their efforts to connect their rudimentary power networks with their neighbours' trunk and/or branch transmission lines. Besides trying to escalate their relevance to the envisioned Subregional power grid, they also seriously count on electricity trade to grow their fiscal revenues and lead to new economic development potentials. Aiming at becoming a "Battery of Southeast Asia", they all seek to accelerate and scale up the development of their richly endorsed hydro and other energy generation resources for export earnings. Yet what remains inadequately explained in the Subregion-wide urge to exploit power trade is how aggressive development of hydro and other forms of generation systems will help enhance social and environmental sustainability. Also insufficiently crafted are policy and administrative frameworks and measures to ensure fair and equitable sharing of benefits among the GMS countries and between developers/investors and affected local communities.[74]

Electricity trading and benefit sharing

Sadoff and Grey[75] classify the diverse types of benefit sharing in transboundary rivers into four groups: (1) benefits to the river; (2) benefits from the river; (3) reduction of costs because of the river; (4) benefits beyond the river. Of the four, the GMS programme-championed direct and indirect economic cooperation activities across the Mekong River Basin fall into Types 2 and 4. Also covered by Type 2 are the hydro development and power trade that the GMS countries have been and will remain eagerly and heavily involved in.[76] Type 4 meanwhile also comprises benefits from non-water sectors such as transport, tourism, human resources development, and integrated efforts for poverty reduction. Political paybacks, on the other hand, are included in Type 3. In view of their broad and complementary scope, Types 3 and 4 benefits should incentivise the GMS countries, and have indeed done so, to participate in the budding Subregional cooperation programme for their own economic growth, at the very least.

The GMS programme, however, has not tapped all the benefit-sharing potentials. Type 1, for example, signifies the importance of and calls for joint commitment to environmental protection and ecological sustainability of transboundary rivers. Yet GMS-initiated or supported development projects seem to suggest that the Subregional programme is concerned more about economic growth than environmental issues. On the other hand, Type 3 may not be very pertinent to the GMS programme or its member countries. For while hydro development remains controversial across the Mekong Basin, there are few publicly expressed worries about dam-related issues being escalated into political crises and/or conflicts. Put differently, the GMS countries have never really been confronted with the challenge of mitigating inter-state political clashes over the Mekong River and shifting their state policy orientation from hostility to cooperation and development, as represented by Type 3 benefits. They could, instead, engage themselves in regional cooperative initiatives almost immediately after restoring domestic peace and stability, as in the case of Cambodia and Myanmar. That the GMS members have not been burdened with serious political disputes over their shared water, and resultant added costs to development, may be further exemplified by the fast and continued per capita GDP growth across the Subregion since the early 1990s (Figure 6.2). At the same time, and relatedly, the intra-Subregion trade has increased from being practically non-existent to 9 per cent of the GMS countries' total import-export volumes (Figure 6.3). With their economic growth averaging 7.5 per cent over the last two decades, the GMS countries have achieved dramatic reductions in poverty and admirable increases in food security.[77] Whether measured by individual national (Table 6.7) or standardised international (Table 6.8) poverty lines, the Subregion has seen a substantial annual reductions in poverty.[78]

What seems clear from the above research findings is that benefits from the Mekong Power Grid may be multidimensional, and that Laos, Myanmar, and Cambodia are likely among the principal beneficiaries of this GMS flagship hydro project. Exporting hydropower to neighbouring countries has, for example, boosted their state coffers as well as energy industries. The significant improvements in government fiscal positions and increases in power trade earnings have in turn enabled the GMS countries to further expand their hydro capacities, and have also allowed them to allocate more resources to other economic sectors. Furthermore, increasing intra-Mekong energy trade will in the long run help the Subregion to gradually ease its dependence on oil and coal in power generation, which are not only environmentally unfriendly, but also subject to price volatility.[79] In fact, the hydropower interdependent and accompanying substitution of fossil fuel generation have already resulted in US $14.3 billion in cost savings across the region.[80]

Facilitated by, but more inspiring than the impressive economic returns thus far, the GMS energy trade has also generated social benefits. Figured prominently in academic and policy discussions on achievements in this regard are improved public, particularly rural, access to electricity and the supporting role of ameliorating energy deprivation in poverty reduction across the Subregion.[81] Attracting equal attention are environmental benefits that are expected from the fast-growing hydro systems and regional power trade in the GMS countries. Although hydro reservoirs are not free of greenhouse gas emissions, for many in the Mekong region, hydropower remains, as illustrated by Table 6.9, part of the clean-energy equation and a climate-friendly alternative to fossil fuel sources.[82] Particularly, a regionally interconnected and coordinated power sector may better condition

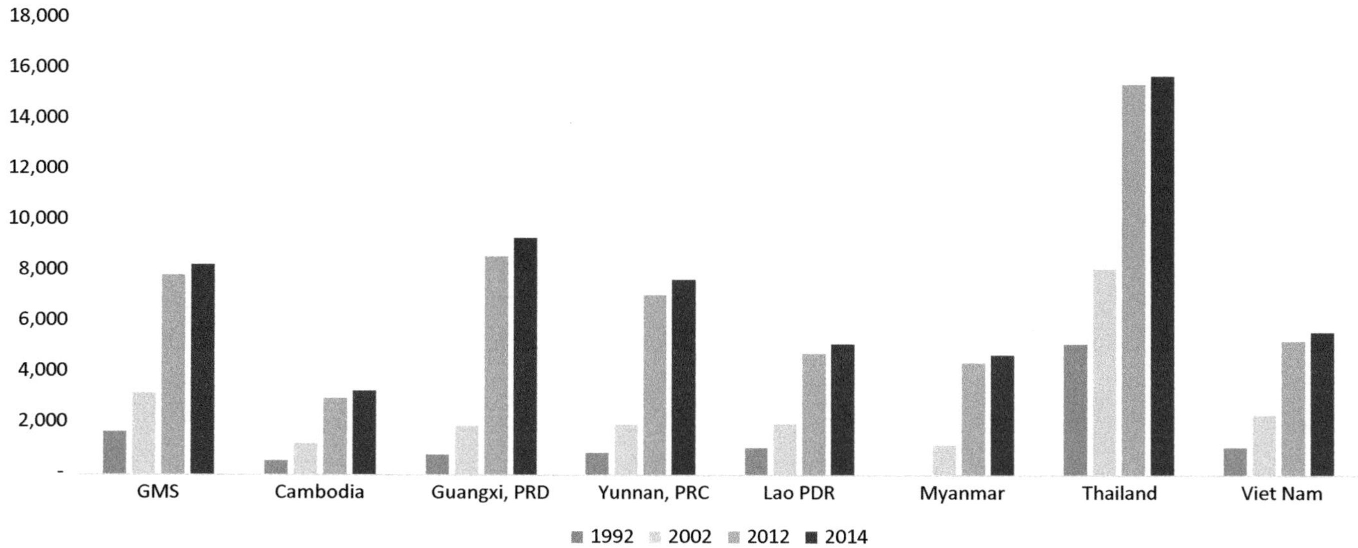

Figure 6.2 GDP per capita at PPP
Source: ADB (2016/August: 9).[83]

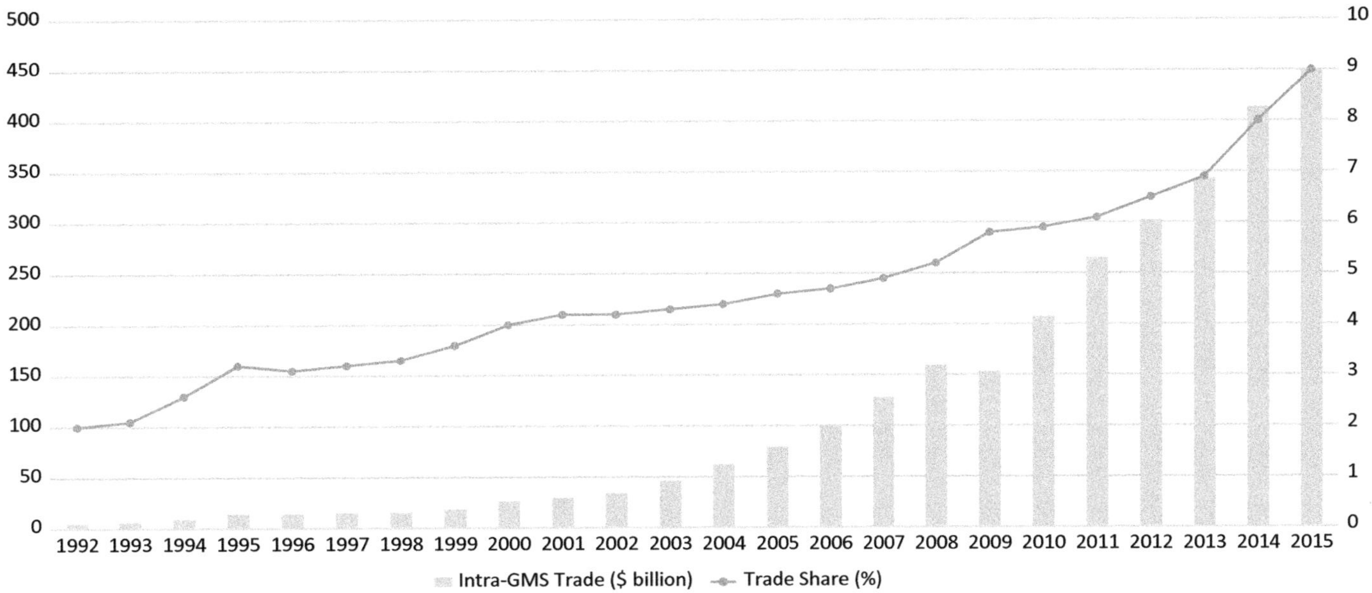

Figure 6.3 Intra-GMS trade (US$ billion and % of GMS total)
Source: ADB (2016/August: 18).[84]

Table 6.7 Progress in poverty reduction – headcount % (national)

Country	*Initial yr*	*Final yr*	*pp. per yr*
Cambodia (1993–2011)	45	19.8	-1.40
Laos (1993–2008)	46	27.6	-1.23
Vietnam (1998–2010)	37.4	14.2	-1.93
Thailand (1988–2010)	42.2	7.8	-1.56
China (2003–10)	6.6	2	-0.66
Yunnan, China (2003–08)	8.2	5.6	-0.52

Source: Madhur and Menon (2014: 11).[85]

Table 6.8 Progress in poverty reduction – headcount % ($1.25-a-day)

Country	*Initial yr*	*Final yr*	*pp. per yr*
Cambodia (1994–2009)	48.6	18.6	-2.00
Laos (1992–2008)	55.7	33.9	-1.36
Myanmar (2005–08)	32.1	25.6	-1.30
Vietnam (1993–2008)	63.7	16.9	-3.12
Thailand (1990–2010)	11.62	2	-0.48
China (1990–2008)	60.2	13.1	-2.62

Source: Madhur and Menon (2014: 11).[86]

Table 6.9 Contribution of hydropower development to CO_2 emission reduction in Lower Mekong Basin by 2030

CO_2 emission	*Estimation*
Total of reduction of CO_2 emission(thermal power plant replacement by hydropower)	75.40 (Million tons/year of CO_2)
CO_2 emissionfrom hydropower dam reservoirs	6.05 (Million tons/year of CO_2)
Net CO_2 emission reduction from hydropower development	69.35 (Million tons/year of CO_2)

Source: The authors' adaptation from data presented in Piseth and Sophearin (2014: 235–9).[87]

hydro projects so that they will be less harmful to the flow regime and water quality of the Mekong River, two essential elements for food security and livelihoods.[88] Moreover, the intra-regional power grid and trade may allow some Lower Mekong Basin countries to optimise potential ecological benefits by importing electricity from their upper stream neighbours and hence minimising human and environmental challenges if they carry out hydro development on their own land. Thailand is a case in point, where public pro-ecosystem, anti-dam campaigns led by environmental non-governmental organisations (NGOs) make it harder to construct new hydropower facilities within its territorial boundaries. The Subregional power grid and electricity trading system help Thailand to meet its persistent and growing demands for electricity.[89]

Nevertheless, controversies and scepticisms over hydropower development remain in many parts of the Subregion. Growing public concerns about socio-environmental impacts reportedly reflect diminishing public confidence in the top-down approach of the GMS programme to intergovernmental decisions on hydro development and energy trade.[90] That there has been a persistent lack of public information and consultation about large-scale dams on the upper Mekong in China's Yunnan Province and Myanmar has made an increasing number of people anxious about sediment blockage, disruption of the river flow, fish migration, eco-degradation, and loss of biodiversity down the stream of the River. In fact, Cambodia's fishery industry and Vietnam's agricultural sector are already feeling the negative impacts of domestic and regional hydropower development. There are increasingly loud warnings that if unchecked, the adverse effects may ultimately threaten food security, trigger economic crises, and undermine the Subregional socio-political stability.[91] Yet while all the GMS countries agree to undertake a transboundary Environmental Impact Assessment (EIA) of the GMS programme's hydro projects, such proposed EIAs have not been carried out due to lack of transboundary enforcement mechanisms.[92] Adding to the uncertainty of environmental impacts posed by hydropower projects along the Mekong is the bigger challenge of adequately compensating the millions of people, either displaced or imposed with changes to their traditional habitats, and more importantly ensuring them a fair share of the benefits of hydro development.[93] If national governments, hydro developers, and Subregional programmes fail to deliver their promised economic "well-being", resettled and affected local communities may face the risks of falling into further impoverishment.[94]

Conclusion

The Mekong Power Grid is still at an embryonic stage of development. All the six member countries pledge to participate in collaborative responses to the socio-economic-environmental-technical challenges associated with hydropower projects and cross-border energy trading in the Subregion. They remain, however, entangled in many unresolved territorial disputes among themselves. Uncertain borders, be they land and maritime boundary disputes between Cambodia and Vietnam, or overlapping claims to a few border villages between Laos and Thailand, or territorial tensions between China and Vietnam, are certainly potential flashpoints that may derail Subregional interconnection and cooperation efforts.[95] Yet by focusing on building an integrated energy market to help accelerate Subregional economic growth, narrow development gaps, and alleviate poverty, the GMS programme, with the support of the ADB, provides an attractive and useful platform for them to negotiate their differences, multilateral objectives, regional priority areas, and Subregional joint projects. Thus while the GMS's ambition and push for hydropower continue to stir controversy surrounding impacts and decision-making processes,[96] the activity-based programme also has encouraging stories about how transboundary rivers can serve as both a source of conflicts and a medium of cooperation and trust building.[97]

Notes

1 UNEP-DHI, *Transboundary River Basins: Status and Trends*, Volume 3, UNEP: DEW/1953/NA, Nairobi, Kenya, 2016, p. xiii, online at http://twap-rivers.org/assets/GEF_TWAPRB_FullTechnicalReport.pdf.
2 S. C. McCaffrey, *The Law of International Watercourse,* Second Edition, Oxford, UK: Oxford University Press, 2007, pp. 16–17.
3 UNEP, "Freshwater Strategy 2017–2021", 2017, online at https://wedocs.unep.org/bitstream/handle/20.500.11822/19528/UNEP-full_report-170502.pdf?sequence=3&isAllowed=y; M. McCracken, *Measuring Transboundary Water Cooperation: Options for Sustainable Development Goal Target 6.5*, Stockholm, Sweden: Global Water Partnership Technical Committee, 2017, pp. 13–16, online at https://www.gwp.org/globalassets/global/toolbox/publications/background-papers/gwp-tec_23_measuring-transboundary-water-cooperation.pdf.
4 UNEP, 2017, op cit.
5 UNEP, "Transboundary Waters Assessment Programme", UNEP/EA.2/1/Rev.1. K1605937/200516, 2016, p. 2, online at https://wedocs.unep.org/bitstream/handle/20.500.11822/17614/K1605937%20INF24.pdf?sequence=8&isAllowed=y.
6 GEF Secretariat, *GEF-7 Replenishment: Programming Directions*, GEF/R.7/15, Brasilia, Brazil: Global Environment Facility Secretariat, 22 December 2017, pp. 51–63, online at https://www.thegef.org/sites/default/files/council-meeting-documents/GEF-7%20-%20Programming%20Directions%20and%20Policy%20Agenda%20-%20GEF_R.7_15.pdf.
7 UNU-INWEH, *Water Security and the Global Water Agenda: A UN-Water Analytical Brief*, Ontario, Canada: United Nations University Institute for Water, and United Nations Economic and Social Commission for Asia and the Pacific, 2013, pp. 6–8.
8 Han Li, "Institutions, economic transition, and urban land expansion in China", PhD dissertation, Department of Geography, University of Utah, 2016.
9 Susanne Schmeier, "Regional cooperation efforts in the Mekong River Basin: Mitigating river-related security threats and promoting regional development", *Australian Journal of South-East Asian Studies*, Vol. 2, No. 2, 2009, pp. 28–52.
10 S. Choi and S. Lee, "Patterns of international relations on hydropower development in the Mekong River Basin", *Peace Studies*, Vol. 22, No. 1, 2014, pp. 389–434.
11 Zhenming Zhu, "Mekong development and China's (Yunnan) participation in the Greater Mekong Subregion cooperation", *Ritsumeikan International Affairs*, Vol. 8, 2010, pp. 1–16.
12 Evelyn Goh, "China in the Mekong River Basin: The regional security implications of resource development on the Lancang Jiang", RSIS-DISS *Working Paper Series*, No. 69, 2004.
13 C. Tubilewicz and K. Jayasuriya, "Internationalisation of the Chinese subnational state and capital: The case of Yunnan and the Greater Mekong Subregion", *Australian Journal of International Affairs,* Vol. 69, Iss. 2, 2015, pp.185–204.
14 F. Urban et al., "An analysis of China's investment in the hydropower sector in the Greater Mekong Sub-Region", *Environment, Development and Sustainability*, Vol. 15, Iss. 2, 2013, pp. 301–24.

15 Hiroshi Hori, *The Mekong: Environment and Development*, Tokyo: United Nations University Press, 2000.
16 M. Kummu and O. Varis, "Sediment-related impacts due to upstream reservoir trapping, the Lower Mekong River", *Geomorphology*, Vol. 85, Iss. 3–4, 2007, pp. 275–93.
17 Y. Zhang et al., "The influence of large dams building on resettlement in the Upper Mekong River", *Journal of Geographical Sciences*, Vol. 23, Iss. 5, 2013, pp. 947–57.
18 C. Piseth and C. Sophearin, "Assessment of power trade benefits from hydropower projects in Lower Mekong River Basin" in P. Han and F. Kimura (eds.), *Energy Market Integration in East Asia: Energy Trade, Cross Border Electricity, and Price Mechanism*. Jakarta, Indonesia: ERIA Research Project Report FY2013, No. 29, 2014, pp. 193–239.
19 C. Weatherby and B. Eyler, "Mekong power shift: Emerging trends in the GMS power sector", *Letters from the Mekong*, 2017, online at www.css.ethz.ch/content/dam/ethz/special-interest/gess/cis/center-for-securities-studies/resources/docs/Stimson-EnergyPublication%20(1).pdf.
20 O. Shrestha and A. Chongvilaivan, "Greater Mekong Subregion: From geographical corridors to socio-economic corridors" in O. Shrestha and A. Chongvilaivan (eds.), *Greater Mekong Subregion from Geographical to Socio-economic Integration*, Singapore: Institute of Southeast Asian Studies, 2013, pp. 1–17.
21 Susanne Schmeier, op cit.; C. W. Nam and K. Y. Nam, "Economic factors shaping private sector development in the Greater Mekong Subregion", *Internationales Asianforum*, Vol. 39, No. 3–4, 2008, pp. 325–41; M. Krongkaew, "The development of the Greater Mekong Subregion (GMS): Real promise or false hope?" *Journal of Asian Economics*, Vol. 15, Iss. 5, 2004, pp. 977–98.
22 M. Ishida (ed.), *Border Economies in the Greater Mekong Subregion*, London and New York: Palgrave Macmillan, 2013.
23 S. Lee, "Benefit sharing in the Mekong River Basin", *Water International*, Vol. 40, Iss. 1, 2015, pp. 139–52; S. Lee and S. Lee, "Cooperation in the Mekong River Basin through benefit sharing", 동남아연구 [*Southeast Asia Research*], Vol. 25, No. 1, 2015, pp. 275–310.
24 A. Haefner, "Regional environmental security: Cooperation and challenges in the Mekong Subregion", *Global Change, Peace & Security*, Vol. 25, Iss. 1, 2013, p. 38; M. Krongkaew, op cit.
25 L. Soliev et al., "The costs of benefit sharing: Historical and institutional analysis of shared water development in the Ferghana Valley, the Syr Darya Basin", *Water*, Vol. 7, Iss. 6, 2015, pp. 2728–32; C. W. Sadoff and D. Grey, "Cooperation on international rivers: A continuum for securing and sharing benefits", *Water International*, Vol. 30, Iss. 4, 2005, p. 422.
26 S. Lee, op cit.; H. Qaddumi, "Practical approaches to transboundary water benefit sharing", *Working Paper* 292, Overseas Development Institute, London, 2008.
27 C. W. Sadoff and D. Grey, 2005, op cit.; C. Sadoff and D. Grey, "Beyond the river: The benefits of cooperation on international rivers", *Water Policy*, Vol. 4, Iss. 5, 2002, pp. 389–403.
28 S. Lee, op cit.
29 M. Kummu and O. Varis, op cit.
30 R. M. Pink, *Water Rights in Southeast Asia and India*, London and New York: Palgrave Macmillan, 2016, p. 127; Han Li, op cit.
31 C. M. Nguyen, "Forward" in GSM Secretariat, *Statistics on Growth, Energy, and Bilateral Trade in the Greater Mekong Subregion*, Third Edition, Hanoi, Vietnam: GSM Secretariat, 2017, p. xi, online at https://www.greatermekong.org/statistics/downloads/gms-statistics-3rd-ed-view.pdf.
32 ADB, *Greater Mekong Subregion Energy Sector Assessment, Strategy and Road Map*, Manila: Asian Development Bank, June 2016, p. 22, online at www.eepmekong.org/index.php/resources/reports-presentations/248-greater-mekong-subregion-energy-sector-assessment-strategy-and-road-map-2016/file; T. Kudo and M.

Ishida, "Prologue: Progress in cross-border movement and the development of border economic zones" in M. Ishida (ed.), *Border Economies in the Greater Mekong Subregion*, London and New York: Palgrave Macmillan, 2013, pp. 3–5.

33 S. Siriprachai, "The Thai economy: Structural changes and challenges ahead", *Thammasat Economic Journal*, Vol. 27, No. 1, 2009, p. 166.

34 Ibid.

35 O. Shrestha and A. Chongvilaivan, op cit.

36 G. Lacombe et al., "Regional assessment of groundwater recharge in the Lower Mekong Basin", *Hydrology*, Vol. 4, Iss. 4, 2017, p. 2.

37 M. Zhou et al., "Evapotranspiration in the Mekong and Yellow River Basins", *Hydrological Sciences Journal*, Vol. 54, Iss. 3, 2009, pp. 625–7.

38 E. E. Wohl, "Hydrology and discharge" in A. Gupta (ed.), *Large Rivers: Geomorphology and Management*, Chichester, UK: John Wiley & Sons, Ltd, 2007, p. 39; Hiroshi Hori, op cit.

39 MRC, *MRC Work Programme 2010*, Vientiane: Mekong River Commission, 2009, online at www.mrcmekong.org/assets/Publications/strategies-workprog/workprogram10.pdf.

40 World Bank Databank, online at http://databank.worldbank.org.

41 ADB, *Greater Mekong Subregion Economic Cooperation Program*, Manila: Asian Development Bank, 2015, online at https://www.adb.org/sites/default/files/publication/29387/gms-ecp-overview-2015.pdf; K. Sakai and T. R. Nguyen, "Coordinating the supply of regional public goods: The Greater Mekong Subregional Program" in A. Estevadeordal et al. (eds.) *Regional Public Goods: From Theory to Practice*, Washington, DC: Inter-American Development Bank and Manila: Asian Development Bank, 2004, p. 424.

42 Swedish International Development Cooperation Agency (Sida), "Transboundary water cooperation in the Mekong", *Water and Sanitation*, August 2015, online at https://www.sida.se/contentassets/1734153ba8e6402a841f8ee2e947de06/18086.pdf.

43 ADB, "Fourth GMS Economic Corridors Forum CONCEPT NOTE", Greater Mekong Subregion Fourth GMS Economic Corridors Forum, Mandalay, Myanmar, 22 June 2012, p. 1, online at https://www.adb.org/sites/default/files/related/31970/ECF-4-Concept%20Note-19-Jun-2012.pdf.

44 ADB, June 2016, op cit.

45 ADB, *Greater Mekong Subregion Power Trade and Interconnection – 2 Decades of Cooperation*, Manila: Asian Development Bank, September 2012, pp. 26–7, online at https://www.adb.org/sites/default/files/publication/29982/gms-power-trade-interconnection.pdf.

46 O. Shrestha and A. Chongvilaivan, op cit.

47 ADB, September 2012, op cit.

48 ADB, *Assessment of the Greater Mekong Subregion Energy Sector Development: Progress, Prospects, and Regional Investment*, Manila: Asian Development Bank, 2013, p. 47, online at https://www.adb.org/sites/default/files/institutional-document/33872/files/assessment-gms-subregion-energy-sector-development.pdf.

49 C. Weatherby and B. Eyler, op cit.; ADB, June 2016, op cit.; Intelligent Energy Systems (IES), *Alternatives for Power Generation in the Greater Mekong Subregion, Volume 1: Power Sector Vision for the Greater Mekong Subregion*, Sydney: Intelligent Energy Systems, April 2016, online at http://awsassets.panda.org/downloads/regional.pdf; World Energy Council, *World Energy Resources Hydropower*, London: World Energy Council, 2016, pp. 38–47, online at https://www.worldenergy.org/wp-content/uploads/2017/03/WEResources_Hydropower_2016.pdf.

50 O. Shrestha and A. Chongvilaivan, op cit.; ADB, *Regional Cooperation and Integration: Experiences in Asia and the Pacific*, Manila: Asian Development Bank Conference Proceedings, March 2012, p. 71, online at https://www.adb.org/sites/default/files/publication/30215/regional-cooperation-conference-2012.pdf.

51 O. Shrestha and A. Chongvilaivan, op cit.

52 ADB, *Evaluation Study: Energy Sector in the Greater Mekong Subregion*, Manila: Asian Development Bank, December 2008, p. i, online at https://www.oecd.org/countries/mongolia/42222387.pdf.
53 D. Roland-Holst and S. Heft-Neal, "Food-water-energy nexus: GMS challenges of growth for 2020 and beyond" in Hasan Moinuddin and Jay Maclean (eds.), *GMS 2020 Conference Proceedings: Balancing Economic Growth and Environmental Sustainability*. Bangkok: Asian Development Bank and Greater Mekong Subregion Core Environment Programme, 2012, p. 487.
54 F. Urban et al., "China's dam-builders: Their role in transboundary river management in South-East Asia" in *Hydropolitics and Conflict Management in Transboundary River Basins: China and Its Neighbours*, special issue of *International Journal of Water Resources Development*, Vol. 34, Iss. 5, 2018, pp. 748–9.
55 D. O. Vasconcelos, "The stumbling blocks to China's green transition", *The Diplomat*, 21 April 2018, online at https://thediplomat.com/2018/04/the-stumbling-blocks-to-chinas-green-transition/.
56 MRC, *Review and Update of the MRC Preliminary Design Guidance for Proposed Mainstream and Significant Tributary Dams of the Lower Mekong Basin*, Vientiane: Mekong River Commission, 7 November 2017, p. 21, online at www.mrcmekong.org/assets/Uploads/DG2018-CN-FINAL-DRAFT.pdf.
57 S. Biba, "China's 'old' and 'new' Mekong River politics: The Lancang-Mekong cooperation from a comparative benefit-sharing perspective", *Water International*, Vol. 43, Iss. 5, 2018, p. 626.
58 C. Weatherby and B. Eyler, op cit., p. 35.
59 Economist Intelligence Unit, "Myanmar's hopes of a new approach to hydropower", *The Economist*, 8 June 2018, online at www.eiu.com/industry/article/2006811184/myanmars-hopes-of-a-new-approach-to-hydropower/2018-06-08.
60 Intelligent Energy Systems, op cit.
61 K. Rabin and C. Madden, "Out of darkness: Myanmar's quest to (em)power its citizens", *Foreign Affairs*, 1 October 2015, online at https://www.foreignaffairs.com/articles/burma-myanmar/2015-10-01/out-darkness.
62 C. Weatherby and B. Eyler, op cit.; ADB, 2015, op cit.; K. Sothear, "Electricity provider says power from Koh Kong Dam not wasted", *The Cambodia Daily*, 21 November 2014, online at https://www.cambodiadaily.com/news/electricity-provider-says-power-from-koh-kong-dam-not-wasted-72780.
63 A. Johnson, "The role for hydropower in the Greater Mekong Subregion's power sector: An interview with Brian Eyler and Courtney Weatherby", *Pacific Energy Summit* series, National Bureau of Asian Research, 4 October 2017, online at https://www.nbr.org/publication/the-role-for-hydropower-in-the-greater-mekong-subregions-power-sector.
64 K. Kouphokham, "Lao PDR Country Report" in S. Kimura and H. Phoumin (eds.), *Energy Outlook and Energy Saving Potential in East Asia*, Jakarta: Economic Research Institute for ASEAN and East Asia, June 2016, p. 194; T. Kyozuka, "Laos pins economic hopes on extra electricity", *Nikkei Asian Review*, 30 November 2015, online at https://asia.nikkei.com/Economy/Laos-pins-economic-hopes-on-extra-electricity.
65 C. Weatherby and B. Eyler, op cit.; A. Johnson, op cit.; ADB, June 2016, op cit.; ADB, 2015, op cit.
66 Intelligent Energy Systems, op cit., p. 90.
67 Ibid., pp. 91–2; ADB, June 2016, op cit.; ADB, 2015, op cit.
68 ADB, September 2012, op cit.
69 S. Lee, op cit; ADB, June 2012, op cit; S. Schmeirer, "Regional cooperation efforts in the Mekong River Basin: Mitigating River related security threats and promoting regional development", *Australian Journal of Southeast Asian Studies*, Vol. 2, No. 2, 2010, pp. 28–52; Economic Consulting Associates, *The Potential of Regional Power Sector Integration: Greater Mekong Subregion (GMS) Transmission and Trading Case Study*, Washington, DC: Energy Sector Management Assistance Programme, 2010,

online at www.esmap.org/sites/esmap.org/files/BN004-10_REISP-CD_Greater%20Mekong%20Subregion-Transmission%20&%20Trading.pdf; J. Dosch and O. Hensengerth, "Sub-regional cooperation in Southeast Asia: The Mekong Basin", *European Journal of East Asian Studies*, Vol. 4, Iss. 2, 2005, pp.263–86; Evelyn Goh, op cit.

70 ADB, September 2012, op cit.

71 T. Ahmed et al., "ASEAN power grid: A secure transmission infrastructure for clean and sustainable energy for South-East Asia", *Renewable and Sustainable Energy Reviews*, Vol. 67, March 2017, pp. 1431–3; P. N. Bao et al., "Integrated approach for sustainable hydropower development in the Mekong River Basin", *Environment and Natural Resources Research*, Vol. 7, No. 1, 2017, pp. 60–1.

72 ADB, June 2016, op cit., p. 9.

73 R. Cronin and C. Weatherby, "Time for a new narrative on Mekong hydropower", *Letters from the Mekong*, 2015, p. 35, online at https://www.stimson.org/sites/default/files/file-attachments/Letters_from_the_Mekong_Oct_2015.pdf.

74 V. Chheang, "The Cambodia-Laos-Vietnam Development Triangle Area", *ISEAS Perspective*, No. 30, June 2018, online at https://www.iseas.edu.sg/images/pdf/ISEAS_Perspective_2018_30@50.pdf; A. Johnson, op cit.; ADB, September 2012, op cit., p. 14; J. Antikainen et al., *Review of the Greater Mekong Sub-Region Regional Power Trade Final Report*, Stockholm: Swedish International Development Agency, 2011; Economic Consulting Associates, op cit.

75 C. W. Sadoff and D. Grey, 2005, op cit., pp. 421; C. W. Sadoff and D. Grey, 2002, op cit., pp. 392–3.

76 D. Arjoon et al., "Sharing water and benefits in transboundary river basins", *Hydrology and Earth System Sciences*, Vol. 20, Iss. 6, 2016, pp. 2135–6.

77 Mekong Institute and ADB, "Harmonizing food safety systems and increasing market access in the Greater Mekong Subregion", GMS Core Agriculture Support Program: *Discussion Paper Series*, No. 1, 2017. p. 2, online at www.gmswga.org/sites/default/files/documents/harmonizing-food-safety-systems.pdf.

78 S. Madhur and J. Menon, "Growth, development and inclusion in the Greater Mekong Subregion: An assessment" in GMS-DAN, *Inclusive Development in the Greater Mekong Subregion: An Assessment*, Phnom Penh: Greater Mekong Subregion Development Analysis Network, February 2014, pp. 10–11.

79 K. H. Do and A. Dinar, "The linkages of energy, water, and land use in Southeast Asia: Challenges and opportunities for the Mekong region", UNU-WIDER *Working Paper*, No. 62, 2016, p. 9, online at https://www.wider.unu.edu/sites/default/files/wp2016-62.pdf.

80 International Energy Agency, *Development Prospects of the ASEAN Power Sector: Towards an Integrated Electricity Market*, Paris: OECD/IEA, 2015, p. 11, online at https://www.iea.org/publications/freepublications/publication/Partnercountry_DevelopmentProspectsoftheASEANPowerSector.pdf.

81 ADB, *Greater Mekong Subregion Atlas of the Environment* Second Edition, Manila: Asian Development Bank, 2012, pp. 185–98, online at https://www.adb.org/sites/default/files/publication/30074/gms-atlas-environment-2nd-edition.pdf; International Centre for Environmental Management, *MRC SEA for Hydropower on the Mekong Mainstream: Summary Baseline Assessment Report*, Vientiane: Mekong River Commission, 15 April 2010, pp. 157–66, online at www.mrcmekong.org/assets/Publications/Consultations/SEA-Hydropower/8-Summary-baseline.pdf.

82 C. Piseth and C. Sophearin, op cit.

83 ADB, *Greater Mekong Subregion Statistics on Growth, Infrastructure, and Trade,* Second Edition, Greater Mekong Subregion Eighth Economic Corridors Forum, Phnom Penh, Cambodia, 3–4 August 2016, p. 9, online at https://www.adb.org/sites/default/files/institutional-document/189958/gms-statistics-2nd-ed.pdf.

84 Ibid., p. 18.

85 S. Madhur and J. Menon, op cit., p. 11.

86 Ibid.
87 C. Piseth and C. Sophearin, op cit., pp. 235–9.
88 C. Weatherby and B. Eyler, op cit.
89 P. Deetes, "The hidden cost of Thailand's electricity", *Bangkok Post*, 19 May 2015, online at https://www.bangkokpost.com/opinion/opinion/565867/the-hidden-cost-of-thailand-electricity.
90 C. Tubilewicz and K. Jayasuriya, op cit.
91 K. R. Olson and L. W. Morton, "Polders, dikes, canals, rice, and aquaculture in the Mekong Delta", *Journal of Soil and Water Conservation*, Vol. 73, No. 4, 2018, pp. 83A-9A; C. Weatherby and B. Eyler, op cit.
92 S. Lee, op cit.; S. Ogden, "Challenges facing cooperation and sustainability on water security and hydropower development in the Mekong River Basin: The GMS response" in Hasan Moinuddin and Jay Maclean (eds.), *GMS 2020 Conference Proceedings: Balancing Economic Growth and Environmental Sustainability*, Bangkok: ADB and Greater Mekong Subregion Core Environment Program, 2012, pp. 276–8; A. Oehlers, "A critique of ADB policies towards the Greater Mekong Sub-region", *Journal of Contemporary Asia*, Vol. 36, Iss. 4, 2006, pp. 464–78.
93 S. W. D. Pearse-Smith, "The impact of continued Mekong Basin hydropower development on local livelihoods", *Consilience: The Journal of Sustainable Development*, Vol. 7, Iss. 1, 2012, pp. 73–86.
94 Y. Zhang et al., op cit; *Vientiane Times*, "Xayaboury dam developers pledge 'well-being' of relocated villagers", 25 August 2013, online at http://wle-staging-mekong.cgiar.org/xayaboury-dam-developers-pledge-well-being-of-relocated-villagers/; T. Scudder, *The Future of Large Dams*, London: Earthscan Publication, 2005.
95 S. Lee and S. Lee, op cit.; J. Dosch and O. Hensengerth, op cit.
96 Tanya Lee. "Time to re-assess Greater Mekong Subregion: Energy sector investments", *International Rivers and Mekong Watch*, September 2015, online at https://www.internationalrivers.org/sites/default/files/attached-files/re-assessing_gms_investments_2.pdf.
97 ADB, *The Greater Mekong Subregion Economic Cooperation Program Strategic Framework 2012–2022*, Manila: Asian Development Bank, 2011, pp. 1–7; P. Sokhem, "Cooperation in the Mekong Basin in implementing Integrated River Basin Management (IRBM): From negotiation stage to a more concrete joint planning and implementation", paper presented at First General Meeting of Network of Asian River Basin Organization (NARBO), Malnag, Indonesia, 24–6 February 2004.

7 Vietnam Mekong River Delta

A regional connection perspective[1]

Bui Quang Binh

Introduction

The Mekong River begins at the base of the Guosangmucha Mountain in China's Qinghai Province. This is the starting point for a 4,350 km journey that ends in southwestern Vietnam. There, the River's 14,800 m^3/second discharge has created a delta of 39,000 km^2 in area and a long coastline that Vietnam shares with Cambodia on the west. On the northeast of the Delta region, Hồ Chí Minh City lies just outside its boundary.[2] Although it is a world-renowned name, the Mekong Delta is more popularly known in Vietnam as "Nine Dragons" because the River breaks up as it enters the country, distributing its water and alluvium through nine channels. Endowed with rich agricultural resources, the "Nine Dragons" Delta has in recent centuries been settled by the Vietnamese people, who have in turn established the region as Vietnam's "rice bowl".

Administratively, the Mekong River Delta comprises 12 provinces (Figure 7.1), whose total population exceeds 20 million relatively evenly distributed across the region. Cần Thơ City, an independent municipality located near the geographic centre of the Delta area, is the fourth largest city in Vietnam. With a population of approximately 1.2 million, Cần Thơ is nicknamed the "western capital" of the country.

Economically, the topography of the delta has created mixed physical environmental conditions for trade. The vast distributary network of rivers and canals, and proximity to the sea, has given the region great advantages with respect to water transport. Yet these same riverine conditions, combined with weak soils typical of delta landforms,[3] have been an obstacle to the development of land transport. As a result, both intra- and extra-regional trade has been inhibited, which has reduced the overall level of regional competitiveness as Vietnam tries to develop economically.

Through examining these physical and economic settings, this chapter outlines the development conditions of the Delta region. The main argument will take the holistic position that development is multifaceted, and therefore the availability of physical resources, the sectoral division of the economy, the socio-economic structure, and the human agency should be taken into consideration as an interconnected whole. Overall, six such factors will be examined both individually and

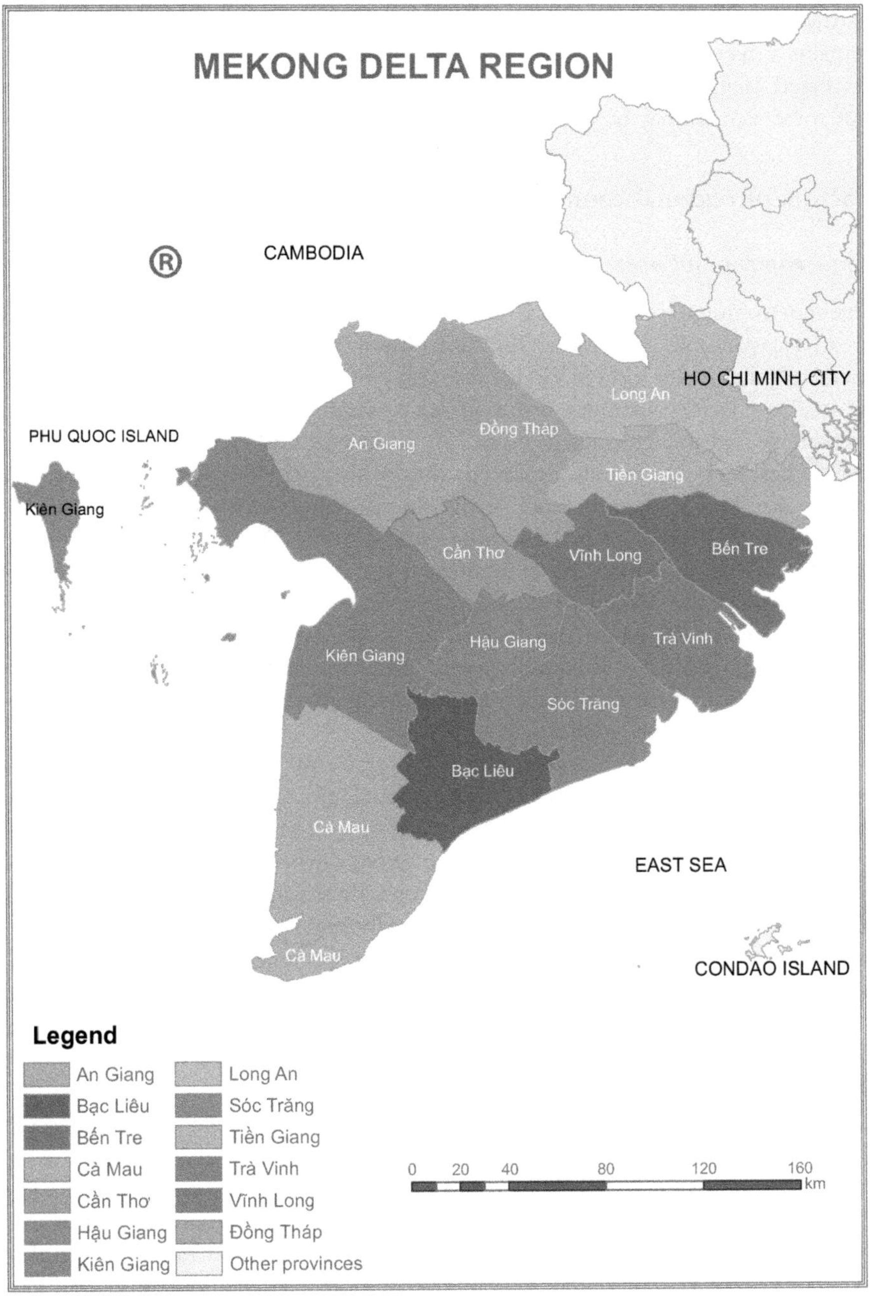

Figure 7.1 Administration map of the Mekong Delta provinces in Vietnam
Source: Adapted from Gobbler at wikivoyage shared

in their connectivity. The goal of the analysis is to show that persistent stasis remains a major challenge facing the Delta region, and that development through increased connectivity will be a complex undertaking to overcome this problem, but some aspects may be possible now.

Factors of regional connection in the Mekong River Delta

Environment and natural resources and comparative agricultural advantages

The environmental and natural endowment of the Mekong River Delta has created favourable conditions for agricultural and aquatic resource development. While many other Vietnamese regions are also blessed with natural riches, the Delta outshines them in scale, volume, variety, and many other measurable factors. Through centuries of occupancy and use, the fertility of the region has been successfully exploited. Meanwhile, with the population relatively evenly distributed in accordance with the natural conditions, an agriculturally based economic structure has also been created in the Delta area. Within the framework, all 12 provinces have adequate natural resources to produce enough goods to meet the immediate needs of their respective residents. Of course, if all the provinces produce not only enough for local consumption, but also the same or similar agricultural and aquatic goods, there would typically be little need or demand for intra-provincial trade. This situation may also result in little enthusiasm for intra-regional connectivity.

As may be expected, however, the Delta region does not fit the above profile completely. Some of the provinces have sufficiently advantageous conditions to develop a commodity, be it rice, shrimp, catfish, or fruit, on an adequate scale to export.[4] Farmers' long-accumulated, time-tested environmental knowledge helps in this production surplus.[5] Again, this favourable situation exists throughout the region, and thus the difference between provinces is not big enough to create a high level of specialisation. Yet given that export commodity prices are vulnerable to national and global market fluctuations, regional advantages are comparative, not absolute. Finding reliable markets for production will thus remain a problem until competitive advantages can augment comparative ones. This applies to both domestic and international export.

Considering the region as a whole, the Mekong River Delta offers the conditions to allow the production of certain groups of agricultural products to be centralised on a sufficient scale to create export economic hubs and sectors. The relatively even disbursement of the population in rural and urban hierarchies may potentially also enhance the overall comparative advantage. Yet raising the level of export production will, more importantly, require an enhanced level of intra-regional connectivity. In this regard, however, the Delta region seems caught up in a chicken-and-egg situation: improved productivity requires improved connectivity, but improved connectivity will likely only result once more income from improved productivity is available.

Rural and urban context

Figure 7.1 above shows the location of the Delta's provinces and their capital cities. These urban locations are by and large centred along the main distributary channels of the Mekong River. With the exception of Cần Thơ City, the urban population is well below one million across the provinces, indicating the overwhelmingly rural character of the region. Population densities are consistent with agricultural conditions, varying between 250–800 people per square kilometre. The two largest, and most distant, provinces, Kiên Giang and Cà Mau, have the lowest population density, illustrating the centralising tendency of agricultural activities in the Mekong River Delta, and the relationship between agricultural extensiveness and the distance from the main distributary channels. Nevertheless, throughout the region, a network of lower-level cities and towns has sprung up, serving as support centres for industrial production, product distribution, and transport. Such towns typically emerge in places where topographic conditions are relatively homogeneous, and their goods, services, locations, and population size dictate their position in the hierarchy of central places.

Cần Thơ City, for example, has a population of 1.2 million and is centrally located within the Delta region. Although a municipality and with a provincial status since 2004, the city functions as the regional administrative capital. The Cần Thơ Bridge over the Hau River distributary directly links the city with Hồ Chí Minh City. Another expressway is also currently being constructed to further improve connectivity.

As mentioned earlier, in addition to Cần Thơ, an increasing number of provincial cities in the Delta are becoming main centres and playing significant roles in the regional connection improvement effort. Among them, the most important cities include M⊠ Tho, Cà Mau, Long Xuyên, and Rạch Giá. These district towns and townships are typically connecting centres at lower levels of the hierarchy. Besides being administrative centres, these regional towns function mainly as centres for product distribution and transport. Their roles as centres of industrial production and support services remain modest and unobtrusive.

Hồ Chí Minh City, on the other hand, dominates the Delta region by its very proximity. Given its status as the nation's former capital and current largest city, connectivity with Hồ Chí Minh City is extremely important for all localities in the Delta.[6] This is especially the case for cities in close proximity, whose specialised urban functions remain linked more directly with Hồ Chí Minh City than Cần Thơ. In contrast, within-the-region connectivity tends to be much weaker. There is certainly no lack of shared understanding that towns are centralised places for connection, and that the urban network is centralised by connecting space. Yet if we consider each town as a connecting subject, the level of resource development and the degree of functional specialisation of these subjects are still low in the Delta area, including that of Cần Thơ City. Therefore, there have not been great and sustainable demands for linking capabilities to be developed among the urban areas in the region; almost all towns are dependent upon their connections with Hồ Chí Minh City.

Failed transportation infrastructure

Waterways have always been the Mekong River Delta's strength. Due to the improvements in recent years, the Delta region is equipped with a relatively complete transportation system of waterways as well as roads and airways. Yet from the perspective which evaluates whether or how effectively the existing facilities augment trade capabilities, many constraints exist. Specifically, the continuous upgrading efforts have been widely recognised as insufficient to allow the rural areas to link up with the provincial capitals and urban centres, or the Delta area with other domestic or international regions. Moreover, while the "Nine Dragons" are dotted with ports and wharves, their cargo handling facilities are often found to be neither up-to-date, nor complete. As a result,, most of the loading and unloading is still done manually. Moreover, the access for large vessels remains constrained by inadequate berthage. Finally, infrequent drainage of the alluvium-laden distributaries is an ongoing problem. Cái Cui Port, servicing Cần Thơ City, is a typical case in point.

In the road system, Highway 1A from Cần Thơ to Cà Mau is considered to be the "spine" of the Mekong River Delta's transportation network. Yet it is currently incapable of handling all the types of container trucks. Beyond this highway the situation worsens. Narrow roads have limited the operation of heavy-duty trucks, increasing the cost but decreasing the frequency of delivery, and thus reducing the region's competitive advantage. The consequence of the poor road system is especially serious for seafood enterprises in the provinces of Sóc Trăng, Bạc Liêu, and Cà Mau. The seafood companies in these three provinces, for example, produce and export hundreds of tons of shrimps each year. Yet they have to use fleets of small trucks to deliver the shipments. Worse still, the freight can only be transported to Hồ Chí Minh City, rather than directly to the designated consumer markets. According to the Vietnam Chamber of Commerce and Industry (VCCI) office in Cần Thơ City, currently 70 per cent of the products exported from the Mekong River Delta are delivered to ports in the Hồ Chí Minh City vicinity.[7] This inconvenient arrangement inevitably increases the costs and time of product delivery.[8]

Due to the riverine character of the Delta, bridges also deserve special mention. Presently, the regional transportation grid incorporates a dense but spatially uneven bridge network. Yet the network is far from adequate, as in many localities freight must be carried across distributary canals by ship. For example, the arterial route from Hồ Chí Minh City to the western Delta urban nodes must pass through M⊠ Tho City and cross the Cho Gao Canal. In recent years, the flow of vessels through this canal has grown to more than 346,000 per annum.[9] Further, of the bridges that do exist, many were built to service an earlier generation of trucks and other types of vehicles. They are now deficient in terms of width and height clearance. Even the newly constructed Cho Gao Bridge has proved to be too narrow to accommodate some types of trucks, although it is high enough to allow for ship passage underneath. Thus breaking-of-bulk from trucks to cargo vessels and back to trucks remains a necessity for much trade even though the canal itself is only about 100 metres wide.

Last but not least, a large amount of imported materials, including fuel, must pass through intermediary ports outside the region before reaching the Delta region. This is mainly due to a lack of availability and access for big vessels in the Delta area. The port at Cái Cui is a particular problem, but all the other Delta ports suffer from inconsistent access. Over the years, there have of course been constant government and commercial efforts to improve the facilities. However, the overall quality has not kept pace with demand, and the general level of connectivity has not reached the synchronisation stage of key water and land transport mediums. This bottleneck represents a major obstacle to the development of the Delta's economy, and exemplifies the commonly held opinion that infrastructure is a vital factor affecting the economic growth and development of virtually all regions.

In sum, an important reason why the Mekong Delta's abundant waterways have yet to make the supposed transport advantage a reality is the absence of suitable ports that are equipped with facilities for cargo handling and storage. Adding to the problem is the fact that unlike some in Hồ Chí Minh City, the ports in the Delta region are not furnished or prepared for large container vessels to dock. Yet the surface transport system is not ready to rise to the challenge and function as a feasible alternative. For the existing road network provides for only small and light vehicles, and hence makes it difficult, if not impossible, for container trucks to manoeuvre through it. Furthermore, the transport capacity of bridges and roads is often not compatible. The inadequate transport infrastructure across the Delta, the insufficient interconnections between regional road systems and waterways, and the almost lopsided dependence on Hồ Chí Minh City all unfavourably impact goods transportation and, in turn, weaken the region's inherent competitive advantages for trade and development. Clearing these "bottlenecks" in the transport circulation on the "Nine Dragons" through upgrading/expanding its infrastructure capacities remains an urgent challenge for the region.

Labour factors

The regional population remains predominantly rural and employed in household-scale agriculture, particularly rice. Most residents have great skills in crop production, perfected through exposure to environmental vagaries over the centuries. But these skills often do not suffice when the national economy is trying to lift itself into manufacturing and service activities.

As may be expected, a growing awareness that cities provide the potential for earning increased income has produced a certain amount of labour-related movement in recent decades. Inter-regional labour movement from the Mekong River Delta to other regions, and sometimes vice versa, has affected the supply of labour for provincial markets, leading to fluctuations of excess or deficiency, both short term and long term. As is typical worldwide, it is young people who are most likely to move. Their increasing discontent with low-skilled agricultural work and impatience with the consequent local inability to improve individual and household income push them to the city. The dominant direction of the young rural-to-urban labour movement in the Delta area should not be hard to guess: Hồ Chí Minh City, and secondarily, the provinces of Southeast Vietnam. In recent years, the shortage of young labour in rural areas of the Mekong River Delta during the harvest has not been uncommon.[10] The obvious logic behind this rather one-sided connection between city and countryside is that compelling economic advantages of urban life overshadow corresponding rewards from struggles with nature in the countryside.

Throughout the world, including Vietnam, efforts to build inter/intra-regional connections for development in general and for economic improvement in particular enable and encourage movement of labour and jobs, which may greatly impact income levels and redistribution, consumption patterns, investment flows, technology transfers, and social networks. For the Mekong Delta, the intra- and extra-regional population distribution and labour movement reflect the commonly-identified connectivity elements in development. Accordingly, a likely implication is that people remaining in the countryside may fall further behind in terms of the consumption of the products that often represent the underlying reason for economic development.

This may indeed become a serious concern for the Delta region. For in spite of compelling motivation to leave, the current population dynamics and migration patterns in the Delta suggest that an excess supply of agricultural labour will occur in the near future. This is due to the fact that most other economic sectors will rely more on an educated and trained labour force, and thus shy away from, or be simply unable to take advantage of the existing vast pool of inadequately educated or trained rural labour. This is particularly true for provincial-level cities. Again, the result will be more movement of the young to Hồ Chí Minh City.[11] The former capital will therefore likely increase its domination over the Delta region, which will be increasingly reliant on the former for economic and social needs.

Capital factors and private sector business development

With respect to capital, it is not surprising to find that a regional economy based on household agricultural production has but limited surplus to be spent on development. The amount of foreign direct investment (FDI) into the Delta is insignificant compared to Hồ Chí Minh City and the country's Southeast region. A certain number of state-owned enterprises (SOEs) – electricity plants, oil and gas companies, and nitrogenous fertiliser production operations – do exist in the Delta area. However neither FDIs nor SOEs play more than a very negligible role in promoting spill-over effects across economic sectors by incorporating complementary local industries.[12]

The majority of the enterprises in the Delta area are privately owned and consequently are small or tiny.[13] In terms of business transactions, the private sector – business-to-business, or B2B, activities – plays a dominant role. In other words, the Mekong River Delta's regional business linkages are based on tens of thousands of private enterprises, formed by millions of individual agricultural producers. Yet these businesses have control of (and access to) very limited resources. Furthermore, direct transactions between producing households and business enterprises, or between private businesses and local cooperative producers, are still relatively uncommon. Thus the ability to connect-up and achieve scales that signify regional development remains low across the Delta.

Another indication of low levels of regional development in the Mekong Delta is the very small number of business enterprises in relation to the population size. The total number of enterprises in the Delta is equal to only one quarter of that in Hồ Chí Minh City, and the per-business amount of capital available is only around 50 per cent that of Hồ Chí Minh City. While the number of enterprises in the Delta slightly exceeds the corresponding number in the five provinces of the Southeast region, the average amount of capital available is only 33 per cent and the average number of employees per business is only about 40 per cent. [14]

The proportion of the region's enterprises in trade and services (mostly retail and small services) is very high; this is followed by construction (mostly civil construction). This situation exists due to low initial investment requirements, little need for skilled labour, and faster capital returns, when compared to other production sectors.[15] It thus follows that while the region specialises in agriculture and fishing, the number of businesses involved in processing or logistic operations for value-added products is disproportionately low. Likewise, modern service industries in the Delta are still very much in their infancy. Although sectoral structural reforms in the period 2006–10 have added momentum to sector specialisation in some provinces, the degree of concentration and specialisation in the region as a whole remains low and has not generated significant economic improvements.

At the household level, connectivity related to production is non-existent. This is also the case for household-private sector connectivity. Obviously, agricultural production based on millions of small and dispersed households cannot be easily integrated. Effective organisation of widely diverse and scattered farming operations is very difficult to accomplish, if possible at all. Equally challenging is any attempt to effectuate a coordinated division of labour in crop production, or to reconcile and standardise quality difference between products.

However, the lack of capital may play a more important role in agricultural household producers' decisions to deal directly with industrial input suppliers and traders, and product purchasers. This common practice among farmers has disadvantaged and handicapped regional connectivity in the Delta region. Put differently, excessive dependence on input suppliers and traders has increased the number and level of intermediaries in the production chain, resulting in raised prices of products, reduced revenues, and weakened competitive advantage. Furthermore, being overly dependent on individuals' direct dealings with suppliers and traders has resulted in a structural inability to negotiate effectively. To gain an equal position with other players and to enhance competitiveness, Delta farmers may need to put more effort in to establishing and participating in household cooperative production networks.

Realistic a solution as this may be, however, suggested models with connectivity potentials, such as *cánh đồng lớn* (vast field),[16] have thus far not been effective. Identified reasons behind their failing to effectuate large-scale connectivity drives or operations include a pervasive lack of confidence among the farmers in the models, inadequate transport facilities and poor infrastructure networks, and management capability shortages.[17] Yet pilot programmes continue to be set up in the Delta region to facilitate the development and application of integrated, or concentrated/centralised, agricultural production models. Thus far, successes have been few.

Successful or not, however, a modern agricultural value chain encompasses more than integrated primary functions of growing, collecting, and transporting. Nevertheless the Mekong River Delta's industries remain underdeveloped. In spite of its long tradition of intensive cultivation, processing and other agriculture-related value-adding industries are mostly at the primary level of development. Within the region, no city has been able to grow into a development centre or to form industrial clusters that enable specialised production to create competitive advantages and move up the value chain. Although the Delta region has designated a few industrial zones, the lack of complementary processing industries means that its export production remains based on cheap low-skilled labour and centred on low value-added products.[18] For the most part, what exists across the region is a consumption market of products imported from Hồ Chí Minh City or overseas. The weak urban-rural connectivity has thus not permitted integrated regional development across the Mekong River Delta.

What needs to be emphasised here, though, is that there are some encouraging, bright spots emerging in this gloomy picture. For example, Long An Province, by taking advantage of its proximity to Hồ Chí Minh City and benefiting from consequent spill-over effects, is on its way to becoming a specialised production centre of garments, electronics, and construction technologies and materials. Meanwhile, Cần Thơ City, the effective regional capital, is set to become a powerhouse in education, training, finance and banking, tourism, and public administration services. Also picking up development momentum is Vĩnh Long City, whose transportation service sector, in particular, has experienced major growth and expansion. Last but not least, the provinces of Kiên Giang, Bến Tre, and Cà Mau have been showing promising signs of progress in aquatic product processing.

Yet the positive momentum created by the frontrunner regions continues to face the risk of being disrupted or stalled by weak inter-sectoral connectivity across the Delta, especially insufficient linkages and synergy between R&D institutes and service providers, and between market management firms and policy agencies. In other words, most enterprises and businesses in the leading economic zones of the Delta region remain small in scale and capacity. They are often not adequately equipped for value-added innovations or activities. Being resource poor, they rely heavily on the coordinated support from R&D, policy and services sectors for modern technology lines, state-of-the-art preservation, storage, and transport facilities, strategic planning, and brands creation. Joint efforts and integrated assistance are, in short, essential to develop high value-added products that are capable of maintaining and expanding domestic and international markets.[19] In the absence of a comprehensive physical and institutional connectivity, both businesses and government agencies are typically able to create and adopt only short-term strategies for immediate profits and gains. The lack of long-term investments has resulted in many rice exporters in the Delta region continuously struggling with a shortage of storage and handling facilities, logistic and marketing support, critical materials supply, and new start-ups or brands.[20] It is not surprising, then, that while Vietnam is now among the world's top rice exporting countries, its rice exporters, including those in the Delta, have not, in the last four decades, created any strong brands.

Governmental management – a mosaic

While Vietnam has been steadily shifting towards a mixed or socialist-oriented market economy, the government still has the potential to play a significant role in development. However, to date the activities of the quaternary sector have been limited. State management agencies and supporting organisations have not been very effective, either, in coordinating regional planning, improving sectoral capabilities, synergising resources for cross-sectoral partnerships, or facilitating market adjustments to support export expansion. Budget constraints and poor results in public investment effectiveness have further prevented many localities from achieving their potential. Cần Thơ City, for example, has been trying to expand its capacity and influence from being the Delta's administrative centre to become a leading innovation hub for other socio-economic functions. Yet its strivings have so far remained more expectant than realistic, due to continued inadequate availability or supply of the required or crucial inputs, especially the capital needed for development.[21]

Although current policies increasingly encourage regional connectivity, present approaches to planning, investing, and managing continue to prioritise operations at the provincial level rather than through regionally coordinated strategies and actions. This may have enabled provincial level government and industries to harvest some immediate benefits, but the yields are often limited and unsustainable, and hence contribute little to the progress of regional synergy development. As for government-to-business (G2B) relations, current state policies have also fallen short of motivating enterprises to invest in agricultural and related business sectors as an effective way to increase resource acquisition potentials.[22]

Investing in rural infrastructure improvements is an important role of the government in Vietnam. Though the National Programme on Building New Rural Areas has achieved some good results, especially in upgrading roads and irrigation systems, its efforts have only gone a small way to providing the necessary conditions for enterprises to work effectively. From a business point of view, investment in agricultural land is effective and profitable only when large-scale land concentration can result from it. Yet the land market in the rural Delta areas is still predominantly made up of small-scale farmers with individual or household ownership titles of their land. Thus sales volumes on the regional land market remain minimal.[23]

Another important role of the government involves developing and executing strategies and implementation plans for penetrating world markets for sales of national products. To date, however, state management agencies in the Mekong

River Delta are yet to make a significant contribution to expanding global market access. Businesses in the region remain in desperate need of better-developed market entry services to help them compete internationally for exports of their major products, which include rice, shrimps, fish, and fruit. Without greater government involvement, most exporting businesses in the Delta region may not be able to break into the international marketplace, cultivate and maintain a stable global demand for their products, or increase their market shares worldwide, at least, not in the foreseeable future.

An additional and equally vital role that the government plays in development focuses on education, training, research, and application of science and technology. In the Delta region, the government has been attempting to fulfil its duties and responsibilities in this regard, but still only to a limited extent. Thus far, the agriculture sector may be among the best noticeable beneficiaries of the government's services, as Cần Thơ University, Cửu Long Delta Rice Research Institute, and the Southern Horticultural Research Institute now have some tailored-made, farming-related research, teaching and training programmes/activities for local communities. Yet up and running as they are, these institutions are constantly challenged by a shortage of trainers/specialists. As a result, the agriculture sector, a key engine of economic growth in the Delta, does not always have its needs met, and its dependence on imported products for carrying out basic operations is yet to be alleviated. Agricultural enterprises, in other words, have to continue importing, among other essentials, fertilisers and cattle-feed, mostly from China.[24]

Towards initial solutions

The Mekong River Delta region of Vietnam, though close to Hồ Chí Minh City, remains a peripheral region when it comes to development. Regional economic development is, of course, a multifaceted, complex process. A weakness in any constituent element may prevent a geographic area from prospering, or even coming into its own. In this sense, "complexity" signifies the concept of "connection". For not only must individual facets of development progress internally, but their external connections with other facets are also necessary and absolutely essential.

Like everywhere else, the Delta's internal development assets and aspects range from strong to weak. Its agricultural resource base, provided by deposited alluvium, has created excellent conditions for farming. Farmers have consequently learned to use and nurse these conditions, and so they have become a strong factor in the development of the region. Yet development in the twenty-first century necessitates a replacement, or an upgrade, of what has until recently been an effective system of subsistence agriculture with one that is capable of penetrating global markets. The transformation first and foremost requires hugely increased levels of business connection between the region and the outside world.

The Delta's regional comparative advantages in agricultural and seafood products have long been noted. Yet the homogeneity of the physical environment has also handicapped development and specialisation at the regional scale. Due to the limited availability of capital and other resources that they can tap, enterprises in the region rarely have the capability to improve infrastructure networks and embark on the specialisation process in agricultural production on their own. In fact, they have not been able to adequately invest in even the most basic activities underlying the supply chain connectivity, such as local sourcing of raw materials, warehouse services, processing facilities, and branding techniques. Of all the links in the Delta's connections to the global value chain, however, the weakest is the supply-demand connectivity, or the lack of export markets for local products. The low supply-demand connectivity in part explains the slow growth of agricultural enterprises across the region both in number and in capacity.[25]

Poor regional economic connectivity is also reflected in the fact that provincial industries in the Delta do not complement each other. Most provinces in the region are at a similar state of development in the areas of technical facilities for processing and creating value-added products, social labour allocation, and functional specialisation among localities. Accordingly, an optimal solution for the weak regional linkage problem may be a higher degree of smart, functional specialisation in all development sectors and spaces. Meanwhile, strategies for regional industrialisation need to focus on the existing strong sectors in order to increase the added value of products and maximise the comparative and competitive advantages of the region. Furthermore, increased functional concentration and specialisation in the main urban centres in the Delta should help activate demand intra-regionally and externally across the country and the world.

Regional connections in the Delta are at present dominated by short-term benefits for specific local districts and businesses holding dominant power there. A resultant weak spot in the regional linkages is the connectivity of entities, including households, enterprises, supporting agencies, and state management bodies. A causal factor behind this situation is that the regulatory framework as it currently stands is simply too weak to coordinate and oversee development and connectivity efforts initiated by scattered producers and commercial firms in the region. There is thus an urgency and need for the creation and consolidation of institutional connectivity and hence capability to coordinate developmental attempts at connection in the Delta.

To accomplish this daunting task requires the government to take a leading role, and to prioritise its involvement in the whole process. Government agencies need to exercise due diligence to ensure that their proposed policy solutions are comprehensive and synchronous, and, more importantly, not skewed by the concerns or interests of individual provinces, but beneficial to the entire region. This further necessitates that regional and sectoral planning and management agencies familiarise themselves with the relevant empirically derived concepts and empirical reality of connection and specialisation for value-added development. In other words, planning and management agencies have to first improve their own capabilities to implement, supervise, and enforce compliance with regional initiatives for improving the Delta's infrastructure networks and promoting its economic growth.

Notes

1 Acknowledgement: this work was supported by the National Program KHCN-TNB. ĐT/14–19/X02, the objective of which is to institutionalise sustainable development in Southwest Vietnam.

2 In Vietnam, the Mekong Delta is often referred to as its southeast region.

3 IMHEN [Vietnam Institute of Meteorology, Hydrology and Climate Change], "Tác động của biến đổi khí hậu lên tài nguyên nước và các biện pháp thích ứng đồng bằng sông Cửu Long" [Impacts of climate change on water resources and adaptation solutions], Hanoi, Vietnam: IMHEN, 2010, pp.1–7.

4 N. T. Binh, *Nông nghiệp vùng đồng bằng sông Cửu Long: thực trạng, cơ hội và thách thức trong bối cảnh hội nhập* [Mekong Delta Agricultural Sector: Statement, Opportunities, and Challenges in the Context of Integration]. Hanoi, Vietnam: Institute of Vietnamese Studies and Development Sciences, Vietnam National University, 2015, online at http://repository.vnu.edu.vn/handle/VNU_123/192.

5 T. V. Viet, "Vai trò và tiềm năng của ngành thủy sản đối với sự phát triển kinh tế của vùng ĐBSCL, Vietnam" [Roles of fisheries in social economic developments in the Mekong Delta, Vietnam]. *Tạp chí khoa học Đại học Cần Thơ* [Can Tho University Journal of Science], No. 27, 2013, pp. 136–44.

6 N.T. Canh et al., *Báo cáo Chính quyền đô thị tại Việt Nam: Nghiên cứu tình huống từ thành phố Hồ Chí Minh và Đà Nẵng* [Report on Municipal Government in Vietnam: Case study of Ho Chi Minh and Da Nang City], Trường Đại học Kinh tế – Luật [Ho Chi Minh City, Vietnam: University of Economics and Law], 2013, p. 8, online at https://asiafoundation.org/resources/pdfs/MunicipalGovermentVietnamese.pdf.

7 Vietnam Chamber of Commerce and Industry, "Phát triển cảng nước sâu: Sức bật của Đồng bằng sông Cửu Long" [Deep water port development: Rebound of Mekong Delta], 2012, online at http://vccinews.vn/news/5943/.html.

8 Luis C. Blancas and M. Baher El-Hifnawi, *Facilitating Trade through Competitive, Low Carbon Transport: The Case for Vietnam's Inland and Coastal Waterways*, World Bank Report 83030, Washington, DC: World Bank, 2013, online at http://documents.worldbank.org/curated/en/800501468320727668/pdf/830300PUB0978100 Box379862B00PUBLIC0.pdf; World Bank, "Green growth demystified: Investing in Vietnam's inland and coastal waterways", Washington, DC: World Bank, 2013, online at https://www.worldbank.org/content/dam/Worldbank/document/EAP/Vietnam/IWT_Policy_Note_EN.pdf.

9 Soc Trang's DARD [Department of Agricultural and Rural Development], "Đánh giá hiện trạng nghề nuôi tôm nước lợ của tỉnh Sóc Trăng và đề xuất giải pháp phát triển bền vững" [Assessment of brackish water shrimp farming in Soc Trang Province and proposed solutions for sustainable development], *Hội thảo: tái cơ cấu phát triển nông nghiệp gắn xây dựng nông thôn mới thích ứng với Biến đổi khí hậu vùng Đồng bằng sông Cửu Long* [Conference Proceedings on Restructuring Agricultural Development and Adapting New Rural Construction to Climate Change in the Mekong River Delta], Soc Trang, Vietnam: Department of Agriculture and Rural Development, 2015, pp. 78–81.

10 D. N. Thanh and N. M. Hieu, "Thực trạng lao động và việc làm nông thôn Việt Nam" [Status of labour and employment in rural Vietnam], *Tạp chí khoa học Đại học Cần Thơ* [Can Tho University Journal of Science], No. 30, 2014 pp. 42–50.

11 N. Q. Nghi et al., "Thực trạng và giải pháp cho vấn đề di cư ở tỉnh Hậu Giang" [Solution to migration problems in Hau Giang Province], *Tạp chí khoa học Đại học Cần Thơ* [Can Tho University Journal of Science], No. 15a, 2010, pp. 283–92.

12 V. T. T. Anh et al., *Báo cáo: Đồng bằng sông Cửu Long Liên kết để tăng cường năng lực cạnh tranh và phát triển bền vững* [Report: Mekong Delta cooperation to strengthen competitiveness and sustain development], 2011, p. 32, online at www.fetp.edu.vn/ca

che/MPP8-545-R21V-DBSCL_Lien%20ket%20de%20tang%20cuong%20nang%20luc%20canh%20tranh%20&%20phat%20trien%20ben%20vung–Vu%20Thanh%20Tu%20Anh%20et%20al-2016-05-12-09001606.pdf.

13 V. H. Dung, "Về vai trò của ĐBSCL và Doanh nghiệp đối với phát triển kinh tế trong Vùng" [Roles of Mekong Delta and enterprise for regional economic development], 2011, online at http://mekongdelta.com.vn/mekongdelta/Admin/Upload/1361525999.pdf.

14 Q. M. Nhut, "Đánh giá các phản ứng chiến lược cuả doanh nghiệp đồng bằng sông Cửu Long trong điều kiện hội nhập kinh tế" [Assessment of possible strategic responses of Mekong River Delta enterprises in the context of international economic integration and cooperation], *Tạp chí khoa học Đại học Cần Thơ* [Can Tho University Journal of Science], No. 12, 2009, pp. 261–9.

15 MPI [Ministry of Planning and Investment], "Tình hình kinh tế-xã hội và đầu tư phát triển vùng đồng bằng sông cửu long năm 2014" [Situation of social-economic and investment development in Mekong Delta, 2014]. *Kỷ yếu Hội nghị xúc tiến thương mại, đầu tư nông nghiệp, nông thôn vùng ĐBSCL* [Conference proceedings on trade promotion, investment in agriculture and rural areas in Mekong Delta], Hanoi, Vietnam: Ministry of Planning & Investment and Ministry of Industry & Trade, 2014, pp. 6–23.

16 *Cánh đồng lớn*, or "vast field", is an applied model designed for the Mekong Delta region, which was adopted by the Vietnamese National Assembly and released in its Resolution No. 21/2011/QH13 in November 2011.

17 L. N. D. Khoi and N. N. Vang, "Giải pháp phát triển ngành thương mại & dịch vụ để thành phố Cần Thơ trở thành trung tâm động lực phát triển đồng bằng sông Cửu Long" [Solutions to develop trade and services to Can Tho City became a dynamic centre of development in the Mekong Delta region], *Kỷ yếu hội thảo khoa học, ĐH Cần Thơ* [Proceedings of Can Tho University Science conference], Can Tho, Vietnam: Can Tho University, 2012, pp. 47–55.

18 P. T. M. Duyen, "Một số giải pháp giảm nghèo vùng Đồng bằng sông Cửu Long" [Solutions to poverty reduction in the Mekong Delta region], *Tạp chí phát triển và hội nhập* [Journal of Development and Integration], Vol. 21, No. 31, 2015, pp. 69–77.

19 N. D. Cung, "Khó khăn của doanh nghiệp: vấn đề và giải pháp" [Difficulty for enterprise: Problems and solutions], *Kỷ yếu Diễn đàn Kinh tế mùa thu 2012* [Proceedings of the 2012 fall economic forum], Hanoi, Vietnam: Central Economic Committee, Vietnam Academy of Social Sciences, and Vietnam Chamber of Commerce and Industry, 2012, pp. 219–36, online at http://dl.ueb.edu.vn/bitstream/1247/9330/1/15_Kho%20khan%20cua%20doanh%20nghiep_Nguyen%20Dinh%20Cung.pdf.

20 V. T. T. Loc and L. N. D. Khoi, "Phân tích tác động các chính sách và chiến lược chuỗi ngành hàng lúa gạo" [Impacts of rice sector policies and strategies], *Tạp chí khoa học Đại học Cần Thơ* [Can Tho University Journal of Science], No. 19, 2011, pp. 110–21.

21 L. T. D. Hai and N. Q. Nghi, "Giải pháp phát triển ngành thương mại & dịch vụ để thành phố Cần Thơ trở thành trung tâm động lực phát triển đồng bằng sông Cửu Long" [Boosting trade and service as a solution to Can Tho City's challenge of becoming a driving force for regional development in the Mekong Delta], *Kỷ yếu hội thảo khoa học, ĐH Cần Thơ* [Proceedings of Can Tho University Science conference], Can Tho, Vietnam: Can Tho University, 2012, pp. 47–55.

22 CIEM [Central Institute for Economic Management], *Xây dựng chính sách đặc thù để thu hút đầu tư tại vùng đồng bằng sông Cửu Long* [Developing Special Policies to Attract Investments to the Mekong Delta], 2011, online at www.ciem.org.vn/Portals/0/CIEM/DeAnTrinhBo/2011/Tom_tat_de_an_DBSCL.pdf.

23 T. T. Dat, "Phân tích hiệu quả kỹ thuật sản xuất lúa theo mô hình cánh đồng lớn tại huyện Thới Lai, TP. Cần Thơ "[Technical analysis of efficiency of "vast field" model for rice production in Thoi Lai District, Can Tho City], Master's thesis on Public Administration, University of Economics, Ho Chi Minh City, 2015.

24 MARD [Ministry of Agriculture and Rural Development], “Báo cáo: Kết quả thực hiện kế hoạch tháng 5 năm 2015 ngành nông nghiệp và phát triển nông thôn” [Report: Results of implementation of the May 2015 plan for agriculture and rural development], 2015, online at www.mard.gov.vn/Lists/appsp01_statistic/Attachments/92/Baocao_T5_2015.pdf.

25 N. X. Dung et al., “Phát triển kinh tế vùng đồng bằng sông Cửu Long giai đoạn 2011–2020” [Economic development of the Mekong Delta in the period 2011–2020], *Tạp chí Phát triển Kinh tế* [Journal of economic development], No. 9, 2011, pp. 62–70.

8 Participatory water governance and impact assessment

A case study of the Hua Na Irrigation project in northeast Thailand[1]

Kanokwan Manorom

Introduction

For years, large-scale water infrastructure projects in Thailand have been subject to controversies over their social and environmental impact on surrounding regions and communities. One central issue behind many of the contentions is the reportedly perpetual lack of reliable and comprehensive assessments and analyses prior to project construction.[2] Another frequently raised concern is the apparently constant exclusion of local perspectives on anticipated benefits, costs, and social consequences of water resources development projects.[3]

To tackle water governance challenges, considerable Thai governmental and societal efforts have been devoted to the formulation and popularisation of a new, participatory approach to project evaluation and impact assessment. In this regard, the evaluation process of the Hua Na (Weir) Irrigation scheme (HNW) in the Si Sa Ket Province of the Northeast region (Isan) of Thailand[4] tells an encouraging story of local knowledge being integrated into the assessment process and of consensus being built between affected communities and other governmental/commercial stakeholders.

The HNW, as discussed in later sections, was approved by the Thai government in the late 1980s and completed in the early 2000s. The operation of the irrigation system, however, was stalled due to protests by local communities as well as non-governmental organisations (NGOs) over the adequacy and properness of the impact assessment.[5] The stand-off continued until 2007 when the Royal Irrigation Department (RID) of Thailand agreed to fund a comprehensive and participatory impact assessment initiative for a better informed decision on the future of the HNW.

The innovative and enabling operational process of the initiative, which was carried out between January 2008 and August 2009, has attested to the possibility of a "People's Impact Assessment" (PIA). More importantly, the HNW experience has illustrated the productive role of PIA in facilitating consensus-based decisions on water resources management and development. Given the mounting pressure along the Mekong for ever more water infrastructure projects, the HNW initiative may also offer an alternative model for decision makers, commercial developers, and local communities in the Subregion to cultivate a sense of shared endeavour so as to more effectively coordinate their respective interests and activities.

To examine the "People's Impact Assessment" attempt in and impact on the decision making for Hua Na (Weir) Irrigation scheme, this chapter will first review the concept of social impact assessment and the perceived desirability of maximal public participation in an assessment process. The theoretical exploration will be followed by an analysis of Thailand's environmental and social impact assessment procedures and the expanding role of public participation in the processes. The third section will be devoted to the study of the HNW and its innovative PIA practice. The chapter will conclude with a discussion of how proactive incorporation of local knowledge and perspectives will ensure the quality of the social-environmental impact assessment of a water development project and hence the local support of its execution.

Social impact assessment and public participation in water governance

According to H. A. Becker, impact analysis (IA) is a "process of identifying the future consequences of a current or proposed action". Social impact assessment (SIA) is meanwhile a major sub-field of impact assessment. Becker further defines SIA as "the process of identifying the future consequences of current or proposed actions, which are related to individuals, organisations and social macro systems".[6] SIA is thus not problem analysis, policy development research, or evaluation research.[7] It instead includes the following five key characteristics:

1 A systematic effort to identify, analyse, and evaluate the social impacts of a proposed project (or policy change) on individual and social groups within a community, or on an entire community, in advance of the decision-making process so that the information from the SIA can improve the decisions made;
2 A means of developing alternatives to the proposed course of action and of determining the full range of consequences of each alternative;
3 An attempt to increase the knowledge of both the project proponents and the impacted community;
4 An undertaking to effectively raise the level of understanding of the community and put the residents in a better position to understand the broader implications of the proposed action;
5 A process equipped to evaluate and, when necessary, mitigate against any negative social impacts likely to occur if a specific action is taken.[8]

The international guidelines and principles for SIA were developed under the auspices of the International Association for Impact Assessment (IAIA) in 2003. They were, however, immediately criticised for overlooking core values such as human rights, justice, fairness, democratisation, freedom from fear, transparency, or the right to use local knowledge and/or to involve locals as decision makers.[9] The guidelines were thus believed not to have been based on a principle of equity, or on the goals of building social and human capital in local communities. Yet people should, argued critics of the guidelines, "have a right to live and work in an environment which is conducive to good health and to a good quality of life" and "to be involved in decision making about the planned interventions that will affect their lives", and local knowledge and experience "are valuable and can be used to enhance planned intervention".[10] Deeming the 2003 guidelines unclear as to whom they were directed towards, critics insisted that SIA principles should stress participation and its facilitation process in clear terms. They also redefined SIA as an inclusive process to analyse, monitor, and manage the intended and unintended social consequences of planned interventions so as to bring about a more sustainable and equitable biophysical and human environment.[11] Since 2003 this definition has been widely cited as a guiding principle of SIA.[12]

In terms of its implementation, SIA is commonly seen as a hybrid of concept and tool that consists of both sciences and political processes.[13] It is, in other words, not simply an evaluation research. Rather, it focuses on the consequences of technological development that can potentially alter physical and/or social conditions. Moreover, in examining unintended consequences, be they caused by private firms or government agencies, SIA is not retrospective but serves as a prospective planning tool to foresee, avoid, and minimise unwanted impacts. In that regard, there are three broadly defined types of SIA projects, which respectively study national- and international-scale impacts, demographic impacts, and collective behaviours of organisations, social networks, and social movements.[14]

While the three types of SIA projects may vary in scale, they all underscore the integral role of public participation in the stages of scoping, formulation of alternatives, profiling, projection, assessment, evaluation, mitigation, and monitoring.[15] Participation of local people in the SIA process is particularly important in addressing the potentially negative consequences of proposed projects.[16] Specifically, community members' perspectives often reflect locally unique social, economic, cultural, and political reaction parameters on adaptations made to past impacts. They may thus help form proper articulations of unintended consequences occurring in the present. They can also provide insight into prospective future impacts. Through direct exchanges of information and perspectives, alternative viewpoints on the consequences of proposed actions or projects may lead to better judgements.[17] Put differently, an informed judgement in SIA is generated only in a deliberative process that enables a genuine engagement of local people and stimulates dialectic exchanges of information.[18]

In practical terms, the participation of local communities in SIA helps enhance the "competence" of "expert knowledge" and the assessment outcome. An inclusive and "fair" SIA process would likely also increase the legitimacy, especially among potentially affected parties, of the appraisal result and hence the intended project. Equally important is the fact that only when an SIA process invites affected communities to tell their side of the story and ensures them an equal say in the final resolution, can it be considered a democratic public decision making endeavour.[19]

When it comes to transboundary water management, public participation in SIA was explicitly introduced in the 1970s. It has steadily became a widespread practice since then, primarily due to the ever more rigorous environmental regulations implemented to improve the outcomes of hydropower dams and other hydro development projects.[20] Today, inclusive, collaborative, and accountable SIA is not only encouraged in water governance, but also requested by international conventions to be guaranteed by state laws.[21] Yet local and indigenous people remain mostly excluded from the SIA process of proposed hydro projects that may affect them. There have certainly been efforts all along to extend and expand public involvement in SIA, but progress is both slow and inadequate.[22]

From his research on river basin management, Molle[23] concludes that one important reason for the unsatisfactory level of public involvement is that social and environmental impact assessment in hydro projects is often conducted in a "conventional" manner that emphasises how the technical apparatus assures growing water demand to be met by supply. Following this "rational" approach, knowledge about water is highly controlled by hydrologists, engineers, and economists, who are supported by the bureaucratic management system. To achieve more sustainable water management solutions, the concept and practice of integrated water resource management (IWRM) should be introduced into the conventional approach.

Echoing the Global Water Partner's definition of water governance,[24] Hirji and Davis further explain that local participation in SIA at the river basin level is necessitated by the fact that governance means that a range of political, social, economic, and administrative systems are in place to develop and manage water resources and deliver water service to all.[25] Meanwhile, the involvement of mixed stakeholders and parties with different scale and level perspectives, note Dore and Label, also indicate that water governance is a very complex issue. They quickly add, though, that multifaceted as water governance may be, its main component should be social justice, knowledge sharing, and participatory democracy, particularly the representation of the civil society.[26]

As for how to critically appraise water governance, Hirji and Davis believe that tools and/or mechanisms for assessing this complex system need to be effective and measurable. Their opinion concurs with that of many international organisations including the World Bank, as they are calling ever louder for the development of operative tools to evaluate the impacts of water utilisation and management prior to the decision-making stage of a proposed project. Citing a 2009 World Bank report entitled *Strategic Environmental Assessment: Improving Water Resources, Governance and Decision-Making*, Hirji and Davis point out that SIA may very well answer the appeal and serve as an effective tool for water management. In their elaboration, they place a specific emphasis on the nearly all-purpose nature of SIA, which allows it to be used in assessing the cumulative impacts of hydro development projects on irrigation, forestry, biodiversity, mining, water supply, fisheries, and human health. Additionally, by advocating and enabling the participation of civil society organisations and institutions, SIA may also help increase the transparency, equity, and hence positive effects of water governance.[27]

As aforementioned, however, problems remain with the SIA process, exemplified especially by the often insignificant recognition, in the final report, of affected local peoples' input (concerns, opinion, knowledge, desire for alternatives) on the impacts of planned projects on their livelihoods. At the decision-making level, SIA is still habitually considered to be only a minor component of a standard impact assessment attempt. A much-commended resolution of the issue is to integrate SIA into the negotiation of legally binding agreements between developers and local people.[28] The legal approach reportedly will reinsure that SIA is a participatory process and hence empower it to influence the decision making on proposed hydropower dams and other hydro projects.

Impact assessments in Thailand: Continuing improvement attempts and lingering issues

Thailand is one of very first countries in Southeast Asia to legislate for a national environmental impact assessment (EIA) process. In 1981, the government abolished the 1975 National Environmental Quality Act (NEQA) and replaced it with the first mandatory provision for EIA, Section 46 of the Enhancement and Conservation of National Environmental Quality Act 1972. Since then, Thailand's EIA laws and regulations have undergone numerous amendments and, partly due to movements for social reform, have incorporated many legislative changes.

An important modification has been the Enhancement and Conservation of the NEQA, enacted in 1992.[29] The Act includes provisions for specifying the type and size of projects required to submit an EIA. It also prescribes procedures for an EIA on intended projects irrespective of whether or not they required Cabinet approval.[30] While the 1992 NEQA has been an improvement on the 1975 version, it still does not contain clear regulations on EIA compliance by small and medium-scale projects with the potential to have social and environmental impacts. They are only required to submit an Initial Environmental Examination (IEE), which is less rigorously examined.[31] Another shortcoming of the NEQA is that EIA remains a government-controlled process and it has put insufficient emphasis on social impact assessment in its procedures. Consequently, there are few avenues for genuine public participation throughout the EIA process – from its inception, when project developers define the scope and formulate the terms of reference, through to the report review process undertaken by government agencies and government-appointed committees.[32]

In Thailand, the bureau in charge of EIA is the Environmental Impact Evaluation Bureau (EIEB) under the Office of Natural Resources and Environmental Policy and Planning (ONEP). The bureau specifies the types of projects that require EIAs, undertakes preliminary reviews of submitted EIAs, and makes recommendations to the Expert Review Committee who deliver final judgements. The EIEB is mandated by law to scrutinise EIAs for 22 types of projects, from oil refineries to hotels. With regard to large-scale dams, Thai EIA regulations require their applicants to produce, and submit at the project feasibility stage, an EIA conducted by registered consultants in accordance with the guidelines issued by ONEP. For example, all dams with a reservoir volume exceeding 100 million cubic metres, or with a surface area above 15 square kilometres, or an irrigated area of at least 80,000 *rai* (12,800 hectares) must submit an EIA suitability statement (EIASS).[33]

Although Thailand's EIA legislation requires dam developers to comply with strict guidelines, the legislation has been criticised by members of civil society for not allowing local people sufficient involvement in the process. Recently, governmental institutions have addressed this issue through legislation. The *2003 Royal Decree on Guidelines and Procedures on Good Governance*, for example, stipulates that arrangements for public hearings for any project must be made prior to its operationalization.[34]

The inaugural Natural Resources and Environment Minister, Praphat Panyachartrak, is also greatly acknowledged for his genuine efforts to upgrade Thailand's EIA procedures.[35] During his short tenure (November 2002–March 2004), Panyachartrak was never shy about his ambition to build Thailand's EIA into a state-of-the-art regime so that it could keep up with the country's rapid economic growth and accommodate the growing demand for public participation. He especially pushed for the poor to have a chance to express their opinions and concerns about the potential impact of proposed projects on local ecological systems and household livelihoods. Promoting the involvement of the poor, Panyachartrak intended to engage local knowledge in project decisions and mitigation plans.[36]

In Thailand, free access to information by people affected by projects such as hydro dams is a constitutional right. Article 58 states that "a person shall have the right to participate in the decision making process of State officials in the performance of administrative functions that affect or may affect his or her rights and liberties, as provided by law".[37] Even more explicitly, Sections B.E. 2540 (1997) and B.E. 2550 (2007) both delineate the concept of "people participation" in the protection of the environment and in the improvement of local livelihoods.[38]

Yet although the Thai government has attempted to improve legislation regarding impact assessment for the past two decades, construction of large-scale water infrastructure projects remains controversial, often even contentious. The central issue is their widespread environmental destruction and social dislocation that have resulted repeatedly in spite of the legislation. The failure to produce comprehensive and reliable assessments and analyses before commencing has been a key weakness and point of controversy.[39]

In theory, an EIA should provide an accurate prediction and assessment of the potential impact of proposed large-scale projects. This information helps determine whether a project should proceed at all. Critics in Thailand argue, however, that political influences on supposedly neutral scientists and specialists frequently result in unduly positive research conclusions about environmental and social impacts.[40] EIA in Thailand, as in many other countries, has thus often been depicted as an exercise to rationalise pre-determined outcomes, rather than a process that provides independent and rigorous analysis upon which sound decisions should be made. In addition, underestimation of the social and environmental costs and exclusion of local perspectives on the anticipated benefits, costs, and social consequences of projects, have led many local communities, NGOs, and academics to mistrust and question the veracity of EIAs.

One salient example of these issues is the Khong-Chi-Mun Inter-basin Diversion Scheme (KCM) in the Northeast region (Isan). This mega-project was first approved by the Thai government in 1989 and transferred to the RID in 2002. The planned goal was for the KCM to divert water from the Mekong River mainstream for storage in the Chi and Mun River Basins. The water diversion was intended to allow at least 18 irrigation projects (weirs and dams) to be constructed in the Northeast, which was considered by the Thai government to be the poorest and driest region of the country.[41] The project was planned to take 42 years to complete and was divided into three phases.[42] The Council of Ministers of the Chatichai government passed a Cabinet resolution to approve the construction and asked the Department of Energy and Development Promotion (DEDP) under the Ministry of Science and Technology to complete feasibility studies by 1992. The study that was later presented suggested that it was technically feasible to irrigate 4.98 million *rai* (796,800 hectares) in 15 provinces of Northeast Thailand. Nevertheless, the KCM project has been continuously debated and heavily criticised by NGOs and academics for its impacts and cost effectiveness. A key point of contention is that the feasibility studies lacked comprehensive environmental and social assessments, and that had the full costs and impact of this project been accounted for, KCM might have never been built.[43]

Contested understandings of costs and benefits associated with large dam projects result in social conflicts at multiple levels and divided communities. Thailand has thus been attempting for decades to create a good impact assessment process. However the issue of participation of local people in the assessment process has yet to be fully addressed. To date, there remain very limited opportunities for local people and the public at large to articulate their concerns about the impact of water infrastructure projects, let alone frame the issues of importance.

Thailand's RID is one of the government agencies mandated to both improve irrigation capabilities and ensure flood protection.[44] In the Northeast region, the RID commenced its development efforts in 1939 with the construction of pilot irrigation tank projects and run-off-river diversions, which caused major changes in the water resources of the region. Nevertheless, until 2002 the RID's irrigation projects had not been severely criticised because their results were generally fruitful and the negative impacts were not extensive.[45]

That began to change after the RID took over the projects of the former Department of Energy and Development Promotion in 2002.[46] Those projects, including the KCM, had been accepted by the government. When implemented, however, they caused acute adverse impacts on local people's lives and the surrounding ecological systems. Thus as soon as it took over the reins, the RID came under pressure from the local people, academics, and NGOs who had long been questioning the efficacy of the projects. Samatcha Khon Chon, or the Assembly of the Poor (AoP),[47] was one such pressure group known for promoting re-evaluation of EIAs from a participatory perspective.

As a response to AoP pressure, the RID began to focus on improving the situation of the most urgent project, HNW project, which was one of 16 water projects opposed by the AoP since 1995. The RID's rectification efforts were targeted at gaining a better understanding of the impact of it on local livelihoods and the ecological system, providing fair financial compensation, and developing a new approach to the EIA legislation.[48] In its attempts to improve the outcomes of the HNW project, the RID accepted the concept of PIA from the 2006 EIA guidelines, which was promoted by the AoP and academics. The following sections will focus on PIA as a consensus-building tool for solving EIA conflicts in the HNW project.

HNW and its controversies

Northeast Thailand in brief

The Hua Na Weir project is located on the Mun River in Isan, northeast Thailand. This region covers an area of 170,218 square kilometres, about one-third of the country's total land space. Sharing a border with Laos and Cambodia, the arid tropical Northeast region is delineated by mountain ranges to the west and south and by the Mekong River to the north and east. Topographically, the Khorat Plateau takes up much of the region's land, with an elevation between 100 and 200 metres above sea level and with a temperature between 19.6°C and 30.2°C. Yet a more important geographic feature of the region is perhaps the Chi and Mun Rivers, two major tributaries of the Mekong that flow through Northeast Thailand.[49]

The agricultural productivity in the Northeast region, however, continues to lag behind many other districts in Thailand because of its soil. In fact, the physical properties of the soil in Isan are believed to be among the poorest in the country, featuring low fertility, sandy composition, and poor water retention. Worse still, many of the large swathes in the region contain rock salt deposits and saline groundwater, resulting in high levels of natural soil salinity. It is estimated that six million hectares, or 34 per cent of Isan's arable land, are affected by salinity, and the problem appears to be escalating.[50] This not only affects the region's annual crop yields, but also throws ever more chunks of its land into the category of being unsuitable for cultivation.[51]

Furthermore, the region has been through a rapid environmental transformation in the last 50 years – from vast tracts of forest into rice paddy fields, 80 per cent of which depend exclusively on rainfall for their water requirements. Thus while the forests were well adapted to the bi-modal rainfall pattern (distinct wet and dry seasons), farmers' adaptation in this rapidly deforested area has been constantly challenged by erratic rainfalls and hence extremes of water scarcity and excess. Due to the low elevation of the region, increasingly frequent flooding has become a particularly serious problem. Worse still, this problem is often exacerbated by artificial features such as roads, canals, weirs, ditches, and dykes that have changed the natural drainage patterns.[52] Among them, hydro dams are perhaps the most striking and consequential man-made alterations of the physical environment in Isan.

The Thai government embarked on the hydropower programme in the Northeast in 1971 when the Lam Dom Noi (Sirinthorn Dam) was completed. To date, the region has 17 dams, with the Pak Mun Dam, completed in 1998, being the latest addition. Despite the large number of dams, however, electricity demand systematically exceeds supply and forces Isan to import power from the national grid and neighbouring countries, particularly Laos.

Moreover, given the importance of agriculture in the Northeast, it is not surprising that every Thai government, upon coming to power, places considerable importance on water resource development as a prime solution to the region's economic growth needs. In the last 70 years or so, successive governments in Bangkok have consecutively invested in over 6,000 irrigation projects of varying types and sizes designed to supply water to 1.2 million hectares. Their shared rationale and justification have all along been that the water development endeavours are an essential means to achieve food security, grow agri-businesses, fight communist insurgencies, and win electoral support.

The above reasoning and logic have surely been applied to many irrigation-hydro schemes carried out in or planned for the Northeast region. Among them, some widely studied large-scale water resource development ventures include the "Accelerated Rural Development Program", "Greening Isan", "Khong-Chi-Mun Water Diversion", and "Water Grid". In planning for them, however, successive Thai governments have been operating on an additional, openly articulated assumption, that is, poverty in the Northeast is drought-induced and can be alleviated through large-scale water projects. Government ventures are based on this questionable assumption.[53]

The Hua Na (Weir) Irrigation project (HNW)

The HNW is one of the projects carried out under the auspices of the KCM. The weir is a channel storage dam which is located approximately 90 kilometres downstream of the Rasi Salai Weir and 160 kilometres upstream of the Pak Mun Dam (Figure 8.1). Initially, the central government claimed that the Hua Na structure would be a 4-metre high rubber weir, which could be deflated during the wet season to minimise flooding. Instead, a 17-metre high concrete dam, over 200 metres in width, with 14 gates, was built, making it the largest dam in the KCM.[54]

The HNW project was approved by the Thai government in 1989. The weir was intended to provide irrigation water to 61 communities in five districts of Si Sa Ket Province, covering 77,000 *rai* (12,310 hectares) of farmland.[56] After more than 2.1 billion baht (7.2 million US$) had been spent, two main canals were completed in 2003, with a total length of 88.85 kilometres. Also completed were the gates of the weir and 21 ditches. The canals and ditches were ready to be used, and about 10,000 households along both canals were able to benefit from the additional water supply. The HNW scheme, however, still lies idle, and the irrigation facilities have yet to be utilised because of the fierce opposition from many communities living along the Mun River. In other words, by joining forces with the AoP and other participating NGOs, local communities have successfully stalled the operation of the dam and forced the government to redo the EIA.[57]

Completed in 1992, the first EIA was conducted by two consultancy companies – Asian Engineering Consultants and TEAM Consulting Engineering and

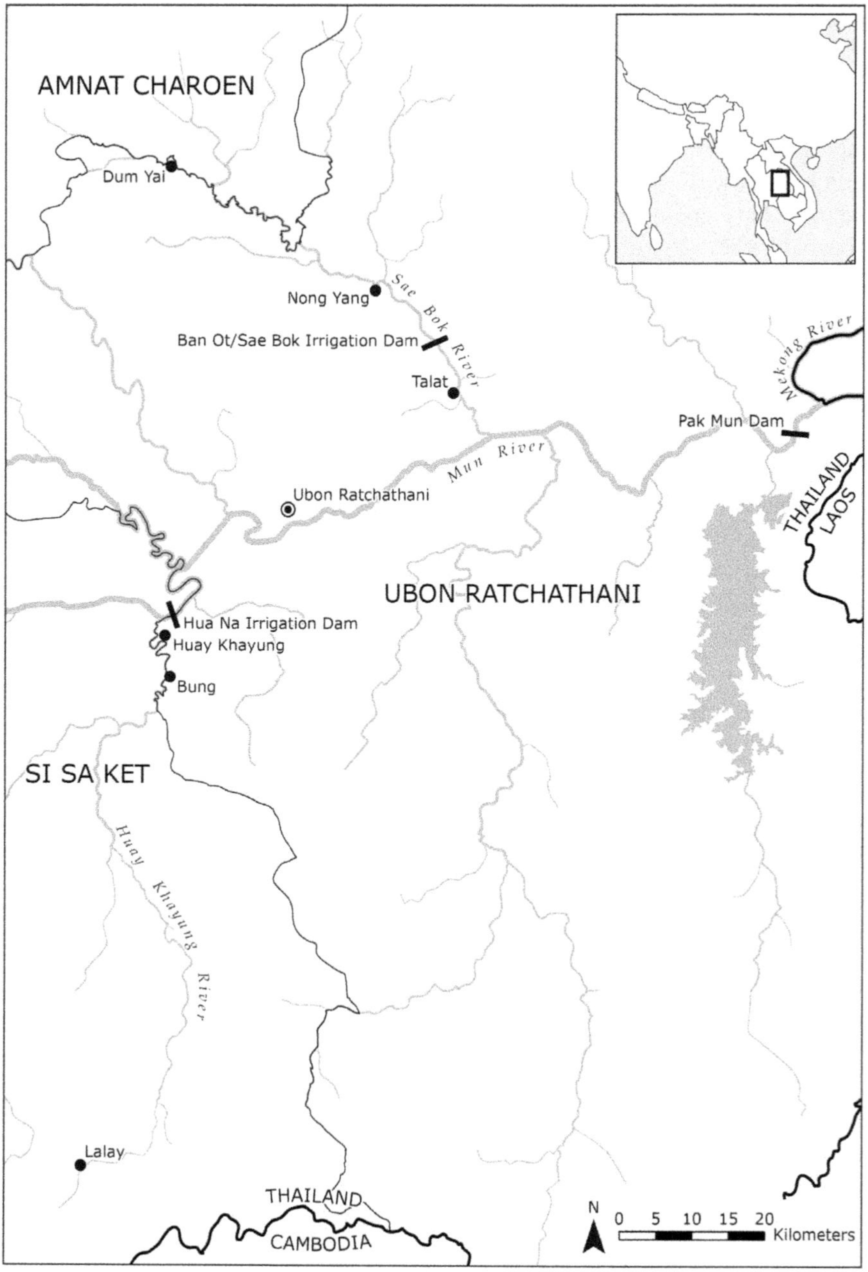

Figure 8.1 Map of Lower Mun River Basin and project area in Northeastern Thailand
Source: Ian G. Baird et al. (2019: 3).[55]

Management. Yet their work was rejected by EIEB because neither the EIA process nor the written report had followed the guidelines and regulations prescribed by the NEQA 1992. Special concerns were raised about the failure to fully engage local people and hence to conduct a proper SIA that included livelihood assessment.[58] For example, the EIA report did not take into consideration the dependence of local people on wetland resources (locally called *pha boong pha taam*) for their livelihoods. Consequently, soil salinity and other farming-related issues were not adequately investigated and discussed. Yet the soil salinity issue has been one of the AoP's primary concerns regarding the KCM project. Yuvaniyama[59] and Sneddon[60] have noted that Isan soil salinity levels may potentially increase throughout the region, estimating that 19.4 million *rai* (3.1 million hectares) of land is at risk. Issues concerning soil salinisation has thus been creating endless debates among academics, government institutions, and NGOs. Sceptical predictions suggest that extensive expansion of irrigated areas would negatively affect the regional ecosystems and thus hurt people's livelihoods. [61]

The scepticism was founded on the experience of the Rasi Salai Weir project, 80 kilometres upstream from HNW. When the Rasi Salai Weir was planned, the government had also promised to build it with rubber so as to minimise its impact. The promise challenged the necessity of an EIA, which was indeed not included in the construction planning process. The government, however, did not keep its promise and built a 9-metre concrete weir. When its gates were closed in 1994, a reservoir stretching 120 kilometres was created, which submerged more than 8,000 hectares of surrounding wetlands.[62] Worse still, the water was too saline to be used for farming, hence the promised irrigation benefits never materialised.[63]

Having seen the disastrous results of the Rasi Salai Weir project, many of the 7,000 households likely to be affected by a functioning HNW joined the communities already negatively impacted by the Rasi Salai Weir and the Pak Mun Dam in calling on the government to address their concerns. Their petition movements were carried out under the umbrella of the AoP, which had submitted three proposals concerning the HNW to the government. The first called for a temporary halt to the project. The second demanded that a complete EIA and SIA be conducted in accordance with the amendment of the NEQA 1992 and other guidelines on impact assessments specified in the 1997 Thai Constitution. The third asked for the provision of just compensation to the affected households. The government accepted all these proposals and ordered the RID to respond to the petitions.[64]

One detail worth mentioning here is that with the support of NGOs the AoP demanded in the second proposal that a complete EIA and SIA be carried out with the full participation of local people. The goals of the request were to: (1) enable local people and NGOs to address their concerns on unintended impacts; (2) create a monitoring framework for all possible future impacts; and (3) find appropriate solutions for any losses incurred. The AoP insisted that all these goals had to be met before the project could begin to operate. The concerted pressure proved successful for, in 2000, the RID agreed to conduct a participatory and open EIA and SIA.[65] It should be noted, however, that not all locals were unified in opposition. A large cohort of farmers was in fact unconcerned about "people's" or any other types of impact assessments. They just wanted to receive the irrigation water promised by the government.

PIA processes in the HNW project

In late 2007, the RID allocated funds for scholars from three local universities (Ubon Rathchathani, Suranaree Technology, and Khon Kean) to conduct a comprehensive assessment of environmental (EIA), social (SIA) and health (HIA) impacts associated with the HNW irrigation project. The RID also hosted meetings for all the parties involved, including the affected people, beneficiary groups, NGOs, Irrigation Department officials, and interdisciplinary researchers. The meeting venue quickly turned into a space for all parties to brainstorm in a participatory manner how to ensure all concerns were being addressed. This exercise became a model for properly incorporating affected/concerned people into technical impact assessments, and hence operationally creating a PIA process. The HNW impact assessment process was later summarised to include four steps.

Step I: Scoping

Scoping, as an exercise, involves establishing the terms of reference for a project. Importantly, it establishes who is included and who is excluded. In the case of the HNW irrigation project, many people could potentially be impacted; and therefore the scoping exercise had to be fully inclusive. Accordingly, numerous meetings, workshops, and focus group discussions were held to deliberate the issues to be assessed. These were attended by technical experts, RID representatives, and a wide range of stakeholders including local officials, the project developer, and villagers (who represented both pro- and anti-project camps). The scope of the assessment was debated intensely. A consensus was reached that the scoping had to cover the concerns of not only the AoP, but also the villagers who supported the project. The impact assessment process was mandated to follow the rules prescribed by the ONEP as well as the 2006 "Guideline for Public Participation and Impact Assessment of Social Environment in Environmental Impact Assessment Process" drafted by the EIEB.

Through their scoping meetings, the participating groups jointly identified the following four key elements of the EIA and SIA of the HNW project:

1 Determining the number and location of people who were dependent on the wetland resource for their livelihoods; assessing the extent to which the dependence of people varied by geographic distance from the river and local ecosystems; and estimating the economic and social value of the wetland resources to local users at the household level.
2 Establishing a large enough spatial scale to incorporate five districts up- and downstream from the HNW and all villages within five kilometres of the Mun River in the impact assessment.

3 Involving villagers both supporting and opposing the HNW in data collection and analysis.
4 Selecting an equal number of villagers from both the pro- and anti-project camps to join the assessment team, and the selection criteria being: (a) a high interest level, (b) good interview and note-taking skills; and (c) a strong interpersonal capability to liaise with other participants on data quality and analysis. (Twenty-two villagers ended up being selected.)

Step II: Data collection and initial report

For a comprehensive PIA process, the philosophy underlying data touches upon both asking the right questions and having a broad community representation in the collection, analysis, and report writing processes. For the HNW irrigation project, data were collected by using a mixed-method approach to achieve comprehensiveness of knowledge, as suggested by the 2006 EIA Guideline. To gather qualitative data, for example, a participatory action research was conducted. The specific techniques used included rural appraisal, focus groups, small group meetings, and workshops. Meanwhile, the quantitative data were obtained through a household survey.

Whether qualitative or quantitative, however, to construct survey and interview instruments properly necessitates professional input and the assistance of experts in this field. Indeed, the participating scholars from the aforementioned three universities were actively engaged in the scoping discussions. When agreement was reached on the issues to be covered in the EIA and SIA for the HNW project, they created drafts of the instrument for the household survey, the set of questions for the focus groups, and the guidelines for interviews. These drafts were then subjected to review and comment by the RID, NGOs, and villagers, and were subsequently revised accordingly. Throughout, a special emphasis was placed on the critical issue of sustainable livelihoods. Viewed through the lens of food security and income, attention was primarily focused on wetland dependency and vulnerability to change in resource availability.

The 22 village members of the assessment team then took over. Their first activity was to contact other villagers about the planned impact evaluation of the HNW project. The survey and interview respondents and the focus group members were thus recruited by knowledgeable locals. Also, because both pro- and anti-project villagers were involved, the fairness of the sampling was satisfactorily guaranteed. Next, the assessment team members, after being trained by the participating experts from the local universities on asking questions and taking short notes, went on to conduct the survey, the interviews, and the focus group meetings. At the end of the collection stage, a large quantity of raw data had been successfully assembled.

It was considered that ideally, in the data analysis phase, the assessment team would link local insights with expert knowledge. One villager who was a member of the research team said that:

> When doing data analysis, the team must realise the significant problems facing the local people. Among them are the impacts of flooding. We know about the extent of our utilisation of wetlands. We have knowledge of local resources. We know what it is going to be like regarding the river, fish, wetland, and how our lives will be affected if the NHW is commissioned. This is because we know the flooding histories in its surrounding areas. We have been faced with this problem from time to time. We know how to deal and adapt with it and how it has damaged us. We urge the assessment team to incorporate our knowledge in the study. We know for sure that the NHW will affect our lives. We will suggest solutions drawn from our local knowledge on flooding adaptation so we will not be harmed too much.[66]

The data from the household survey were enumerated by students majoring in Social and Development Studies at the Faculty of Liberal Arts in Ubon Ratchathani University (URU). The Statistical Package for Social Sciences (SPSS) was used on the quantitative data; and the output was analysed by URU faculty members. Meanwhile, all raw qualitative data were sorted, grouped, and classified according to the assessment themes, again by URU scholars.

During the analysis, the bio-physical data collected by the participating academic experts and the socio-economic data collected by both the experts and the village team were integrated. The collection and analysis of environmental baseline data by the bio-physical team were run parallel to the work done by the social team. The social team identified key wetland resources utilised at the household level as sources of food and income. The social analysis of people's use of river resources also included an assessment of both the social and economic benefits of river goods to households. Furthermore, there was a variety of opportunities built into the process for the different teams to share information, particularly on the types of resources being used.

For example, the data on the history of flooding severity were obtained from local villagers. This knowledge was integrated by the social team as a preliminary step in assessing the likely consequences of changes to critical resources that the HNW irrigation schemes would cause. The social team then turned to the bio-physical team for assistance in conducting further statistical analyses. The latter in turn entered the locally collected social and economic data on the inundated areas into its database containing flood information over 100 years. The simulations that followed created numerical models to help predict the inundation extent when the flood water levels reached 112, 113, 114, 115, 116, and 117 metres above mean sea level (MSL). The bio-physical team presented these models to villagers at several meetings and workshops for their feedback and input on the relative severity of flood water impacts. The simulation models also stimulated vigorous discussions among representatives from the Steering Committee on Monitoring the Participatory Impact Assessment (SCMPEIA), RID, NGOs, assessment teams, and stakeholders. The agreement reached stipulated that the water volume after the completion of the HNW had to be sufficient to provide for the dry season and that the optimal water level was 112 metres above MSL.[67]

The preliminary PIA report was drafted in language that was appropriate to the reading levels of local people and the public. A month was then spent on meetings with and workshops for NGOs, pro- and anti-project villagers, and other stakeholders in the communities. The meetings gave the entire local population the chance to ask questions, make comments, and get answers about the preliminary report. The workshops provided great clarification opportunities for both the assessment teams and stakeholders, enabling them to come to a final agreement on the contents of the report. The document was then submitted to the SCMPEIA and RID, which subsequently noted their approval of the PIA approach adopted.

Step III: The final report – a people's consensus

All those involved in the above HNW assessment initiative were fully aware that in order for their final PIA findings, conclusions, and recommendations to be sealed with the stamp of approval, they had to be presented in the form of a baseline report. Not surprisingly, the assessment team had to revise the initial report discussed above according to the comments from SCMPEIA, NGOs, villagers, and other stakeholders. The interactive meetings among these stakeholders were constructive in addressing key concerns about the potential impacts of the HNW project.

Most importantly, such gatherings soon became a space for negotiations between the pro- and anti-project groups. A consensus was eventually reached on water allocation and the project management with regard to inundation levels, compensation, and monitoring of the implemented programmes. All this was reflected in the final report, which was presented at a Cabinet meeting by the RID and SCMPEIA in late 2009 and approved by the Cabinet in 2010. On 16 November 2010, the Cabinet appointed the "Committee on Resolution for the Hua Na" to monitor the implementation of the development plan.[68]

Step IV: Implementing and monitoring the mitigation plan

The PIA report and the government approval of it ignited a significant change to the status quo. In other words, people's participation had now become mandatory in the implementation and ongoing management of the HNW irrigation project. Immediately, a joint committee consisting of RID staff, local people, and academics was formed to operate the HNW. The committee decided to take a basin-wide approach to coordinating water flows from the HNW with the Rasi Salai and Pak Mun Dams. A plan was then prepared to enforce mitigation measures to contain the potential negative impacts of the irrigation scheme.

At the same time, the AoP and other involved NGOs offered creative ideas on how people's involvement in the HNW could be continued after the project was completed and the irrigation mechanisms began to function. They worked out specific ways in which affected local people and national/regional NGOs, such as the Sustainable Agriculture Organisation and the Wetland Organisation, could be involved in crafting major mitigation proposals, plans, and measures for relevant water resource development projects. Specific participation tactics and tools were also suggested for local people and NGOs to utilise in pushing government agencies to engage them in the implementation of mitigation plans and measures. Public engagement was confidently expected to help create a sense of ownership and belonging among the local people in the development of the project. Yet local people would need budget support, training, and up-to-date information which the government and academics could and should supply.

Given that the HNW project was already completed, impact monitoring became more important for all those involved. During their discussions, the assessment team, SCMPEIA, NGOs, and stakeholders, especially affected villagers, reached agreement that the monitoring review of long-term impact factors must be undertaken every three years by an independent team. People's participation would continue to be a key principle of its membership selection. The team would be required to function by agreement on key tasks and responsibilities in monitoring long-term impacts and compensation payments. The results of the review must be reported to all stakeholders.

Conclusion

The innovative PIA process conducted for the HNW project has exemplified two important elements in the relationship between the PIA and water governance. First, according to the literature, the goal of water democratisation for a given spatial area requires an effective water governance policy.[69] A vital aspect of the policy concerns the proper scale of water development projects in relation to community involvement. This explains why top-down large-scale projects in Northeast Thailand, such as the KCM and the Pak Mun Dam, were controversial and created adversarial relations between the state and civil society. Key factors associated with their poor performance included technical problems (topography, sandy soils, salinity, high evaporation), economic constraints (low commodity prices, labour shortages), social shocks (forced resettlement), and inadequately designed distribution systems. As a result, few surrounding villages had benefited from those large-scale irrigation schemes. The lack of meaningful consultation with and involvement of local villagers in the decision-making and construction processes saw many of the local people, who were the intended beneficiaries, not even taking up the big-budgeted opportunity to irrigate their lands. These large-scale schemes thus failed to deliver the anticipated benefits and the billions of dollars spent on the under-performing infrastructure were wasted.[70]

It goes without saying that government economic policies concerning water resources development projects and their management have also produced positive impacts on ecosystems and human livelihoods in Northeast Thailand. Yet the fact that political controversies often occur upon the announcement of water development projects suggests loudly and unequivocally that the standard impact assessment tools cannot convince all parties involved about the findings of cumulative unintended impacts. For more persuasive EIA results and mitigation solutions, the impact assessment efforts should, as proven by the HNW experience, attach greater significance to setting proper spatial scales, adopting interdisciplinary approaches, seeking and incorporating local knowledge, and insisting on inclusive, participatory, and responsive processes. An effective coordination among these elements is meanwhile an essential requirement for a meaningful PIA, which in and of itself is a constructive tool for integrating the typically separate techniques of environmental and social impact assessment.

A second example set by the PIA of the HNW project for those involved in impact assessment and water governance is that conducting a PIA does not slow down project planning and implementation. Rather the PIA is a useful tool for evaluating, in advance, different problems, perspectives, and interests because it allows people at the grassroots level and the wider public to interactively participate in the impact assessment process. In other words, given that the value and legitimacy of an impact assessment hinges on the inclusion of the voices of all the stakeholders, the PIA is an innovative tool in collecting in-depth information from and about affected communities for effective decision making and water governance. As pressure mounts not only in Northeast Thailand but throughout the Mekong Sub-region for medium and large water infrastructure projects, the PIA initiative in the HNW project may provide insights into alternative, less contentious and hence more effective EIAs and SIAs to better mitigate negative environmental and disruptive social impacts.

Since PIA facilitates a genuine participation of an extensive range of stakeholders in the planning and implementation of water resource projects, it has been positively received by local people, NGOs, and developers in Northeast Thailand. Whether the entire HNW experience can be duplicated across the Mekong Sub-region, PIA should be encouraged in all hydro projects and irrigation schemes on the River in the six countries. For the process helps create a governance space where impacted local people can frame and articulate their needs, values, and priorities. Facilitating the participation of *all* stakeholders in project assessments and impact mitigation monitoring and reporting, PIA helps direct more decision making and planning attention to the links among river flows, ecosystems, and people's livelihoods. This should better enable an intended hydro/irrigation project to address and minimise its potential negative impacts, and hence contribute to its execution and progress.

Notes

1 This chapter is supported by the CPWF PN 67 on "Improving Mekong water allocation" under MPOWER 2008–2009. My deep thanks go to David S. Hall for helping me to reshape my thoughts and rethink the story telling of the subjects and the field data and enthusiastically urging me to rewrite this chapter for the second time. My thanks also go to François Molle and John Dore who made some very useful comments on this chapter.

2 P. Sivaruk, *EIA: State of Knowledge, Problems and Alternatives*, Bangkok: Thailand Research Fund, 2002.

3 Kanokwan Manorom, "People's EIAs as a new approach for water governance: Case of Hua Na Irrigation project in Northeast Thailand", *CPWF Project Number 67 Working Papers*, 2010, p. 161.

4 The full report of the original project was entitled *Social Impact Assessment of Hua Na Irrigation Project of Si Sa Ket Province in the Northeast Region of Thailand*. For details of the project and the report, see Kanokwan Manorom, 2010, op cit.
5 Sanan Choosakul, *Community Rights Studies: A Case of Mun-Chi River Basins*, Bangkok: Thailand Research Fund, 2006.
6 H. A. Becker, "Social impact assessment", *European Journal of Operational Research*, Vol. 128, No. 2, 2001, p. 312.
7 K. Finsterbusch, "State of the art in social impact assessment", *Environment and Behavior*, Vol. 17, Iss. 2, 1985, pp. 193–221.
8 J. R. Burdge and R. Robertson, "Social impact assessment and public involvement process", *Environmental Impact Assessment Review*, Vol. 10, Iss. 1–2, 1990, pp. 81–90.
9 F. Vanclay, "SIA principles: International principles for social impact assessment", *Impact Assessment and Project Appraisal*, Vol. 21, Iss. 1, 2003, pp. 5–11.
10 Ibid., p. 9.
11 F. Vanclay, "Principles of social impact assessment: A critical comparison between the international and the US document", *Environmental Impact Assessment Review*, Vol. 26, Iss. 1, 2006, p. 10.
12 F. Vanclay et al., *Social Impact Assessment: Guidance for Assessing and Managing the Social Impacts of Projects*, Fargo, ND: International Association for Impact Assessment, 2015, p. 95.
13 R. W. Freudenburge, "Social impact assessment", *Annual Review of Sociology*, Vol. 12, 1986, pp. 451–78.
14 H. A. Becker, 2001, op cit., pp. 316–17.
15 J. R. Burdge and R. Robertson, op cit.
16 D. R. Becker et al., "A participatory approach in social impact assessment: The Interactive Community Forum", *Environmental Impact Assessment Review*, Vol. 23, Iss. 3, 2003, pp. 367–82; M. Gismondi, "Sociology and environmental impact assessment", *Canadian Journal of Sociology*, Vol. 22, No. 4, 1997, pp. 457–79; H. A. Becker, *Social Impact Assessment: Method and Experience in Europe, North America and the Developing World*. London: UCL Press, 1997; T. Weble et al., "Public participation in impact assessment", *Environmental Impact Assessment Review*, Vol. 15, Iss. 5, 1995, pp. 443–63; F. N. Laird, "Participatory analysis, democracy and technological-decision making", *Science Technology Human Values*, Vol. 18, No. 3, 1993, pp. 341–61; R. B. Reich, "Public administration and public deliberation: An interpretive essay", *Yale Law Journal*, Vol. 94, Iss. 7, 1985, pp. 1617–41.
17 S. E. Daniels and G. B. Walker, *Working through Environmental Conflict. The Collaborative Learning Approach*, Westport, CT and London: Praeger Publishers, 2001.
18 Daniel Yankelovich, "How to achieve sounder public judgment" in Daniel Yankelovich and Will Friedman (eds.), *Toward Wiser Public Judgment*, Nashville, TN: Vanderbilt University Press, 2010, pp. 25–32; Daniel Yankelovich, *Coming to Public Judgment: Making Democracy Work in a Complex World*, New York: Syracuse University Press, 1991.
19 T. Weble et al., op cit. pp. 443–4.
20 H. A. Becker, 2001, op cit.; R. W. Freudenburge, op cit.
21 United Nations, *Water Management: Guidance on Public Participation and Compliance with Agreement*, Geneva: ECE/UNDP Network of Expert in Public Participation and Compliance, 2000.
22 M. B. Lane et al., "Sacred land, mineral wealth, and biodiversity at Coronation Hill, Northern Australia: Indigenous knowledge and SIA", *Impact Assessment and Project Appraisal*, Vol. 21, No. 2, 2003, pp. 89–98; C. O'Faircheallaigh, "Making social impact assessment count: A negotiation based approach for indigenous peoples", *Society and Natural Resources*, Vol. 12, Iss. 1, 1999, pp. 13–60; B. J. Howell, "Folklife, cultural conservation, and environmental planning" in Michael Owen Jones (ed.), *Putting Folklore to Use*, Lexington, KY: University Press of Kentucky, 1994, pp. 94–114; I.

Nottingham, "Social impact reporting: A Maori perspective – the Taharoa case", *Environmental Impact Assessment Review*, Vol. 10, Iss. 1–2, 1990, pp. 175–83.

23 F. Molle, "Scales and power in river basin management: The Chao Phaya River in Thailand", *The Geographical Journal*, Vol. 173, Iss. 4, 2007, pp. 358–9.

24 Cited in P. Rogers and A. W. Hall, "Effective water governance", *TEC Background Papers* No. 7, 2003, Stockholm: Global Water Partnership Technical Committee, p. 7.

25 R. Hirji and R. Davis, *Strategic Environment Assessment: Improving Water Resources Governance and Decision Making*, Washington, DC: World Bank, 2009.

26 J. Dore and L. Label, "Deliberation and scale in Mekong Region water governance", *Environmental Management*, Vol. 46, Iss. 1, 2010, pp. 60–80.

27 R. Hirji and R. Davis, op cit.

28 C. O'Faircheallaigh, "Effectiveness in social impact assessment: Aboriginal peoples and resource development in Australia", *Impact Assessment and Project Appraisal*, Vol. 27, Iss. 2, 2009, p. 107.

29 NEQA, *Enhancement and Conservation of the National Environmental Quality Act*, Government of Thailand, 1992, online at www.krisdika.go.th/wps/wcm/connect/cb9fc5004e34c615bdfbfdf7e6da8c7c/ENHANCEMENT+AND+CONSERVATION+OF+THE+NATIONAL+ENVIRONMENT+QUALITY+ACT%2C+B.E.+2535+%281992%29.pdf?MOD=AJPERES&CACHEID=cb9fc5004e34c615bdfbfdf7e6da8c7c.

30 B. Pichyakorn, "Thailand water resources development: A review of the existing policy and legislation framework" in Robert A. R. Oliver et al. (eds.), *Mekong Region Water Resource Decision-Making: National Policy and Legal Frameworks vis-a-vis World Commission on Dam Strategies and Priorities*, Bangkok: Chung Wicha Press, 2006, pp. 64–5.

31 F. Molle and P. Floch, "Megaprojects and social and environmental changes: The case of the Thai 'water grid'", *A Journal of the Human Environment*, Vol. 37, Iss. 3, 2008, pp. 199–204.

32 P. Pantumsinchai and T. Panswad, "Improvement of EIA process in Thailand", *Environmental Engineering Association of Thailand Yearbook and Directory 2004*, Bangkok, 2004, pp. 45–8.

33 ONEP, *Environmental Impact Assessment in Thailand*, Bangkok: ONEP, 2015, pp. 85 and 91, online at www.onep.go.th/wp-content/uploads/22.EIAbookAugust2015.pdf.

34 Office of the Council of State, "Rule of the Office of the Prime Minister on Public Consultation, E.E. 2548 (2005)", *Government Gazette*, Vol. 122, Part 73, Special Iss. 55d, 2005, online at http://thailaws.com/law/t_laws/tlaw10785.pdf.

35 F. Molle and P. Floch, op cit., p. 200.

36 F. Molle et al., "The 'greening of *Isaan*': Politics, ideology and development in the northeast of Thailand" in F. Molle et al. (eds.), *Contested Waterscapes in the Mekong Region: Hydropower, Livelihoods and Governance*, London and Sterling, VA: Earthscan, 2009, p. 274.

37 Asian Legal Information Institute, *Constitution of the Kingdom of Thailand 2007*, n.d., online at www.asianlii.org/th/legis/const/2007/1.html.

38 Thailand Environmental Governance Coalition, *Environmental Governance Indicators Toolkit*, 2008, p. 8, online at www.accessinitiative.org/sites/default/files/tai_citizens_toolkit_eng_thailand_env_institute.pdf; Office of the Council of State, op cit.

39 Sarawuth Chesoh, "Environmental impact assessment of power development project: Lessons from Thailand experiences", *Asian Social Science*, Vol. 7, No. 9, 2011, p. 122; P. Sivaruk, op cit.

40 P. Pantumsinchai and T. Panswad, op cit., pp. 45–8.

41 F. Molle and P. Floch, op cit.

42 Kanokwan Manorom, 2010, op cit., pp.161–2; Kerry Lee Shannon, "The social and environmental impacts of the Hua Na Dam and Khong-Chi-Mun project: The necessity for more research and public participation", paper presented at *Water in Mainland Southeast Asia Conference*, organised by the International Institute for Asian Studies,

Netherlands, and the Centre for Khmer Studies, Cambodia, 29 November–2 December, 2005, pp. 1–2.

43 C. K. Sretthachau et al., "Social impacts of the Rasi Salai Dam, Thailand: Loss of livelihood security and social conflict", submission to the World Commission on Dams Public Hearing on *Large Dams and Their Alternatives in East and Southeast Asia: Experiences and Lessons Learned*, 26–7 February 2000, online at www.livingriversiam.org/3river-thai/rs/rsd_wcd_e1.htm.

44 M. Kaosa-ard et al., *Water Resource Management Policy in Thailand*, Bangkok: National Research Council, 2001.

45 F. Molle and P. Floch, op cit.

46 In 2002, the Thaksin government passed the law on Bureaucratic Restructure and the Administration Act, creating six new ministries to increase efficiency and accountability. Many existing departments were meanwhile dissolved or merged with one another. DEDP was among those being eliminated, and some of its programmes related to water resources were transferred to the RID. For details, see F. Molle and P. Floch, op cit.

47 The AoP was established in 1995 and has become the most powerful and striking civil society organisation in the political movement of Thailand. The group is composed of many people organisations including the Peasants Federation (*Sahapan chaona chaorai*). The members of the AoP are from around the country, and are mostly villagers affected by development projects or poor people living in urban areas. These people have long been suffering from state development projects in the areas of water, land, forest, and urban development. The main aims of the AoP are to negotiate with the state over development alternatives, strengthen civil society power, and share civil society's knowledge and address its concerns about development at the policy and practice levels. The group is especially vocal when it comes to management and assessment of medium- and large-scale hydro dam projects and carrying them out in a sustainable manner. For details, see P. Pintoptaeng, *Kan muang bon thong thanon. 99 wan samatcha khonchon* [Politics on the street: 99 days of Assembly of the Poor], Bangkok: Krirk University Press, 1998.

48 C. K. Sretthachau et al., op cit.

49 Sawadee.com (a), "Geography: Northeast (Isan)", n.d., online at http://isan.sawadee.com/geography.html; Sawadee.com (b), "Weather: Northeast (Isan)", n.d., online at http://isan.sawadee.com/weather.html.

50 William Milne-Home, "Salinity management in south-eastern Australia, north-eastern Thailand and Lao PDR" (ACIAR Project No. LWR/1997/150, January 2001–March 2005) in D. Pearce and D. Tempeton (eds.), *Adoption of ACIAR Project Outputs: Studies of Projects Completed in 2005–06*, Canberra: Australian Centre for International Agricultural Research, 2010, pp. 37–40, online at https://www.aciar.gov.au/file/74666; N. Hall et al., "Adapting modelling systems for salinity management of farms and catchments in Australia and Thailand", *Mathematics and Computers in Simulation*, Vol. 64, Iss. 3–4, 2004, pp. 320–2.

51 Charles Keyes, *Finding Their Voice: Northeastern Villagers and the Thai State*, Chiang Mai: Silkworm Books, 2014, p. 9; H. Gebhardt, "The impact of internationalisation processes on the region of Isan – the examples of international migration and transnational tourism", paper presented at the 7th Southeast Asian Geography Association (SEAGA) International Conference 29 November – 2 December 2004, online at http://www2.geog.uni-heidelberg.de/media/personen/gebhardt/isan.pdf.

52 Kosit Lorsirirat and Hideji Maita, "Soil erosion problems in Northeast Thailand: A case study from the view of agricultural development in a rural community near Khon Kaen" in Hideaki Marui (ed.), *Disaster Mitigation of Debris Flows Slope Failures and Landslides*, Tokyo: Universal Academy Press, 2006, pp. 675–86; F. Molle and P. Floch, op cit.

53 P. Floch and F. Molle, "Irrigated agriculture and rural change in Northeast Thailand: Reflections on present developments" in Rajesh Daniel et al. (eds.), *Governing the Mekong: Engaging in the Politics of Knowledge*, Petaling Jaya, Malaysia: SIRD, 2013, p. 195; F. Molle and P. Floch, op cit.

54 DEDP, *Hua Na Weir Project*, Bangkok: Department of Energy and Development Promotion, 1996.
55 Ian G. Baird et al., "What about the tributaries of the tributaries? Fish migrations, fisheries, dams and fishers' knowledge in North-Eastern Thailand", *International Journal of Water Resources Development* (forthcoming 2019), online at https://www.tandfonline.com/doi/pdf/10.1080/07900627.2019.1611549?needAccess=true.
56 DEDP, op cit.
57 AoP, *Siphok panha sammacha kon chon* [Sixteen problems of the Assembly of the Poor], Bangkok: Assembly of the Poor (AoP), 2000.
58 Sanan Choosakul, op cit.; AoP, op cit.
59 Arunee Yuvaniyama, "Management of problem soils in northeast Thailand" in S. P. Kam et al. (eds.), *Natural Resource Management Issues in the Korat Basin of Northeast Thailand: An Overview*, Manila: International Rice Research Institute, 2001, pp.147–56.
60 Chris Sneddon, "Reconfiguring scale and power: The Khong-Chi-Mun project in Northeast Thailand", *Environment and Planning A: Economy and Space*, Vol. 35, Iss. 12, p. 2241.
61 F. Molle and P. Floch, op cit.; Sanan Choosakul, op cit.
62 C. K. Sretthachau et al., op cit.
63 Sanan Choosakul, op cit.
64 Ibid.; AoP, op cit.
65 Kanokwan Manorom et al., *Social Impact Assessment of Hua Na Irrigation Project of Si Sa Ket Province in the Northeast Region of Thailand*, Ubon Ratchathani,Thailand: Ubon Ratchathani University Research Project, 2009.
66 Field research note, 15 March 2008.
67 Kanokwan Manorom et al., 2009, op cit.
68 Kanokwan Manorom et al., "Finding common ground: Co-produced wetland zoning in Northeast Thailand." *CSDC Project Blogs*, 12 August 2015, online at www.csds-chula.org/project-blogs/finding-common-ground-co-produced-wetland-zoning-in-northeast-thailand.
69 L. Susskind, "Water and democracy: New roles for civil society in water governance", *International Journal of Water Resources Development*, Vol. 29, Iss. 4. 2013, pp. 666–77; R. Hirji and R. Davis, op cit.; M. Keskinen, "Water resource management and impact assessment in the Mekong Basin: Which way to go?", *AMBIO: A Journal of the Human Environment*, Vol. 37, No. 3, 2008, pp. 193–9; J. Dore, "The governance of increasing Mekong regionalism" in M. Kaosa-ard and J. Dore (eds.), *Social Change in the Mekong Region*, Bangkok: White Lotus, 2003, pp 405–40; H. J. Lim and S-Y Tang, "Democratization and environmental policy making in Korea", *Governance: An International Journal of Policy, Administration and Institutes*, Vol. 15, Iss. 4, 2002, pp. 561–82; C-P. Tang and S-Y Tang, "Democratizing bureaucracy: The political economy of environmental impact assessment and air pollution prevention in Taiwan", *Comparative Politics*, Vol. 33, No. 1, 2000, pp. 81–99.
70 Kanokwan Manorom and David Hall, *Water Poverty in Northeast Thailand*, Bangkok: Stockholm Environment Institute Asia, 2008.

9 China and the Mekong

Domestic hydro politics

Xin Chen

Introduction

On 7 October 2011, a post on Tianya.cn, a popular online forum in China, broke the news that two Chinese cargo ships had been attacked on the Mekong River in the Golden Triangle two days before, and that all 13 crew members were killed and dumped in the water.[1] The "explosive revelation" and subsequent updates, complemented by grisly photos of the sailors' gagged and bound bodies floating in the Mekong, quickly turned a tidal wave of Chinese media and public attention to the "golden", but hitherto often unnoticed, waterway linking China with continental Southeast Asia.[2] In March 2013, the same tragedy and the "Mekong River" hit the spotlight again in China. The central issue in this round of public uproar was the live coverage on Chinese state television of the final preparations for execution by lethal injection of a Burmese drug lord and his three accomplices from Thailand and Laos, all of whom were convicted of murdering the Chinese sailors. According to a microblogging vote on chinanewsweek.com, 60 per cent of the Chinese netizens polled believed that it was inappropriate to televise this, or any, execution live, as it "signifies power more than the spirit of law".[3] Then in July 2014, the words "Mekong River" resounded throughout China again, when a 34-episode TV drama series based on the murdered Chinese sailors was aired in the prime time slot of China Central Television-1. Entitled *The Big Case on the Mekong*, the murder-investigation drama became an immediate smash hit among the Chinese and amassed close to 450 million views in the first run of the series.[4]

At the same time, however, the public mind across the Mekong region seemed to be, and still does, focused very much on something else, that is, China's dam-building on the upper reaches of the River, named Lancang in Chinese, and its impact on downstream countries. There have, of course, long been questions both in and outside the region about the environmental risks of the dams and reservoirs straddling the upper Mekong in China's Yunnan Province. Yet the record droughts and water woes that gripped the countries downstream in 2010 and early 2016 have ostensibly brought the concerns of China's "manipulating [of] natural waterways" into much sharper focus in the region.[5]

Not unexpectedly, Chinese officials and other opinion leaders vehemently challenged the blame. They argued that "Mekong River Commission CEO Jeremy

Bird does not think China's dams have caused the droughts",[6] that "sharp reductions in rainfall in recent years are induced primarily by climate change in general and the prolonged effects of El Nino in particular",[7] and that "China's Yunnan Province on the upper Mekong has not been spared by the record droughts since 2010, either".[8] Yet these arguments have not been very effective in dispelling the prevalent notions of China posing "dam threats", "water threats", "hydro-hegemonic threats", "Mekong-choking threats", "environmental threats", or "Subregion encroachment threats".[9] Nor has China's sharing its upstream hydrologic data with countries in the lower Mekong basin since 2003,[10] or releasing water from a number of its dams in 2010 and early 2016 to "help" its downstream neighbours "fight" the drought,[11] managed to reframe the "threat" accounts into a "China opportunity" narrative.[12] In fact, rather than assuaging rising criticism of its dam projects, China's "benevolent" drought-relief action in early 2016 aroused scepticism in the region over whether the effort was also intended to "grease" the inaugural summit of the Beijing-supported Lancang-Mekong Cooperation (LMC) mechanism that was held one week after the water release.[13]

The pros and cons of Chinese involvement with the Mekong River are incredibly complex. This is not just the case for regional relations between the Mekong-sharing countries and China. Domestically, the proper course of action has also been hotly debated for years. This chapter examines the major positions in China's domestic hydro politics. The examination suggests that there are no perfect solutions; any action will displease many. Maintaining the status quo will remain the likely course of political action until such time as a severe crisis demands a draconian response.

China as a threat or an opportunity

The widespread and deepening mistrust towards China has been fuelling serious concerns in Chinese policy and research circles over the potential for "water threat" to escalate into "water conflicts" and "water wars" between China and its Mekong neighbours.[14] A more fundamental worry, however, is that even without imminent confrontation, the hype of water politics is sufficiently damaging already, as it "invites" and "validates" greater involvement of extra-regional players and interest in Mekong affairs.[15] Chinese pundits believe that increasing extra-regional influences further complicate China's bilateral and multilateral relationships in the Subregion, which in turn hinders the attainment of Beijing's "Two-Ocean" policy objectives.[16] This prospect is seen as troublesome because the "Two-Ocean" initiative, or gaining access to the Indian Ocean through engagements with the Mekong countries, is deemed vital for the development of China's Subregion-adjacent, but still landlocked and poverty-stricken southwestern provinces.[17] The initiative is particularly meant for these "gateway" provinces to work towards establishing Lancang-Mekong Subregional value chains and advancing them into synergistic economic networks in Southeast Asia and beyond.[18] On a broader level, the "Two Ocean" endeavour is expected to enable China to break free from its perceived maritime encirclement of the "island chains monitored by the West in the Pacific".[19]

To prevent dam-building controversies from spiralling to destructive levels, Chinese policy commentators, academic analysts, and interested netizens typically suggest that China infuses greater transparency into its hydrological data sharing with the other Mekong countries.[20] They also opine that if trans-boundary water resources development is tinged with "original sin", China should pivot its attention from "going-it-alone projects" to "joint ventures" when it comes to utilising and conserving the River.[21] They further urge China to take a "leading", but "non-aggressive" role in creating "public goods" across the Subregion.[22] The internal push for China "doing more" and "doing better" has arguably culminated in Beijing's advocacy for the newly launched Mekong-states-only LMC mechanism, the endorsement of which is packaged with multi-billion dollar concessional loans and funds for development and poverty alleviation projects in the Subregion.[23]

Meanwhile, growing regionwide misgivings and cynicism about China being able to "make" as well as "break" drought and about the Mekong countries being at risk of "drowning" in Beijing's LMC "generosity"[24] have also prompted spasms of national soul-searching among Chinese pundits and interested members of the public. They ask out loud, for example, why after decades of avowing a "peaceful", "sustainable", "responsible" rise, China seems ever more readily equated, by even "Third World countries", with "old-fashioned Western colonial powers", and its global/regional initiatives with "resource looting" schemes.[25] They also wonder aloud why China's "neighbourly offer" of "free rides on its development" has yet to be greeted with concrete regional responses to its envisioned Mekong "community of common interests and destiny".[26] Likewise, why has the neighbouring Subregion, which enjoys both close economic ties and "friendly political bonds" with China,[27] ended up dealing a most costly blow to Beijing's "neighbourhood diplomacy", namely, the "sudden suspension" of the US$3.6 billion Myitsone hydroelectric dam project in Myanmar paid for by the Yunnan branch of the China Power Investment Corporation in a joint venture with the Burmese government?[28]

It may be no exaggeration to state that these self-reflective questions, whether asked literally or rhetorically, touch the crux of challenges facing China in the Mekong Subregion. Yet judging by the persistent and emerging concerns and criticism about China's involvement in water resources development along the Lancang/Mekong River, it may also be reasonable to query the efficacy of the solution proposals of greater "data sharing", more "joint ventures", increased "public good" provisions, and the like. The latter observation may then beg the question: Why have Chinese pundits not yet aligned or come up with more effective answers to China's challenges in the Mekong region? Or, what else may China do to effectuate its aspiration of making water resource-related matters in the Subregion "add value to, rather than cause trouble for, its neighbourhood diplomacy"?[29] Or, how should Beijing press forward with its bilateral and multilateral engagements with the Mekong neighbours so that they will function as not only "security shields" of China's southwestern borders, but also "test grounds for cultivating its image as a responsible great power"?[30]

Interestingly, however, while Chinese foreign policy experts, Subregional affairs specialists, and interested online critics seem baffled about these issues, a glimpse into China's domestic debates and contending narratives about its own dam boom in recent years may hold some clues as to why it has been difficult for it to get out of a tight spot in the Mekong water/hydro politics. China has reportedly the highest number of dams in the world, with over 98,000 of them sitting on nearly all its rivers and including virtually all types and sizes of dam.[31] Also, similar to that of other emerging economies, including those in the Mekong region, the boom in China's hydro dam construction was prompted and has been sustained by many commonly recognised development factors, such as industrialisation and economic growth, efforts to reduce poverty through access to electricity, urbanisation, lifestyle changes, and global warming concerns. Likewise, China's thriving hydropower development has been accompanied by many regionally well-documented problems and concerns. Ready examples include dam construction posing "tradeoffs with livelihood and ecosystems", the energy sector becoming ever more "neoliberal-oriented", profit-driven private investors assuming greater roles, narratives of "good" water resources development and management constructed by asymmetrically empowered stakeholders, the implementation of "equitable benefit-sharing" charged with unequal representation of economic interests, and voices of affected local communities inadequately featured in deliberations on dam building.[32] All this suggests that an examination of China's domestic discussions about the widespread damming of its own rivers may shed some revealing light on its hydropower policies, strategies, and practices in the Mekong Subregion, which seem to have helped perpetuate regional doubts about China: A threat or an opportunity or both?

Humanitarian or animaltarian concerns

When measured against the UN Millennium Development indicators of access to and delivery of basic needs and infrastructure services, the Lancang/Mekong region remains "characterised by high poverty and limited development".[33] In their efforts to uplift the living conditions of their citizens, most countries along the River fix their gaze on its hydropower resources as a key avenue for providing economic growth. Correspondingly, both governments and commercial developers/investors have been outlining and implementing ambitious plans for building dams and reservoirs on the Lancang/Mekong mainstream and tributaries.[34] Due to its size, however, China outnumbers all its Mekong neighbours in its poverty-stricken population and outpaces them in hydropower development, and by an astronomical margin. On both counts, the characterisation largely reflects the reality in Yunnan, the Chinese province lying on the upstream of the Lancang/Mekong River.

In 1999, when China began to shift its attention from the economic growth in its coastal regions to that of the western hinterland, its official statistics reported 11.22 million people living in acute poverty in Yunnan Province.[35] In the following 15 years, China's "Great Western Development Programme" saw this figure cut in half, to 5.74 million in 2015. The inspiring progress, notwithstanding, Yunnan is still home to the second largest impoverished population in the country,[36] and 44 per cent of the poor are from rural ethnic minority communities.[37] This has resulted in the provincial, district, and county governments all assigning primary importance to poverty reduction. Moreover, while there is ample public acknowledgement that communities and families still in chronic poverty are probably the "toughest row to hoe", after decades of rapid economic growth in China, Yunnan officials at all levels publicly avow that their Province will meet the national 2020 deadline for eradicating rural poverty.[38] This promise is further elaborated to mean that by 2020 all permanent residents in poor rural areas will have secured access to adequate food, clothing, shelter, and health care, and 14 years of compulsory education, through secondary level. In addition, the growth rate of the rural poor's annual per capita disposable income will surpass the provincial average, and key performance indicators of public services will approach the national median.[39] But how will these ambitious goals be realised and financed?

Yunnan is located on the south extension of the Tibetan Plateau, with 94 per cent of its area being mountainous or semi-mountainous. Accompanying the "formidable" geographical feature are frequent natural disasters, such as earthquakes, droughts, floods, and mudslides. All this is widely believed to have greatly affected rural people's livelihoods, hampered their production capabilities, and allowed them little chance to exit poverty through subsidy/relief-fund-assisted conventional farming.[40] It is thus not surprising that Yunnan government's action plan fully embraces the principle of "development-oriented poverty reduction" marketed by the central government for the rural poor across China. Equally unsurprising is that by taking this approach, the action plan highlights the development of physical infrastructure, especially electricity, as an essential facilitating agent of economic growth and social development.[41]

It goes without saying that physical infrastructure is among the most basic of all necessities of daily life, economic growth, and broad-based prosperity. Yet for many in Yunnan's policy circles, a continuous expansion of the Province's hydroelectricity generating capacity and transmission networks offers a particular potential for not only physically enabling, but also financially supporting economic and social endeavours widely considered indispensable for rural poverty eradication. Put differently, there is an entrenched view among policy elites and opinion leaders in Yunnan that developing the rich hydro resources embedded in the mighty Lancang/Mekong, Nujiang/Salween, and Jinsha/Yangtze Rivers descending from Tibet into the Province allows for upgrading the still pervasive weather-dependant farming in poor areas to irrigated agriculture, and ensuring reliable and sufficient power supply to households, emerging industries, and services there as well.[42] Moreover, given that "Yunnan leads China in hydropower capacity",[43] supporters for its development concur in the belief that unlocking the full potential of the water resources should help boost the government revenue, as the Province may increase its sale of "clean energy" to the national "West [region]-to-East [coast]-Electricity-Transfer" grid.[44] Here "east" refers to China's eastern provinces, some of which are not on the coast. In addition, hydroelectricity development is anticipated to be accompanied by infrastructural spin-offs, such as roads/highways and transmission networks, and to create construction, technical, and management job opportunities for the rural poor.[45] Last but not least, corporate taxes from power companies are emphasised as a crucial and the most readily available source of pooled funds to deliver the promised big-ticket poverty-alleviation items, including clean water, adequate housing, universal health care, quality education, radio-film-television networks, and fibre optic broadband services.[46] As an attempt to quantify prospective tax revenues, a frequently cited researcher from Yunnan notes that if the poverty-stricken Nujiang Prefecture could be paid four Chinese cents less in compensation (less than US$0.01) per kilowatt hydropower of the 90 billion kilowatts planned to be generated within its territory, its annual income would be 3.6 billion Chinese yuan (US$530 million). If this money were divided into four equal amounts to help with local government revenue, poverty reduction efforts, infrastructure development, and environmental care, the 270,000 rural poor, about half the Prefecture's population, could receive 900 million yuan (US$130 million) a year from the corporate tax coffers.[47]

Yet districts in China that are rich in hydro energy resources are often renowned also for their unique natural environments, imperative ecological functions, high species diversity, delicate geological conditions, and sensitive ecosystems.[48] This is especially true in the case of the area covered by the "Three Parallel Rivers", Lancang/Mekong, Nujiang/Salween, and Jinsha/Yangtze. This area is classified as China's richest biodiverse region and largest plant/animal gene bank. It is moreover signified as a vital ground to which many animal species in continental Asia owe their origins and evolutionary changes. It is further acknowledged as encompassing the most types of ecosystems per unit area on Earth and generating many of the best botanical specimens in the world. Satisfying UNESCO's requirements of being exceptional in geological, ecological, biological, and aesthetic importance, the Three Parallel Rivers area was inscribed on the World Natural Heritage list in 2003.[49]

Yet while it took the Natural World Heritage Committee only "18 minutes" during its 2003 session to decide to accept China's nomination of the Three Parallel Rivers,[50] the debate fuelled by this decision among the Chinese about developing or conserving the area has been going strong ever since. The Rivers' "defenders" have been appealing to the public and lobbying government agencies and geology/environment research institutions for limiting hydro dams to an unavoidable minimum. They emphatically denounce the growing "jungles" of dams and stepped cascades that "have chopped up" many Chinese rivers into "chains of sausages" and, in turn, radically altered the breeding habitats and biological corridors of many fish and other aquatic species.[51] They argue even more passionately against "uprooting" the 20 plus ethnic minorities, who "have for generations lived on and nurtured" the water and land of the Three Parallel Rivers.[52] They tirelessly advocate that instead of massive human displacement and resettlement for hydropower dams, Yunnan Province should leverage the Rivers' "multi-colour valley culture" composed of unique and diverse ethnic traditions, festivities, myths, legends, and religions, as an alternative and more "accommodating" approach to poverty alleviation.[53] They seize virtually every opportunity to remind Chinese central and local officials, scientists, developers, and the public that China owes it to the world to preserve the Three Parallel Rivers Heritage site,[54] to downstream communities and countries not to turn the "shared" water resources into a "tragedy of the commons",[55] and, most importantly, to China's coming generations to leave behind some untampered, "naturally flowing" rivers.[56]

In responding to criticisms of and opposition to extensive dam construction, which are often from China's still small but increasingly vocal green groups, Chinese supporters of greater and faster hydropower development on the Lancang/Mekong, Nujiang/Salween, and Jinsha/Yangtze Rivers agree that the prevalent and persistent poverty in Yunnan Province is caused by a range of factors and hence necessitates multi-part solutions.[57] They also subscribe to the argument that China's "development-driven poverty reduction" programme should tap into not only natural, but also ethnic cultural resources, and should be built on the concept of sustainability.[58] They further accept the rationale that positive changes in China's environmental and cultural "attention deficits" may help improve its image and credibility across the Mekong Subregion.[59]

Nevertheless they challenge those in the anti-dam camp by asking bluntly, given the harsh natural conditions and limited exploitable resources in much of the Three Parallel Rivers area, how will the locals get out of poverty, if they "cannot touch the mountains or the rivers"?[60] They cynically invite hydro-dam opponents to "name" the dozens of rare fish species in the Rivers that the latter "care more about than the thousands upon thousands of impoverished humans living on the banks".[61] They discredit campaigns for replacing hydro development with eco-cultural tourism, claiming that those movements are built mostly on "outright ignorance" of the often delicate ecological balances, unobliging geographical conditions, and still underdeveloped physical infrastructure at many supposed attractions, none of which are compatible with a large number of visitors.[62] In a tongue-in-cheek manner, they further suggest that "green tourism" campaigners should, instead, simply move in with the locals and "reside permanently" in the "untouched" wilderness, with its "slash-and-burn" life style as well as "authentic" cultures.[63]

Dam supporters are, in addition, often very emotional when arguing that whatever concerns environmentally focused individuals and institutions may have, it is just "unfair" that communities at the Three Parallel Rivers continue to struggle for their basic needs, while the rest of China is already living in "relative comfort" and "relative affluence".[64] What is more "frustrating" and "absurd" for them is that the locals at the three Rivers are "beggars" holding a "golden rice bowl", or "sitting on rich water and hydropower resources".[65] Carrying their argument further, they contend categorically that the success of China's war on poverty hinges upon Yunnan's progress in poverty reduction.[66] Thus "pro-poor growth" is, and has to be, ranked not only the highest priority of many district officials in the province, but also "the most important indicator of their good governance".[67]

Given that Yunnan has the second largest poor population in China, the pressure of poverty indeed often exceeds the pressure of environmental protection for virtually all its local government entities. Likewise, while "environment", "sustainability", "good neighbour diplomacy", "acting as a responsible big country" have been co-opted into China's public policy and public discourse on development and growth, the issue of poverty heavily skews Chinese debates about the extensive hydropower programme in Yunnan on the upper Mekong more towards "humanitarian concerns" than "animaltarian/plant-tarian welfare".[68] This, however, does not mean that hydro dams' environmental, ecological, and river-system footprints are disregarded or sidelined in Chinese politics and public narratives of water resource development and governance in the Three Parallel Rivers area. In fact, shortly after its World Heritage inscription in 2003, a significant controversy arose among Chinese scientists, the power industry, environmentalists, policy advisors, and interested members of the public over whether hydropower could be accepted or classified as "clean" and/or "green" energy.[69] Yet while questions and uncertainties about adverse impacts of hydro dams in Yunnan on local and downstream ecological and environmental systems have become more pronounced, the debate about them seems increasingly dominated by the dilemma, or trade-offs between "local sacrifice" and "national/global benefits", or the impacts of dams on the local ecology versus those on China's pollution "crisis" and its carbon-reduction commitment to the world.[70]

Small self or big "we"

On 30 October 2011, a screenshot of a real-time air quality index from the US Embassy in Beijing was widely circulated on the popular Chinese microblogsite, Weibo. The message sparked immediate outcries from Beijing officials and some online commentators over potential "exaggerations" and attendant "political intentions" of the "American data".[71] The pollution-weary public, on the other hand, anxiously struggled to make sense of the tweeted air quality readings, the discrepancies between them and China's officially announced figures, the government's explanatory reasoning, and social media speculations. All this saw the Chinese terms for "AQI" or air quality index, "$PM_{2.5}$" or particulate matter with a diameter of 2.5 micrometres or less, "burst table" or pollutant concentration exceeding the range, "AQI colour-coded guide", and "toxic haze alert" making their way almost instantly into the vocabulary for everyday life in urban China.[72]

More acute public awareness and discontent about the worsening air quality and related health risks have subsequently resulted in outpourings of netizen-coined non-technical but sarcastic catch phrases for pollution. One such expression that came into prime popularity in late 2014 was "Marathon smog", referring to the 34th Beijing International Marathon held on 19 October that year, at which many runners had to wear heavy-duty mask filters to cope with the "slight to moderate" haze as noted by the event organisers, or the "hazardous" smog as reported by the US Embassy and Western media outlets.[73] A few weeks later, "Marathon smog" was replaced by two other online buzzwords, "APEC blue". In contrast to the earlier phrase, however, the new expression was inspired by the clear sky and clean air seen in Beijing during the 2014 APEC summit held in mid-November, less than a month after the marathon. As the rare and transient "blue" was effectuated by temporary government restrictions imposed for the Summit on cars and construction sites in Beijing and on environmentally unfriendly factories in surrounding areas, Chinese netizens also jokingly and cleverly equated "APEC" to "air pollution eventually controlled".[74] Yet the new explanation of the acronym proved indeed only a wordplay, as the "APEC blue" was followed by a "Two Sessions blue" in Beijing and many provincial capitals in the spring of 2015, when the annual plenary and branch sessions of the National People's Congress and the Chinese People's Political Consultative Conference were held.[75] Then in late August and early September of the same year, the "Two Sessions blue" was again replaced by a two-week "Military Parade blue" during the commemoration of the seventieth anniversary of the end of World War II and China's anti-Japanese war.[76]

Amusing and even satirical as such phrases may sound, their proliferation and immense popularity bear testimony to a pervasive and growing sense of public anxiety and impatience over deteriorating air quality particularly in China's urban areas. With 56.1 per cent of China's population now living in cities and towns,[77] and with $PM_{2.5}$ pollution having already evolved into the fourth leading cause of premature deaths,[78] the Chinese government has few other options but to act on public concerns. It has thus not only incorporated some of the cynical pollution-related phrases into its official rhetoric, but also promised to work towards turning the APEC and other brief "blue" phrases into a permanent "China blue".[79] Furthermore, while many local officials reportedly do not mind, or may even prefer, simply occasioning temporary, events-driven, shock-treatment-style "political blue skies" to ease public pressure over air pollution,[80] the central government has been loudly declaring in its 12th (2011–15) and 13th (2016–20) Five Year Plans, and other climate/environment policy initiatives, to take aggressive actions for the fulfilment of China's promises to peak its carbon emissions by 2030, to bring its carbon intensity of GDP down 40 – 5 per cent below 2005 levels by 2020 and down 60 – 5 percent by 2030, and meanwhile to increase the share of non-fossil energy of the total primary energy supply first to 15 and then 20 per cent.[81]

The government's carbon reduction pledge and the public's growing discontent over the air quality have given rise to high hopes among Chinese hydropower advocates that the development of the water resources in China, especially its southwestern provinces, will pick up speed.[82] Chinese environmentalists and dam opponents, on the other hand, continue to seriously question the prospect of hydropower as a "green saviour" of the world's largest carbon emitter.[83] They go even further, arguing that hydro dams and reservoirs can in fact be significant sources of both water and air pollution, as they reduce the flow rates of rivers, alter their seasonal temperature, hence compromise their self-purification capacity, cause overloads of nutrients, encourage algal blooms, aggravate biological decay, and produce methane or greenhouse gas emissions.[84] Also, dams and reservoirs expand surface areas of rivers and thus facilitate greater evaporation and higher salt concentration.[85] Moreover, slow-moving rivers with large stationary bodies of water typically trap gravel and other sediments. To alleviate the problem of sedimentation and to maintain reservoir capacity, note Chinese environmentalists, more and more dams are often built "higher and higher up the stream". This practice has "chopped up" many Chinese rivers and, in turn, degraded wetlands, ecosystems, and aquatic habitats along their routes as well as at dam sites.[86] Meanwhile, "filtered" water probably travels faster when discharged from dams and thus adds to the risk of downstream river-bed erosion and embankment collapse, resulting in less water inflows to lakes in the case of the former and more floods in the case of the latter.[87] Referring to the seemingly ever more frequent occurrence of landslides, mud/debris flows, torrential storms, and severe droughts in some of China's major river basins, Chinese critics of "escalated" and "disorderly" hydropower development sound a note of warning: "If humans do not let rivers run their natural course to their natural rhythm, rivers will not let humans escape livelihood disruptions, either."[88]

In answering these concerns and criticisms, Chinese hydropower apologists concede that "development" is almost always "accompanied by damage", and that few, if any, forms of "clean/renewable energy" can stay completely clear of negative environmental effects.[89] Yet they vigorously argue that if there are only "comparatively good" energy sources, their pros and cons should be weighed primarily on how they impact "national" and "societal" interests, rather than on "trendy assumptions" or "narrowly" defined concerns of/about a specific locale. It thus logically follows that the "worthiness" of hydropower ought to be judged first and foremost in the context of China's deteriorating air quality, increasing health risks, and the ensuing public demand, international pressure, and policy commitment for radical emission reductions by 2030.[90]

Clean/green and necessary or neither

Aside from the basic principles, Chinese dam supporters also vehemently dispute the allegation that hydropower development brings "grave" and "irreparable" damage to the ecological balance and environmental stability of many waterways. They particularly cite studies conducted in Canada and Switzerland to point out that greenhouse gas emissions from hydropower reservoirs are 1/300 of that from fossil fuels in the best cases and 1/17 at the worst end of the spectrum.[91] They also emphasise that because the water quality required by reservoirs and hydropower stations is generally higher than the existing conditions of many Chinese rivers, hydro development may in fact help curtail the still rather common practice in China of using rivers and other waterbodies as open sewers for domestic and industrial waste.[92]

They back up this claim with references to successful hydropower schemes in the developed world, stressing that the water resource utilisation rate in 22 industrialised countries, including America, Japan, Norway, and Switzerland, is over 80 per cent, and yet there have been few public complaints and scientific reports about environmental and human risks.[93] They thus insist that Chinese hydro development critics are not only misleading, but also missing the point, as the main reason for the much greater environmental impact of China's 35 per cent water resource utilisation rate is "inadequate planning", "sketchy rules and standards", and "poor project governance".[94] The crux of the problem, in other words, is that the national hydropower development policy tends to swing between "promoting", when growth is the dominant pursuit, and "withdrawing", when environmental and resettlement problems and complaints become overwhelming.[95] Evasive hydro development guidelines arising from the "policy pendulum" have in turn made it possible for local government agencies and hydropower companies to "routinise" their irregular practices of "consent without environmental impact assessment", "construction without authorisation", "capacity expansion without approval", "pollution first, abatement later", and "polluting while conserving".[96]

Not giving in, however, Chinese conservation departments and green groups retort that irrespective of the environmental effects of hydro projects, dam supporters still need to "face up" to China's "new normal" of slow economic growth, shrinking electricity demand, and ever worsening overcapacity of the energy industry.[97] They press even harder on the issue of "excessive" supply of electricity in Yunnan Province on the upper Lancang/Mekong River, and its hydropower stations "abandoning" more and more water since 2012 to alleviate overcapacity. They eagerly share with the public the data from the hydropower industry indicating that the total worth of daily abandoned hydro water in Yunnan during a flooding season can reach 330 million kilowatt hours, or 100 million yuan (about US$14 million) "lost in vain" in a single day.[98] However, that still does not suffice to ease the pressure, since provincial and district economic offices are showing more "compassion" towards local energy-intensive firms, despite their environmental records, and towards efforts to bring into Yunnan more "three high" businesses and enterprises, namely, high power consumption, high emission, and high contamination.[99] Chinese green groups worry that such electricity-oversupply-curbing attempts will expose Yunnan's delicate environment to more risks and meanwhile aggravate overproduction problems in other industries locally and nationally.[100] For them, a better and cut-to-the-chase solution is to introduce "restraint" as well as "order" in hydropower development in Yunnan and other southwestern provinces.[101]

Predictably, Chinese dam supporters scoff at these arguments, claiming that those who "demonise" China's hydroelectric development have "overlooked" the "single most consequential" fact that the build-up of overcapacity is in coal-fired power generation rather than from renewable sources.[102] They further blame Chinese environmental journalists and advocacy groups for "abetting" the primary "culprit" behind China's worsening smog by working persistently since 2003 to "defer" hydropower development on the Nujiang/Salween River. They affirm that the energy and environmental "cost" of shelving that initiative is "2,000-plus extra railway wagons of coal being mined, transported and burnt every day in China".[103] All this, they continue, translated into an 8.7 per cent jump in the total generating capacity of coal in 2014, twice the increase of that year's national electricity consumption,[104] and in addition breaking the ground for the construction of four new coal-burning power plants a week in 2015.[105] Worse still, with the "green identity" of hydropower still in dispute, this "new" energy industry is often pressured to "subsidise" the "established" and "overcrowded" coal-fired power sector by operating below capacity or "donating" proceeds via local governments.[106]

To halt the "explosive surge" of coal power, Chinese dam supporters call for eco-conscious journalists and green groups to stop "hyping false environmental claims" and "vilifying" hydroelectric projects.[107] They also urge dam opponents to unify their environmental intentions and effects by joining in the effort to turn China's power generation overcapacity into a facilitating factor for restructuring its energy sector.[108] Their notion of "restructuring" is further elaborated to include restricting the increase of coal-fired generating units and reducing the market share of coal power to make room for the growth of the hydropower industry,[109] currently accounting for less than one-fifth of the country's total electricity production.[110] To achieve that goal, Chinese dam supporters plead with green groups to join forces in pushing for a level playing field on the supply side of the energy market so that the hydroelectricity industry can have a chance to grow and perfect its power quality and environmental record. Considering the high investment costs, massive relocation expenses, tough environmental demands, and long construction cycles of hydroelectric stations, dam defenders also invite journalists and advocates in the opposition camp to join with them in appealing for greater policy support for hydro development. They maintain that the removal of structural/systemic constraints and availing of public endorsement will be essential for the hydropower industry, and wind and photovoltaic power suppliers for that matter, to "ripen into" a reliable electricity provider and hence shake off its reputation as an at-the-mercy-of-element, "junk" energy source that requires coal power as a standby back-up.[111]

However, there is no sign that eco-advocaters are convinced. Nor does the rampant controversy over the "cleanness" and "greenness" of hydropower appear to be abating across China. On the contrary, "inciting" petitions to "demolish" dams remain loud and constant,[112] and their developers/contractors stay "trapped" in an "are-we-builders-or-destroyers personality disorder".[113] Moreover, with dam critics and supporters both trying to claim the "environmental high ground", such idioms as "ecosystem first", "eco-civilisation", "ecological conservation redlines", and "lucid waters and lush mountains are themselves precious assets" are now incorporated in the official, public, and corporate development narratives on hydropower.[114] At the same time, the attainment of the quantified emission reduction targets pledged to the world and the risk of increased social unrest over smog-choked cities are commonly viewed as a "Sword of Damocles" hanging over China's central and local governments.[115] In fact, the paramount concern about the eruption of massive "smog-mask protests" in urban areas has already seen some cities trying to introduce a real-name registration system in the selling and buying of surgical face masks.[116] Even if no large surgical-masked crowds have taken to the street, the fact that heavy smog occurs increasingly frequently and blankets ever more cities is worrisome enough for Chinese leaders and dam supporters to continue pressing forward with hydropower development and the rhetoric of "big we" outweighing "small we" in nature conservation, and "global eco-environmental resilience and sustainability offsetting local eco-environmental disturbances".[117]

But who are the "small we" who make sacrifices in order for the "big we" to have better breathing air and the "bigger we" to mitigate climate change? Typically, as may be guessed, the group bearing the brunt of adverse, but supposedly necessary, side effects of hydro development in China is the locals living downstream from hydro dams or relocated to make room for hydropower stations. Chinese critics, supporters, and stakeholders of hydropower projects, for their part, all act as the spokesperson for local interests. The way in which they talk over each other and presumptuously about/to dam-affected communities has, however, often served to advance their respective visions and agendas rather than to reconcile locals' economic, social, and ecological concerns over hydro development. That in turn has compromised the effectiveness of numerous efforts undertaken in Yunnan and across China to help alleviate local poverty, reduce nationwide air pollution, and cap China's carbon emission through unlocking hydroelectric potentials.

Stakeholders or local communities

Hydro development, especially the initiation, planning, approval, and construction of large projects, typically involves multiple stakeholders with diverse interests, who compete at various spatial scales to influence public deliberations and narratives on "good" water resource governance.[118] Key players in Chinese hydropower decision making include the National Development and Reform Commission, the National Energy Administration, water conservancy agencies, local governments, power companies, the Ministry of Environmental Protection, green advocates, and the media.[119] A widely held view suggests that participating in China's hydro politics, local governments think primarily of "growth", power company "profits", green non-governmental organisation (NGO) "eco-environments", and state organisations' "balance".[120] Yet "balancing" or reconciling these different foci or expectations has proved challenging.[121] Specifically, efforts towards compromise among contending interests of the many stakeholders seem to have remained largely an academic exercise, but with real and often consequential effects on the life and environment of those living at or close to hydropower development sites.[122]

Environmental agencies and advocates

As mentioned earlier, the key parties featured in China's hydropower decision making may be divided, at a more general level, into pro- and anti-dam camps. Not surprisingly, the main forces of the latter group are both state and non-governmental conservation agencies and organisations. Many of their leading members are journalists, and their critical voices broke into China's mainstream media in 2003, when they began to argue, as a collectivity, against some large hydro schemes proposed for the Three Parallel Rivers region in Yunnan.[123] The rapid growth of social media networks has since redoubled the number of avenues available for them to accelerate public awareness of and engagement in their environmental assessments of specific hydro projects and their conservation campaigns as a whole.[124] Tapping into the powerful tools available in the digital domain, high-flying Chinese environmental NGOs have also been actively cultivating networks with overseas green movements. One of the best-known cases is perhaps the "Protecting China's Last Ecological River – Nujiang/Salween" campaign initiated in 2003 by the environmental group, Green Earth Volunteers. Not only did its petition against damming the River collect signatures from more than 80 NGOs in over 60 countries,[125] but the ensuing national debate on hydro development and eco-sustainability in West China also gained international traction through the *New York Times, Le Monde,* and *Asahi Shimbun*, among others.[126]

Like green movements across the world, enlisting both mainstream and social media resources to inform and mobilise public opinion has enabled Chinese environmental and conservation advocates to build momentum for their endeavours and, more importantly, to prevail over dam supporters in stopping some controversial large hydropower schemes in the Three Parallel Rivers area.[127] Their media-savviness, for example, played an important and instrumental role in their effective coordination of the 2003 national campaign against damming the Nujiang/Salween River. In early 2004, put under pressure by the impressive display of public opinion, Premier Wen Jiabao personally stepped in to suspend the cascade hydro venture planned for the River.[128] This endorsement of the central government has in turn seen the headline theme, "Controversy over hydro development on the Nujiang/Salween River", included as an expository essay question in China's national public servant exams.[129] Furthermore, Chinese green advocates' effort to galvanise the public into making the environment a high-priority concern has also helped them win their defamation lawsuits against those dam supporters who call them "pseudo-conservationists", "media abusers", "liars", "sympathisers of colour revolutions backed by hostile foreign interests".[130]

Yet Chinese environmental agencies and advocates' "single-issue", namely, anti-dam, approach to China's multi-dimensional hydro politics seems to be an effective way for them to choose their battles, but is not sufficient to win them, let alone the war.[131] For example, when they took issue in 2003 with central/local economic and energy departments and power companies on the latter's proposal to carry out massive hydro development on the Nujiang/Salween River, they detailed how some hydropower projects on the parallel-running Lancang/Mekong River had failed to deliver the promised "better living and better farming" to the locals.[132] They have since also been arguing that the still pervasive poverty in Yunnan Province is perpetuated by many interacting factors and thus cannot and will not be eradicated by simply building large hydropower stations on its three major rivers.[133] They have yet, however, to substantiate their envisioned "alternative" and "uniquely Yunnan" paths to economic growth and poverty reduction.[134] Similarly, they have been speaking out loud, perhaps rightly so, about energy policies being only a component, rather than the whole of the fight against air pollution and climate change. However, they have not spelt out their aspired "policy integration" which would embrace and deal with concerns about the integrity and sustainability of the environment, resources, economic prosperity, and socio-cultural development.[135] Furthermore, they constantly caution against China becoming "obsessed" with expanding its hydropower industry and hence "marginalising" other possible measures and sources to increase its energy security. This, they believe, would lock China in the tendency to "sacrific[e] ecology for energy".[136] Yet they do not go into the specifics of the risks, or provide a comprehensive roadmap out of them. They are thus often labelled by dam supporters as "environmental extremists", and their argument of "hydro development inevitably harming ecological health" decried as an "anecdotal slogan" or "unscientific dogma".[137]

All this may help explain why, on the one hand, "environmental protection", expressed as facts, beliefs, assumptions, judgements, and/or contentions, arguably gained its stature of "natural justice" in China during the 2003 Nujiang/Salween campaign to stop dam building on the River.[138] Plus, Chinese green advocates have since been able to avail themselves of the favourable sentiment and the powerful Web 2.0 tools to increase their appeal among the Chinese and cultivate public information sharing, collective thinking, and creative problem solving in their movement.[139] On the other hand, however, many Chinese conservation officials and promoters lament that in their war on environmental harms, they often fight like "Don Quixote", or "tragic heroes with little sense of accomplishment".[140] Indeed, while still relishing their "satisfaction" over helping to halt the Nujiang/Salween Dam in 2004, for example, many Chinese green groups found their nerves frayed again by the National Energy Bureau's "13th Five-Year Plan for Hydopower Development" unveiled in early 2016, as it has "shortlisted" all the Three Parallel Rivers in Yunnan for large hydro dams.[141]

Yet what is worse than the projection or speculation that suspended projects like the one proposed for the Nujiang/Salween River may make a comeback is the cruel reality that the construction of smaller-scale hydro stations has never been stopped on the tributaries of the Nujiang/Salween and other major rivers in Yunnan. In fact, the victory of the 2003 anti-damming-Nujiang/Salween River campaign, argue some Chinese opinion leaders, might have encouraged local governments and power companies to shift their attention to smaller hydro projects and tributary waterways. The Nujiang [Salween] Prefecture, for example, registered 30 small hydropower stations in 2003, with a total installed capacity of 80,000 kilowatts. By the end of 2015, however, the number of stations jumped to 95 and the number of kilowatts to 1.25 million, or 15 times more than that of 2003, when the damming of the River's mainstream was halted.[142]

Local governments

It is generally recognised that a key driver of the fast-track hydro energy growth across Yunnan is the local government at both the provincial and district levels.

Certainly, in the political structure of China today, governments at all levels consist of not only finance, energy, and economic development agencies, but also conservation departments. Yet Chinese studies suggest that the latter, like their green NGO counterparts mentioned above, while winning in the court of public opinion, are often frustrated because they are able to do little more than merely take note of or complain about the environmental impacts of hydro projects.[143]

In contrast, local finance, energy, and economic development agencies in Yunnan, and China as a whole, may occasionally lose public opinion battles on river damming. Nonetheless, their governmental portfolio functions and responsibilities for local GDP growth, job creation, poverty reduction, energy security, and expansion of renewable power generation allow them to uphold their policy position that provinces like Yunnan can "afford neither environmental missteps in nor further delays of hydro development".[144] Furthermore, taking advantage of their administratively granted mandate, they have been incessantly lodging appeals with higher administrative agencies for support for greater and faster hydro development in their constituent regions. In that regard, they are open and firm about their opposition to "allowing" the "rich" water resources in "poverty-stricken" and "revenue-scarce" Yunnan to flow away "unproductively".[145] They are frank about their great interest in increasing provincial and district revenues through hydro development to cover their spending commitments. They commonly state that had it not been halted, the proposed cascade of dams on the Nujiang/Salween River would have brought 90 billion Chinese yuan (US$ 13 billion) of investment into the district, which, in turn, would have added 5.2 billion yuan (US$0.7 billion) to the annual national tax revenue, 2.7 billion yuan (US$0.3 billion) to the provincial/district tax pool, and 450,000 jobs to the labour market.[146]

The constant pressure over GDP records and financial obligations for the provision of public goods, facilities, and services has also seen the provincial and district governments in Yunnan regularly sending lobby groups to Beijing, and inviting officials and scientists from the Environmental Protection Ministry (EPM) for "field studies" in Yunnan.[147] Their efforts to "expose" executives and researchers from EPM to the economic and living conditions of the locals have proved particularly worthwhile. In the case of Nujiang/Salween River Dam proposal, for example, conservation scientists from EPM were reported to be "overbearing" when they first met with their counterparts on Yunnan's lobbying teams in Beijing. At times when discussions became contentious, they even accused the latter of being "bought off" by local governments and developers. Yet their disapproval of damming the River and other major waterways in Yunnan softened significantly after their field research trips. Some of them even became completely silent on the matter.[148]

Unsurprisingly, the acquiescence of higher-level environmental officials and scientists and the constant fiscal challenge in achieving local economic objectives and delivering social and infrastructural services have encouraged the provincial and district governments in Yunnan to "turn a blind eye" to those developers who have taken the liberty of starting preliminary works for the cascade of dams on the main course of the Nujiang/Salween River even with the "suspension" ruling still in place.[149] On a much broader scale, the fiscal pressure has reportedly compelled local governments across the province to go after any and all possible revenue-generating hydro projects with or without environmental implications. That the provincial government holds the authority to grant permissions for small and medium-sized hydropower plants has also been accommodating to the almost uncontainable urge of prefecture and lower-level officials to attract ever more hydropower investments to their jurisdictional locales.[150]

That, of course, does not mean that local officials do not have to concern themselves with environmental assessments or the public, especially green groups' oversight of how they execute the assessments. To a certain degree, the decade-long halt of the initiative to dam the mainstream of the Nujiang/Salween River, regardless of persistent efforts to reverse the decision, also points to the fact that considerations of environmental compatibility have played a role in hydropower decisions in Yunnan Province.[151] Yet when it comes to exercising their inspection and approval authority over small and medium-sized hydro projects, the local government agencies involved are repeatedly faulted for having too little an appetite for exploring a "reconciling point" between economic growth and environmental protection.[152] Widely characterised as letting their "bum guide their mind", they are expressly criticised for often either selectively following their own standards and procedures in evaluating and auditing the environmental compatibility of hydro projects, or elaborating their own rules in a way that *privileges* developers and their expeditious actions. [153] This GDP/revenue-oriented, "flexible" decision-making style is commonly believed to have encouraged hydro developers to "rush to stake river claims", aspire to preferential treatment and cursory environmental reviews, cut corners in environmental compliance, and/or go into operation without permits.[154]

Hydro developers

Being key for-profit stakeholders in China's hydro development, Chinese state-owned and private hydropower companies have never hesitated to make known that they see hydro projects as "gold reservoirs".[155] Informed by such a mindset, they have leapt at any opportunity to be contracted to build and manage storage dams and power plants on any Chinese river. They have, in particular, been vigorously appealing to state economic and environmental authorities and enthusiastically echoing dam supporters in their call for development-friendly policies and decisions in favour of major hydro initiatives on mainstreams of China's principal river systems.[156] They have also been eagerly and forcefully currying favourable considerations from local governments for carrying out small and medium-sized hydropower projects on all dammable rivers and tributaries.

For Chinese hydro developers, the attractiveness of small and medium-sized hydro projects, lies largely in the fact that they are subject to only local governments' scrutiny/approval processes and environmental standards. These are often negotiable and adjustable, and hence looser as well as simpler than those applied to large hydro ventures at both national and provincial levels. Small and medium-sized projects also stay ahead of public opinion more easily. Limited public attention and flexible/neighbourly appraisals typically translate into more prompt construction starts. In addition, the manageable scale of small and medium-sized hydropower projects means that they generally take less time to complete. Once in full operation, smaller hydropower projects, say, of 700 million yuan (US$100 million), can purportedly turn into "banknote printing machines" in just five to ten years. Such a payback period, according to Chinese official media, is much shorter than that of large-scale works.[157]

Besides enjoying relatively low thresholds for approval, a quick returns on investment, and lasting high profitability, locally governed small and medium-sized hydro projects are also structurally shielded from environmental liability risks. The relentless pursuit of local governments for growth, revenue, and jobs persuades their economic development bureaus, investment promotion agencies, finance divisions, public utilities offices, and other departments overseeing hydro development to put into practice a commonly held notion in China's market-oriented reform, that is, central/local governments "set the stage" for corporates to "put on their shows".[158] To fulfil their facilitation roles in hydro development, local government agencies, as indicated earlier, appear almost obligated not to fully or strictly enforce the state's or their own environmental policies, regulations, and accountability mechanisms. When they deem it necessary, they do not hesitate to turn a blind eye to hydro developers' environmental shortfalls, as long as the latter can deliver their side of the bargain, namely, to bring in capital, complete their projects, contribute to tax revenues, and create jobs. [159]

However, being stakeholders themselves in hydro development, local governments are not willing or ready to cover hydro projects' environmental costs. They have, rather, habitually, and often effectively, pushed for the state/society to "pick up the tab".[160] As might be expected, this nearly perfect deal for developers through which they may pocket their projects' yields and essentially socialise the environmental losses and risks incurred, has fuelled wave after wave of "gold rush" of hydro development throughout China. In the water-resource-rich Yunnan Province, for example, virtually all the six major river systems have been densely dammed up, except for the mainstream Nujiang/Salween and that perhaps for the time being only.[161]

Beneficiaries as they may be, however, hydro developers have not been totally insulated from the negative effects of the rapid overcrowding of hydropower stations in Yunnan and the ensuing intensified intra-industry competition. In fact, an increasing number of them have been swept into rising "tides" of ownership transfers, mergers, voluntary close-downs, and bankruptcies.[162] Yet outpacing hydro development planning and project appraisal processes, the dam rush and the pursuit of instant returns by hydro developers, arguably emboldened and enabled by local governments' own socio-economic calculations, have resulted in additional, more severe and largely unnecessary environmental issues. That has, in turn, seen hydropower continue to fare as badly as coal power with many of the public, when they are asked to identify preferred energy sources.[163] Still, by far the most seriously affected by the "great" but disorderly "leap forward" in China's hydropower sector have been the locals who live along and/or just off many of the dammed rivers, and yet who often seem to have the least say in decisions about hydro projects.[164]

Local people

It is commonly accepted in China that dam-induced/forced human displacement and relocation are as "monumental" a hurdle as ecological conservation/compensation in hydropower development.[165] There is also a broad consensus across the Chinese public and professional communities that problems arising from development-related resettlement boil down to one fundamental issue, the distribution of costs and benefits.[166] Yet while their interests are acknowledged as a central concern in hydro development, dam-affected people continue to play little or no essential part in shaping the debates and decisions about hydro projects in their immediate neighbourhood.[167] Likewise, it is widely recognised that in the social media era, the largely "local" issue of population resettlement can easily flare up and be stretched across socio-political frontiers.[168] Apprehension about community discontent evolving into social agitation has indeed resulted in a steady improvement in resettlement payments across China. Hydro relocation compensation in many cases is reported to constitute nearly half of the total project costs.[169] Yet the average people in dam-affected areas remain the worst-off group of all involved, constantly getting the raw end of hydro development deals.[170]

Ironically, however, local people and communities in dam-affected areas suffer no shortage of "champions" of their interests. As a matter of fact, key Chinese hydropower stakeholders from the government, the industry, and green groups all claim to have the locals' livelihoods at heart. In pressing their respective agendas, the self-styled spokespeople typically insist and act on their diverse, and often contending, interpretations and representations of "the will of the local people". Pro-dam government agencies, for example, are unequivocal in their conviction that impoverished rural people in water-resource-rich regions aspire to build a "new socialist countryside" through hydropower development. They are equally confident that "new" should be understood as meaning well-off and up-to-date.[171] Environmental organisations, on the other hand, expand the definition of "locals" to include "future generations",[172] and profess to act on behalf of both groups when campaigning to curb the "great leap forward" in China's hydro development.[173] They further argue that the "slash-and-burn" lifestyle continues in regions like the Three Parallel Rivers because it is an "organic" component of the local "primordial ecosystems" and has been "enjoyed" by people living there for thousands of years. It should thus be "respected" and left "undisturbed".[174] Such contending narratives on dam-affected people and their needs, while serving competing agendas for China's hydro development, often obscure the central issue, namely, fair and adequate compensation and guaranteed delivery to the displaced. As a result, dam-affected locals are frequently left short-changed by virtually all the key stakeholders in hydro development.

Among the many issues faced by rural displaced/resettled families and communities in China, the all-too-common but exceedingly challenging issue is the disruption of their survival means and activities of daily living. [175] Numerous Chinese government, green group, media, and academic studies, for example, indicate that as more hydropower projects are built, or even just planned, the "higher" farmers tend to be relocated above river basins, and their replacement land is at a still higher altitude. With hydro dams already seriously restricting flow rates of rivers, resettlement arrangements as such result in farmers being not only unable to exploit the natural gravitational force of rivers in watering their fields, but also forced to pay for the installation of multi-level pumping irrigation mechanisms. They have then to budget for the operation of the pumps, as their sacrifices for hydropower development are rarely translated into electricity concessions to help ease their outgoings on utilities. Yet not all of their replacement land is suitable for their customary high-value crops, nor can it deliver adequate yields immediately to cover these and other additional production-related expenses. Thus in struggling to make ends meet, relocated farmers sometimes find themselves having no other choice but to leave some of their land uncultivated, which in turn further affects their discretionary income from farming.[176] Moreover, even when they can raise enough funds to pay for the extra irrigation charges, the timing and amount of water that they can have access to are probably still at the discretion of hydropower plants. This is particularly true in the event of severe droughts and flooding when their crops are subject to either extremely insufficient or hugely excessive water released from hydropower stations.[177]

Another constant challenge faced by displaced farmers is that the cash compensation from hydropower developers does not even cover the cost of re-establishing their livelihoods, let alone enable them to create development opportunities or cultivate income-generating capacities to better their overall household and community welfare. One widely identified reason for the scanty resettlement compensation is that too many provincial and district government agencies try to claim a share of the spoils. Some broadly circulated reports reveal that in extreme instances, only 2 out of every 100 yuan of cash compensation "trickle" downward to the displaced families.[178] In many cases, to get a new and moderately adequate roof over their heads, dam-affected farmers often have to supplement the heavily pruned cash compensation with their own savings.[179] To make matters worse, they usually have to leave behind their established sideline farming businesses/activities, which are often indispensable source of income for them to meet their essential living expenses.[180]

When faced with these complaints, Chinese dam-supporters are often quick to point out that hydropower projects bring with them huge demands for tertiary-sector services. Such demands, they maintain, should provide affected farmers with business opportunities to earn more extra income than their traditional sideline farming undertakings have offered.[181] Yet continuous media reports and academic studies indicate that in many poverty-stricken areas, hydro projects are unable to live up to dam-supporters' promises of producing development spillovers conducive to improving local communities' "hematopoietic capabilities" to self-generate and sustain economic growth.[182] When service-sector demands dry up with the completion of dam construction and the operation of hydropower plants, locals in many dam-affected areas fall back into deprivation and poverty.[183] The resultant popular discontent casts a long shadow over hydropower development across China. According to surveys conducted in Yunnan by green groups, for example, 93.6 per cent of local respondents in dam-affected areas are sceptical about benefiting from hydropower projects; 66 per cent are unsatisfied with the compensation that they have received; and 67.6 per cent have serious doubts as to whether they can entrust their interests to local governments.[184]

There has certainly been no lack of public recognition in China that ordinary farmers in dam-affected areas are often not on an equal footing with government agencies or developers in sharing the benefits arising from hydro projects.[185] There have also been numerous policy and academic discussions about equitable benefit-sharing.[186] Suggestions emerging from the deliberations include hydro developers supplementing one-time land/cash compensation with long-term dividend stocks,[187] the central government stepping up pressure on electric grid companies to at least treat hydropower fairly if not prioritise it over coal,[188] government agencies at all levels compulsorily earmarking proportions of hydro tax revenues for relocation assistance to farmers, and each affected district building a dam-induced migration database for local government agencies and hydro developers to assess the post-relocation welfare of farmers and their communities.[189]

Even if carried out, however, these and other similar suggestions are perhaps not much more than a starting point for meaningful improvements in the livelihoods of relocated farmers. Yet tossed among competing interests in hydropower development, contending narratives about its environmental impacts, and conflicting visions of its links with poverty alleviation, these proposed amendments, basic as they may seem, have remained largely an aspiration, especially in poverty-stricken provinces and districts like Yunnan and the Three Parallel Rivers. Consequently, with public debates still going strong in China on its growth models, economic structures, value orientations, resource governance, and development dividend distribution, dam-affected communities in poor rural areas continue grappling with the "resource curse" and corresponding "richly-endowed poverty".[190]

Conclusion

China's worsening smog crisis and daring global pledge to peak its greenhouse gas emissions by 2030 have seen the Chinese government turning ever more determinedly towards hydropower as a pathway and solution.[191] With China's economy confronted with mounting downward pressure, hydro projects, especially mega schemes, are also expected to "inject cardiac stimulants" into growth vitality and momentum by boosting demands for labour, cement, steel, and other raw materials,.[192] At the same time, however, there is increasing scepticism in the Chinese public attitude towards "narrowly equating" water resources to hydropower and "banking exclusively" on energy policies to address pollution and climate change.[193] That ordinary locals are often shut out of project decision making and the beneficiary club has invited further questions about whether massive hydropower development is "inevitably correlated" with rural poverty reduction, or it is simply another "resource trap" for the already economically vulnerable.[194] These contentious issues have consequently subjected virtually all large dams proposed or launched in recent years to waves of vociferous opposition across China.[195]

When it comes to China's transboundary rivers, hydro-dam controversy has been even more intense, especially since 2013 when Beijing began fleshing out its neighbourhood-diplomacy agenda. Not surprisingly, China's foreign policy analysts participating in the debate focus much of their attention on hydro development in Yunnan Province, which sits on the upper stream of four out of the five major rivers running through mainland Southeast Asia,[196] including the Langsang/Mekong. Many of these Chinese analysts openly concede that the prospects are not optimistic for China to win over public opinion in the downstream countries on its massive hydro development in Yunnan, or on its involvement in water resource development across the Subregion.[197] In elaborating the "popularity deficiency" issue, they candidly debate whether China's hydro behaviour towards shared water resources reflects too closely the "dated", "self-interested" theory of "absolute territorial sovereignty";[198] whether China's hydropower rush has "shifted" the carbon footprint onto the lower Mekong countries[199] and inflicted economic and livelihood disruption on downstream communities;[200] whether Chinese "outbound" hydro developers are too "eager" to take advantage of incomplete regulatory mechanisms in some Mekong countries to "dodge" their environmental obligations;[201] whether China-invested hydro projects have benefited elite interest groups and corrupt officials in the Subregion but allowed few cuts of the "cakes" for needy locals;[202] whether China will help turn the Mekong into "fragmented ecospheres" through its expected 40 per cent share of the planned hydrological works on the River's mainstream and tributaries.[203]

Chinese policy analysts' debates and green groups' opposition, notwithstanding, growing public outrage over air quality and cynicism about "political blue skies",[204] or "campaign-style" pollution control,[205] will probably motivate Beijing to press forward with its plan to get hydropower capacity to 9 per cent of China's primary energy mix by 2030.[206] At the same time, however, the unsettled domestic "conceptual/moral disputes" and "special interest rivalries" on the balance between economic development and environmental protection suggest that China's "hydro-dam urge" will also remain fuelled by GDP growth concerns, revenue generation pressures, and profit maximisation desires.[207] This, in turn, means that in the foreseeable future, there are no feasible solutions to many of the issues pertaining to China's hydro development along the Mekong. Similarly, the countries in the Subregion may continue to feel entangled in the dilemma of wanting to engage with China for development cooperation, but agonising over the reality of having a giant economy and resource demander controlling the headwaters of their Mother River.[208]

Notes

1 RUAN Changan, "Zhongguo chuanyuan mei fandu, jie fei huo jie chuan yun du" [Chinese sailors were not involved in drug trafficking, robbers likely hijacked boats to ship drugs], *Huaxi dushi bao* [West China city news], 10 October 2011, p. 4.

2 SHANG Xi, "Meigong he13ming yuxi zhongguo chuangyuan quanbu yunan" [The 13 ambushed Chinese crew members were killed], *Jing hua shibao* [Beijing Times], 11 October 2011, online at http://world.huanqiu.com/roll/2011-10/2070355.html.

3 HUANG Bingfu, "Yangshi zhibo Rukang sixing zhi zheng: fazhi jingsheng yu xa ji jing hou" [Debate over live coverage of execution of Naw Kham: Promoting rule of law or killing the chicken to scare the monkey], ndnews.oeeee.com, 21 May 2013, online at http://ndnews.oeeee.com/html/201305/21/62961.html; "Zhibo sixing, wangmin reyi" [Televising execution live: A most talked about topic among netizens], *Wen Wei Po*, 2 March 2013, p. A12.

4 SHAO Ming, "Jiang hao zhongguo gushi: dianshiju *meigonghe da an* de sixiang yu yishu fenxi" [Tell the China story well: Messages and artistic expressions], *Wenyi lilun yu piping* [Theory and Criticism of Literature and Art], Iss. 6, 2014, p. 75; GUO Hongping, "Yong yiliu de biaoda zhanxian yiliu de gushi: wei jianshe pingan zhongguo fazhi zhongguo tigong qiang you li de jingshen zhizhu" [First class story, first class performance and powerful spiritual support for peace and rule of law], *Jiancha ribao* [Procuratorate Daily], 26 August 2014, p. 1.

5 Thitinan Pongsudhirak, "China's its own worst enemy in regional relations", *East Asia Forum*, 31 March 2016, online at www.eastasiaforum.org/2016/03/31/chinas-its-own-worst-enemy-in-regional-relations; CAO Haili, "Meigonghe de zhongguo weiji gongguan" [China's PR crisis management in the Mekong region], *Xin shiji zhoukan* [New Century Weekly], Iss. 15, 2010, p. 86.

6 LI Yingqing, "Jiduan tianqi yu xiujian daba wuguan: zhuanfang meigonghe weiyuanhui shouxi zhixingguan Jeremy Bird" [Extreme wealth has nothing to do with dam-building: Exclusive interview with Mekong River Commission CEO Jeremy Bird], *China Daily*, 12 June 2010, online at www.chinadaily.com.cn/dfpd/2010-06/12/content_9971087.htm.

7 TONG Guoqing, "E erni yinfa meigonghe sanjiaozhou ganhan daozhi haishui daoguan" [El Nino has caused drought and salt water intrusion in the Mekong Delta], *Zhongguo haiyang bao* [China Ocean News], 6 April 2016, p. A4; SUN Guangyong and WANG Yuexi, "Meigonghe liuyu ganhan buguai zhongguo shuiba" [Chinese hydro-dams are not blamed for the droughts in the Mekong Basin], *Huanqiu shibao* [Global Times], 6 April 2010, p. 3.

8 ZHOU Lei, "Fasheng zai meigonghe shang de 'wenhua duanliu'" ["Cultural disconnection" along the Mekong], 21ccom.net, 24 March 2016, online at www.21ccom.net/html/2016/zlwj_0324/2735.html; TANG Yonglin, "Langcangjian kaoyan zhongguo 'heliu waijiao'" [Lancangjiang River testing China's "water diplomacy"], *Nanfang zhoumo* [Southern Weekend], 1 April 2010, p. D20.

9 LI Chenglin, "'Zhongguo huanjing weixie lun' de chuanbo tiedian ji yingdui: yi lancangjiang-megonghe xiujian shuiba yulun weiji wei li" [Responding to the spread of "China environmental threat theory": A case study of the crisis in public opinion on Langcang-Mekong damming], *Duiwai chuanbo* [International Communications], Iss. 2, 2016, pp. 36–8; LI Zhifei, "Kua guojie heliu wenti yu zhongguo zhoubian guanxi" [Transboundary rivers and China's relations with its neighbours], *Xueshu tansuo* [Academic Exploration], No. 1, 2011, pp. 30–1.

10 YANG Jun et al., "Zhe bushi zhongguo jianba de quo, duo guo zhuanjia cheng meigonghe ci quyu hanzai shi quanqiu qihou bianhua dao de gui" [China is not to blame for the drought in the Mekong subregion, experts from many countries note it is caused not by global climate change], *Qianjiang wanbao* [Qiangjiang Evening News], 4 April 2010, p. B1.

11 DING Xuezhen, "China meets Mekong River nations on joint action", *Global Times*, 23 March 2016, online at www.globaltimes.cn/content/975405.shtml.
12 HONG Juhua and LUO Huasong, "Zhongguo yu dongnanya diyuan huanjing he kuajing heliu hezuo" [Geopolitical environment and transboundary water cooperation between China and Southeast Asia], *Shijie dili yanjiu* [World Regional Studies], Iss. 1, 2015, pp. 31–5.
13 Catherine Wong, "Releasing water from China's dams 'won't wash away mistrust' over Mekong", *South China Morning Post*, 18 April 2016, online at www.scmp.com/news/china/diplomacy-defence/article/1936766/releasing-water-chinas-dams-wont-wash-away-mistrust; Thitinan Pongsudhirak, "China's 'water grab' and its consequences", *Bangkok Post*, 25 March 2016, p. A8.
14 LI Zhifei, "Shui ziyuan waijiao: zhongguo zhoubian anquan goujian xin yiti" [Water diplomacy: New issues in China's effort to build security in its surrounding regions], *Xueshu tansuo* [Academic Exploration], No. 4, 2013, p. 28.
15 REN Na, "Meiguo jieru da meigonghe ci quyu yu zhongguo de yingdui" [US involvement in the Mekong subregion and China's response], *Dongyue luncong* [Donyue Tribune], Iss. 12, 2014, p. 118; LI Zhifei 2011, op. cit., p. 27.
16 LUO Shengrong, "Aobama zhengfu jieru meigonghe diqu hezuo yanjiu" [On Obama government's intervention in Mekong regional cooperation], *Dongnanya yanjiu* [Southeast Asian Studies], Iss. 6, 2013, p. 52.
17 WANG Zhimin, "Xinan zhoubian diyuan taishi yu 'nanfang sichou zhi lu' xin zhanlue" [Geopolitical situation in China's southwestern neighbouring area and "Southern Silk Road" strategy], *Dongbei ya luntan* [Northeast Asia Forum], Iss. 1, 2014, pp. 98–101.
18 CHEN Wenling, "Yi changxiao jizhi tuijin 'yi dai yi lu' jianshe" [Developing effective, enduring mechanisms to promote "one belt one road" initiative], *Guangming ribao* [Guangming Daily], 15 April 2015, p. 16; ZHOU Shixin, "Zhongguo he dongmeng zai da meigonghe ci quyu de hezuo" [China-ASEAN cooperation in the Greater Mekong Subregion], *Dongnanya zongheng* [Around Southeast Asia], Iss. 1, 2011, p. 15.
19 CAI Penghong, "Hu lian hu tong zhanlue yu zhongguo guojia anquan: jiyu diyuan zhengzhi shijiao de hu lian hu tong" [Interconnection strategy and China's national security: A geopolitical perspective], *Renmin luntan xueshu qianyan* [Frontiers], Iss. 7, 2015, pp. 57–62.
20 LI Qing, "Lun zhongguo zhudong canyu lancangjiang-meigonghe liuyu zonghe guanli" [On China actively participating in comprehensive management of the Mekong River], *Zhongnan caijing zhengfa daxue yanjiusheng xuebao* [Graduate Journal of Zhongnan University of Economics and Law], No. 2, 2014, p. 18.
21 Hong Luori, "Meigonghe, wuxu de shui ziyuan zhengduo zhan" [The Mekong River: Development in chaos], Hong Luori (blog), sina.com, 30 January 2013, online at http://blog.sina.com.cn/s/blog_7c0a1e3b01014gac.html.
22 LU Guangsheng, "Quyuxing guoji gonggong chanpin yu GMS hezuo de shenhua" [Regional public goods and deepening GMS cooperation], *Journal of Yunnan Normal University (Humanities and Social Sciences)*, Iss. 4, 2015, pp. 133–7.
23 Xinhua, "China to provide loans to Mekong neighbours", *Shanghai Daily,* 24 March 2016, p. A10.
24 Paritta Wangkiat, "Drowning in generosity", *Bangkok Post*, 27 March 2016, p. 10.
25 WANG Yizhou, "Zhongguo waijiao de chuangzao xing jieru" [China's diplomacy and creative involvement], *Beijing reibao* [Beijing Daily], 15 February 2016, p. 16.
26 XIAO He, "Tuidong meigonghe wu guo jinyibu canyu lan mei hezuo, zhongguo waijiao huo ying yousuo qushe" [Pushing the other five Mekong countries to further participate in LMC: Chinese diplomacy may have to make trade-offs], thepaper.cn, 7 April 2016, online at www.thepaper.cn/newsDetail_forward_1453399.
27 LU Guangsheng and JIN Zhen, "'Yidaiyilu' kuangjia xia da meigonghe ci quyu hezuo shengji ban" [Upgrading GMS cooperation within the framework of the "Belt and Road Initiative"], *Guoji zhanwang* [Global Review], Iss. 5, 2015, pp. 71–2.

28 LI Xinmin, "Qiujie Mixong kunju: zoujin miandian tanfang yi jiang shuidian xiangmu zhenxiang" [Understanding the Myitsone standstill: Finding facts in Myanmar about the hydroelectric project], *Jingji cankao bao* [Economic Information Daily], 2 September 2013, p. A6.

29 GUO Yanjun, "Meigonghe shui ziyuan zhili de xin quxiang yu zhongguo yingdui" [New trends in the governance of the Mekong water resources and China's responses], *Dongfang zaobao* [Oriental Morning Post], 17 January 2014, p. A14.

30 LU Guangsheng, "Guoji gonggong chanpin yu zhongguo – da meigonghe ci quyu guojia guanxi" [International public goods and China – relationships among the countries in the Greater Mekong Subregion], *Chuangxin* [Innovation], No. 3, 2011, p. 8.

31 GUO Jun, "Daba tuyi: women gai zenmeban?" [Retirement of dams: What shall we do?], *Zhongguo nengyuan bao* [China Energy News], 17 November 2014, p. 22.

32 Naho Mirumachi, "Wicked problems, messy analysis, clumsy solutions?" World Peace Foundation, 23 April 2015, online at https://sites.tufts.edu/reinventingpeace/2015/04/23/wicked-problems-messy-analysis-clumsy-solutions.

33 R .Edward Grumbine et al., "Mekong hydropower: drivers of change and governance challenges", *Frontiers in Ecology and the Environment*, Vol. 10, Iss. 2, 2012, pp. 92–3.

34 B. I .Liangliang, "Jiada zhongguo canyu da meigonghe ci quyu ziyuan hezuo kaifa lidu de zhengce jianyi" [Policy recommendations for increasing China's participation in collaborative development of resources in the Greater Mekong Subregion], *Zhongguo keji luntan* [Forum on Science and Technology in China], Iss. 4, 2013, p. 81.

35 CHA Hongwang, "Fazhan zhong de pinkun wenti yanjiu: jiyu yunnan shaoshu minzhu diqu anli fenxi" [Poverty during development: a case study of ethnic minority areas in Yunan], *Journal of Yunnan Minzu University (Social Sciences)*, No. 1, 2012, p. 105.

36 YI Shui, "Tuopin luo shang 'yige dou buneng shao'" [No one should be left behind" on the path to poverty alleviation], *Chuangzao* [Creation], Iss. 6, 2015, pp. 12–13.

37 LI Jixue et al., "Bu rang yige xiongdi minzu diaodui (2)" [No ethnic group will be left behind, part 2], *Zhongguo caijing bao* [China Financial and Economic News], 2 June 2016, p. 2.

38 YIN Chaoping and TAN Jingchun, "Quebao 2020 nian 574 wan pinkun renkou tuopin" [Making sure to lift 5.74 million of impoverished people out of poverty by 2020], *Yunnan ribao* [Yunnan Daily], 1 December 2015, p. 1; NING Jizhe, "Shishi fupin gongjian gongcheng" [Implementation of poverty-relief programmes], *Jingji ribao* [Economic Daily], 18 November 2015, p. 3.

39 ZHENG Yi, "Yunnan shishi fupin kaifa '63683' xingdong jihua" [Yunnan is implementing "63683" poverty eradication action plan], *Zhongguo xianyu jingji bao* [China County Times], 1 July 2016, p. 4.

40 LI Jixue et al., "Saiyun zhinan, kenan gongjian: Yunnan caizheng zhichi tuopin gongjian jishi (1)" [Yunnan, on the south of rosy clouds: government working hard to finance poverty relief, part 1], *Zhongguo caijing bao* [China Financial and Economic News], 31 May 2016, p. 1.

41 Yunnan Provincial Government, "Yunnan sheng nongcun fupin kaifa gangyao (2011–2020)" [Outline of development-oriented poverty reduction programme for rural areas in Yunnan], *Yunnan ribao* [Yunnan Daily], 21 February 2012, p. 6.

42 YANG Qing, "Guanyu woguo xinan diqu shaoshu minzu pinkun di zhou shuili fupin kaifa gongzuo de sikao" [Irrigation and poverty reduction in districts inhabited by ethnic minorities in Southwest China], *Zhongguo shuili* [China Water Resources], Iss. 23, 2015, pp. 15–17.

43 GUI Junsong, "Shui dian shi 'hao' nengyuan" [Hydropower is "worthy" energy], *Zhongguo nengyuan bao* [China Energy News], 9 July 2012, p. 1.

44 MA Sha et al., "Yunnan xi dian dong song dianliang po 5000 yi" [Yunnan's contribution to west-to-east electricity transmission project exceeding 500 billion kilowatt hours], *Zhongguo dianli bao* [China electricity news], 9 September 2016, p. 2; HU

Hongyun, "Yunnan dianli reng xu zhengce 'chongdian'" [Yunnan electricity industry still needs encouraging policy to help "re-charge"], *Zhongguo shuiwu bao* [China Taxation News], 29 June 2015, p. B1.

45 WANG Yonggang and DUAN Xiaorui, "Huaneng Lancangjian: yi zeren jian hexie ying weilai" [Huaneng Group at Lancangjiang River: Corporate responsibility, social harmony and winning future], *Yunnan ribao* [Yunnan Daily], 4 June 2016, p. 5.

46 Yunnan Daily Commentator, "Yaoding mubiao bu songjin" lun quanli tuijin guopin gongjian yu xianyu jingji fazhan" [Sticking to poverty reduction and rural development goals], *Yunnan ribao* [Yunnan Daily], 21 June 2016, p. 1; LI Jihong, "Wudongde shuidian zhan kaigong jianshe" [Wudongde power station broke ground], *Yunnan ribao* [Yunnan Daily], 25 December 2015, p. 1.

47 HUANG Chao, "Zhongguo daba xiehui xueshu nianhui zai Kunming juxing: zhuanjia jianyi jinkuai qidong Nujiang shuidian kaifa" [China dam association opened annual conference in Kunming: Experts suggest beginning hydropower development on Nujiang River as soon as possible], *Yunnan xinxi bao* [Yunnan Information], 4 November 2013, p. 2.

48 WU Xiaoqing, "Shuidian p.k huangbao" [Hydropower development player killing/PK environmental protection], *Zhongguo nengyuan bao* [China Energy News], 26 September 2011, p. 19.

49 SHAN Guo, "Bei canshi de san jiang bing liu shijie ziran yichan di" [Encroachments into World Natural Heritage site, Three Parallel Rivers], *Zhongguo zhoukan* [China Weekly], Iss. 9, 2016, p. 52.

50 WANG Yongchen, "Wu chu shijie yichan chi 'huangpai'de jingshi" ["Yellow card" warning against five Natural World Heritage sites], *Lüse zhongguo* [Green China], Iss. 8, 2004, p. 3.

51 SU Xiaozhou et al., "Changjiang gan zhiliu bei shuidianzhan qie cheng wanduan 'xiangchang'" [Hydropower stations have cut Yangtze mainstream and tributaries into thousands of "sausages"], *Jingji cankao bao* [Economic Information Daily], 30 June 2016, p. A5.

52 WANG Yongchen, "Shijie ziran yichan de guangrong yu mengxiang" [Glory and dreams of World Natural Heritage], *Zhongguo keji huabao* [China Science and Technology Pictorial], Iss. 5, 2004, pp. 20–1.

53 "Yunnan gejie renshi jiu Nujiang shuidian kaifa de jianyan shu" [Suggestions from people from all walks of life in Yunnan on hydropower development on Nujiang/Salween River], 12 September 2014, online at www.chinaelections.org/article/915/236418.html.

54 YI Chengchen, "Gongcheng huo jiang jiao ting: pandian Nujiang dabai shi duo nian lai 'shang' yu 'xia' zhi zheng [Construction may be halted: taking stock of more-than-10-year debates over whether to build dams on Nujiang/Salween River], *China Radio International Online*, 14 April 2016, online at http://news.cri.cn/20160413/2d443d53-fa0a-1bfd-52fa-9e02c763e9a0.html.

55 YUE Yueguo, "Shuidian kaifa yuanhe pin yin zhenglun?" [Why hydropower development continuously fuels disputes and controversies], *Zhongguo huanjing bao* [China Environment News], 15 May 2012, p. 1; JIA Lin, "Xinan guoji heliu de liuyu gongtong kaifa falv jizhi" [Legal frameworks for joint development of international rivers in southwest China], *Shengtai jingji* [Ecological Economy], Iss. 7, 2010, pp. 163–6.

56 CHEN Shuisheng, "Cong Nujiang shuidianzhan kaifa kan zhongguo gonggong zhengce moshi bianhua" [Hydropower development on Nujiang River and changes in China's public policy models], *Dongfang zaobao* [Oriental Morning Post], 13 January 2015, p. 11.

57 LIU Sufen, "Yunnan sheng tishu pinkun yuanyin fenxi ji duice ranjiu" [Poverty in Yunnan: Causes and solutions], *Xueshu tansuo* [Academic Exploration], No. 5, 2007, pp. 39–44.

58 QIN Guangrong, "Zai tiaozheng zhong tuokuan ditan yingyi fazhan zhi lu" [Broadening low-carbon development during economic transition], *Qiu shi* [Seeking truth], Iss. 6, 2010, pp. 37–9.

59 LI Chenyang, "Lancangjiang-meigonghe hezuo: jiyu, tiaozhan yu duice" [Lancang-Mekong cooperation: Opportunities, challenges and solutions], *Xueshu tansuo* [Academic Exploration], No. 1, 2016, p. 25; ZHOU Lei, "Fasheng zai meigonghe shang de 'wehhua duanliu'" ["Rupture of cultural flows" on the Mekong], 21ccom.net, 25 March 2016, online at www.360doc.com/content/16/0325/11/267810_545110788.shtml; LIU Zhi, "Huanjing zhengzhi shijiao xia de da meigonghe ci quyu shui ziyuan hezuo kaifa" [Environmental politics and collaborative development of water resources in Greater Mekong Subregion], *Journal of Guanxi University (Philosophy and Social Sciences)*, No. 5, 2013, pp. 3–6.

60 ZHAO Dachun and YE Jianping, "Furao de pinqiong: paihuai zai kaifa yu baohu liangnan zhong de Nujiang" [Poverty in natural resource-rich areas: Nujiang caught in the dilemma of development and conservation], *Jingji cankao bao* [Economic Information Daily], 5 February 2010, p. 5.

61 XUAN Yucai, "Shan buneng dong, shui beneng dong, rang Yunnan za baohu shengtai? [How can Yunnan protect environment if it cannot touch mountains or rivers?], people.com, 7 April 2005, online at http://politics.people.com.cn/GB/30178/3303095.html.

62 ZHANG Boting and WU Shiping, "Nujiang shuidian kaifa de biyao xing" [It is necessary to develop hydropower at Nujiang], *Zhongguo zhoukan* [China Weekly], Iss., 8, 2016, p. 50; and JIAN Guangzhou, "Nujiang shuidian xiangmu: Yitiao shengtai he de kaifa yu baohu nanti" [Nujiang hydropower project: A challenge of simultaneously developing and protecting an ecological riber] *Dongfang zaobao* [Oriental Morning Post], 2 April 2004, online at http://finance.sina.com.cn/g/20040402/1357699714.shtml.

63 LI Ziliang "Nujiang 'zheng' ba" [Dam debates at Nujiang], *Liaowan xinwen zhoukan* [Outlook Weekly], Iss. 49, 2004, pp. 27–8.

64 SONG Guocheng, "Zhongguo shuidian kaifa guandian de lunxi" [Contending opinions in China on hydropower development], in YANG Zisheng and WU Demei (eds.), *Zhongguo shui zhili yu ke chixu fazhan yanjiu* [Governance and Sustainable Development of Water Resources in China], Beijing: Social Sciences Academic Press, 2013, p. 61.

65 CHEN Yong, "Shangshu fagaiwei: Nujiang shuidian kaifa 'fuhuo' qianliu" [Submitting written statements to Development and Reform Commission: Subsurface currents of Nujiang hydropower development "resurrection"], *Jingji guancha bao* [The Economic Observer], 12 April 2010, p. 9.

66 WANG Yonggang and HU Xiaorong, "Jiji tuijin fupin da shuju pingtai jianshe" [Actively building poverty-reduction mega data platform], *Yunnan ribao* [Yunnan Daily], 26 November 2015, p. 2; ZHANG Renwu, "Guanyu Nujiang shuidian kaifa anli yanjiu de Beijing ziliao [Background information on case studies about hydro development on Nujiang], *Beida weiming BBS* [Peking University Campus Forum], 2005, p. 6, online at https://bbs.pku.edu.cn/new/bbs/article/showpost/CB/4624419.

67 KONG Dejing, "Gonggong zhengce zhiding zhong de liyi qunti fenxi: yi nujiang shuiba jihua wei li" [Interest groups in public decision making: Case study of Nujiang dam projects], *Shehui kexue luntan* [Tribune of Social Sciences], Iss. 1, 2011, pp. 207–8.

68 DENG Quanlun, "Nujiang shuidian kaifa fuhuo" [Resurrection of hydropower development on Nujiang River], *Da jingmao* [Foreign Trade and Economy], Iss. 2, 2013, p. 55; YI Chengchen, op cit.

69 LI Bo et al., "Zhongguo jianghe de 'zuihou' baogao" ["Last" report of rivers in China], *Guoji heliu jianbao (zhuankan)* [World rivers bulletin (special issue)],

October 2014, p. 15; ZHANG Ke, "Shuidian 'kexue fazhan' zhi zheng" [Debate over "scientific development" of hydropower], *Diyi caijing ribao* [China Business News], 8 July 2009, p. C3; SUN Danping, "Is the dam construction in the sunrise or at the sunset?" *Lüse zhongguo* [Green China], January 2004, p. 24.

70 ZHANG Boting, "Nujiang gezhi shinian gei women dai lai le shenme?" [What did shelving Nujiang hydro development for 10 years bring us?], *Zhongguo nengyuan bao* [China Energy News], 11 March 2013, p. 22.

71 David Roberts, "How the US Embassy tweeted to clear Beijing's air", *Wired Opinion*, 6 March 2016, online at https://www.wired.com/2015/03/opinion-us-embassy-beijing-tweeted-clear-air; WANG Shuo, "Beijing huanbaoju cheng mei zhu hua shiguan chaozuo $PM_{2.5}$ zhishu" [Beijing Environmental Protection Bureau claiming US Embassy hyping $PM_{2.}$ index], *Jing hua shibao* [Beijing Times], 4 November 2011, online at http://news.qq.com/a/20111104/000096.htm.

72 HUANG Han, "Wangluo fu quan yu gongmin huanjing xingdong" [Internet empowerment and citizen environment actions], *Xuexi yu tansuo* [Study and Exploration], Iss. 4, 2014, p. 53.

73 LI Laifang, "Cong wumai baodao kan zhong xi fang xinwen jiazhiguan" [Reports on smog: News values applied by Chinese and Western media], *Dui wai chuanbo* [International Communications], Iss. 11, 2014, pp. 53–4.

74 WANG Yan, "Shejiao meiti weiji chuanbo de huayu fenxi moshi – yi APEC lan de weibo reyi weili" [Analytical approaches for studying narratives used in crisis communication on social media: Case study of heated discussions about APEC blue on microblogging sites], *Zhongguo chuban* [China Publishing Journal], Iss. 15, 2015, p. 75.

75 YUAN Yuan, "'Lianghui land' yu qingjie mei" ["Two sessions blue" and clean coal], *Zhengquan ribao* [Securities Daily], 5 March 2015, p. B3.

76 DAI Li, "Yuan 'yuebing lan' bu zhishi huainian" [Hoping "Military Parade blue" not to become only a cherished memory], *Jieneng yu huanbao* [Energy Conservation and Environmental Protection], Iss. 10, 2015, pp. 36–7.

77 LI Ping, "Wo guo chengzhen hua lü dadao 56.1%" [China's urbanisation rate has reached 56.1%], *Shenzhen tequ bao* [Shenzhen Special Zone Daily], 20 April 2016, p. A15.

78 WANG Gengchen and WANG Pucai, "Zhongguo $PM_{2.5}$ wuran xianzhuang jiqi dui renti jiankang de weihai" [$PM_{2.}$ pollution in China and its harm to human health], *Keji daobao* [Science and Technology Review], 32 (26), 2014, p. 76.

79 YAN Junqian, "Rang 'APEC lan' chengwei 'zhongguo zhi lan'" [Make "APEC blue" into "China blue"], *Jinrong jingji* [Finance and Economics], Iss. 6, 2015, pp. 29–30; SUN Xiuyan, "Qing ba 'APEC lan' liu xialai" [Please do not let "APEC blue" go], *People's Daily*, 17 November 2014, p. 17.

80 SHI Qingling et al., "Wumai zhili zhong de 'zhengzhixing lantian': laizi zhongguo difang 'lianghui'de zhengju" ["Political blue skies" and solutions to smog: evidence from local branch sessions of China's National People's Congress and Political Consultative Conference], *Zhongguo gongye jingji* [China Industrial Economics], Iss. 5, 2016, p. 41.

81 XIAO Qiang, "2030nian zuoyou tan qiangdu xiajiang liu cheng yu" [Carbon intensity will be reduced by more than 60% around 2030], *Zhongguo nengyuan bao* [China Energy News], 6 July 2015, p. 1.

82 JI Hongmei, "Jian pai chengnuo daobi shuidian kaifa tisu" [Emission reduction commitments force hydropower development to speed up], *Zhongguo kexue bao* [China Science Daily], 18 October 2012, p. 7.

83 Beth Walker and Liu Qin, "China's shift from coal to hydro comes at a heavy price", *China Dialogue*, 27 July 2015, online at https://www.chinadialogue.net/article/show/single/en/8093-China-s-shift-from-coal-to-hydro-comes-at-a-heavy-price.

84 JIN Jing, "Shuidian huodian wuran zhi zheng" [Disputes on pollution of hydropower and fossil-fuel power], *Guanxi dianye* [Guangxi Electric Power], Iss. 1, 2011, pp. 14–15.

85 YUAN Songhua, "Shuidian yu shengtai fazhan de 'duihua'" ["Dialogues" between hydropower and ecological development], *Zhongguo touzi* [China Investment], Iss. 7, 2005, p. 44.
86 YANGZHOU wanbao, "Shuidian wuran bi huodian geng yanzhong?" [Does hydropower cause more pollution than fossil fuels?], *Yangzhou wanbao* [Yangzhou evening news], 4 January 2011, p. B5.
87 YAN Dingfei and ZHONG Yuhao, "Daba lan sha, jianghu shihen? Changjiang xin mafan" [Dams trapping sediments and upsetting natural balances between rivers and lakes? New troubles for the Yangtze River], *Nanfang zhoumo* [Southern Weekend], 2 April 2015, online at www.infzm.com/content/108614.
88 WU Jinmin, "Kongzhi changjiang gan zhi liu shuidianzhan jianshe shuliang" [Construction of hydropower stations on the Yangtze River and its tributaries should be controlled], *Nengyuan yanjiu yu liyong* [Energy Research & Utilisation], Iss. 4, 2016, p. 16.
89 WU Jie, "Dang shuidian zaoyu yaomo hua" [When hydropower is demonised], *Guoqi* [China SOE], Iss. 8, 2011. p. 85.
90 GUI Junsong, op cit.
91 ZHANG Boting, "Daba pingfan de quzhe licheng" [Hydro dams' tortuous path to vindication], *Nengyuan* [Energy], Iss. 4, 2014, p. 79.
92 CUI Xuan and HUANG Changcheng, "Shuidian 'qingjie nengyuan' Zhengyi" [Controversies over hydropower as "clean energy"], *Zhongguo minhang bao* [CAAC News], 10 January 2011, p. 6.
93 CHEN Yuanxin, "Shuidian da fazhan zhengyi ye buduan" [Hydropower development speeds up and controversy continues], *Dianqi gongye* [China Electrical Equipment Industry], Iss. 10, 2011, p. 9.
94 LI He, "'Pao ma quan shui' shui lai guan" [Who regulates "pre-emptive competition" for water resources], *Keji ribao* [Science and technology daily], 24 May 2012, p. 6.
95 CCTV, "Shuidian maoli kan bi 'mei laoban' shengtai pohuai shui maidan" [Hydroelectricity as profitable as fossil fuel power, but who pays for ecological destruction], *Jingji ban xiaoshi* [Economics 30 minutes], 4 August 2011, online at www.cnr.cn/gundong/201108/t20110804_508323007.shtml.
96 YANG Haixia, "Shuidian kaifa xu pojie huanbao nanti" [Hydropower development needs to puzzle out environmental problems], *Zhongguo touzi* [China Investment], Iss. 4, 2013, p. 39.
97 QIE Jianrong, "Huyu yifa bianzhi 'shi san wu' nengyuan guihua huanping" [Appeal for passing environmental assessment act for China's "13th Five-Year Plan" for energy], *Fazhi ribao* [Legal Daily], 13 June 2016, p. 6.
98 FAN Xiao, "Zhongguo nengyuan xuqiu bing bu xuyao ruci da guimo de shuidian kaifa" [China's energy demand does not require hydropower development at such large scale], *Green Earth Volunteers*, 9 October 2016, online at www.chinagev.org/index.php/greenpro/environmentview/5392-zhonggbuxuyaorucidag.
99 CHEN Fangmiao et al., "Wo guo shuidian kaifa tezheng fenxi yu fazhan jianyi" [Characteristics of hydropower growth in China and suggestions on its further development], *Huanjing baohu* [Environmental Protection], Iss. 7, 2016, pp. 49–50.
100 LI Bo et al., op cit., p. 51.
101 WANG Xinxin, "Minjian huanbao zuzhi jianyi 'shi san wu' nengyuan guihua shenzhong shangma shuidian kaifa" [Environmental organisations recommend caution in proposing new hydropower initiatives in "13th Five-Year Plan" for energy], *Zhongguo qingnian bao* [China youth daily], 26 December 2013, p. 5.
102 ZHANG Boting, "Dianli channeng guosheng de shen ceng ci yuanyi shi nengyuan jiegou ehua" [Deeper reason for electricity generation overcapacity is structural failure of the power sector], *Zhongguo jingji zhoukan* [China Economics Weekly], Iss. 32, 2015, pp. 76–7.
103 ZHANG Boting, op cit, 11 March 2013.

104 GAO Zhu and LI Na, "Shuidian qishui shui zhi guo?" [Who is to blame for hydropower plants abandoning water?], *Gongren ribao* [Workers' Daily], 4 May 2016, p. 6.
105 YUAN Tianyi, "Duo chong yinsu jiqi huodian shenpi baofa shi zengzhang" [Multiple factors sparked explosive growth of coal plant approvals], *Zhongguo zhanlue xinxing chanye* [China Emerging Strategic Industries], Iss. 1, 2016, p. 66.
106 WANG Tao and QIN Chuqiao, "Fengdian hangye ni qidong shou li jiti weiquan – difang ganga xuanzeti: qi feng jiu huo" [Wind power industry planning to take collective action for the first time to uphold rights – local governments'awkward choice: Abandoning wind power to save coal fire], *Nanfang zhoumo* [Southern Weekend], 31 March 2016, online at www.infzm.com/content/116222.
107 ZHANG Boting and WU Shiping, op cit., p. 51.
108 ZHAN Ling, "Huanbao Zhengyi wei xi Nujiang shuidian kaifa didiao qianxing" [Amid environmental disputes, Nujiang hydro development pressing forward quietly], *21 shiji jingji baodao* [21st Century Business Herald], 15 November 2013, p. 18.
109 ZHANG Boting, "Xin changtai xia kan shuidian qishui" [Economic new norm and hydropower stations abandoning water], *Zhongguo dianli qiye guanli* [China Power Enterprise Management], Iss. 11, 2015, p. 17.
110 WANG Xinmao, "Dianli gongye yao jiji tuijin gongjice jiegou xing gaige" [Power industry should actively push forward structural reform on supply side], *Zhongguo nengyuan bao* [China Energy News], 15 February 2016, p. 2.
111 JING Ran, "Shuidian da yuejin hou de ganga" [Great leap forward in hydropower development and awkward aftermath], *Zhongguo dianli qiye guanli* [China Power Enterprise Management], Iss. 23, 2015, p. 95.
112 ZHU Xinmin, "Dui daba jianshe zhengyi de zhexue sikao" [Philosophical reflections on disputes over dam construction], *Shui ke zhi sheng* [Voice of IWHR], Iss. 1, 2016, online at www.iwhr.com/zgskyww/ztbd/cbw/djzc/webinfo/2016/06/1461063796298310.htm; XUE Xiuhong, "Xiao shuidian wu zheng shangma shengtai pohuai yinfa dizhi zaihai" [More undocumented small hydropower stations in operation, ecological destruction triggering geological disasters], *Zhongguo gaige bao* [China reform news], 15 August 2011, p. 5.
113 GUI Junsong, op cit.
114 ZENG Hongjun, "Yue dong de 'lüse yinfu'" [Vibrant "green notes"], *Dangdai dianli wenhua* [Electricity and Culture Today], Iss. 11, 2015, pp. 15–9.
115 LI Qing, op cit, p. 19.
116 XU Qi, "Shi ming zhi neng lan de zhu shui" [Few can be stopped by real-name registration], *Zhongguo huanjing bao* [China Environment News], 29 May 2013, p. 5.
117 WANG Nannan, "Sanxia gongcheng: shengtai huanjing yingxiang li da yu bi" [Three Gorges Project: Eco-environmental benefits outweigh harms], *Zhongguo shuili bao* [China Water Resources News], 22 January 2015, p. 5.
118 Naho Mirumachi, op cit.
119 YANG Shisheng, "Nujiang shuidian 'fuhuo' beihou tuishou" [Nujiang hydropower "resurrection": backstage driving force], *Huaxia shibao* [China Times], 9 May 2016, p. 5.
120 CCTV, op cit.
121 MA Weihui, "Nujiang shuidain shisan zai shengsi jie" [Thirteen-year life and death catastrophe of Nujiang hydropower], *Huaxia shibao* [China Times], 27 June 2016, p. 6.
122 See, for example, ZENG Sheng, "Kaifazhe yu shengtai huanjing zhijian de jinhua boyi fenxi" [Evolutionary game dynamics between hydropower developers and eco-environment], *Xibu luntan* [West Forum], Vol. 23. No. 5, 2013, pp. 72–8.
123 PAN Congxia and CHEN Ming, "Yi chang shuidian kaifa koushui zhan" [A war of words on hydropower development], *Nandu zhoukan* [SM Weekly], 20 March 2009, pp. 42–4.
124 TONG Zhifeng, "Hulianwang, shehui meiti yu zhongguo minjian huanjing yundong de fazhan (2003–2012)" [Internet, social media and development of environmental

movement in China (2003–2012)], *Shehuixue pinglun* [Sociological Review of China], Vol. 1, No. 4, 2013, pp. 52–62.

125 BI Liangliang, op cit., p. 81.

126 WANG Yongchen, "Zai zhongguo xibu jianghe kaifa zhong jianshou yulun jiandu zhengduo huayuquan" [Sticking to public scrutiny and fighting for a voice in the development China's west], *Di 12 jie xin shiji xinwen yu yulun jiandu yantaohui lunwenji* [12th new century media and public opinion scrutiny conference proceedings], Guangzhou, China: Sun Yat-sen University, 2012, p. 202.

127 ZHA Daojiong, "A political ecology of hydropower development in China" in Nathanial Matthews and Kim Geheb (eds.), *Hydropower Development in the Mekong Region: Political, Socio-economic and Environmental Perspectives*, London and New York: Routledge, 2015, pp. 35–6.

128 Christina Larson, "Green activists feel sting of Chinese government crackdown", *Yale Environment 360*, 30 June 2011, online at http://e360.yale.edu/feature/green_activists_feel_sting_of_chinese_government_crackdown/2421.

129 DENG Quanlun, op cit., p. 54.

130 YE Xiaoli, "Pipan jingshen he zhuanye suyang: cong shehuixue de shiye kaoliang meiti 'di tan' baodao" [Critical spirit and professional competence: media coverage of "low carbon" from a sociological perspective], *Meiti guancha* [Media Observer], Iss. 1, 2011, p. 31; and PAN Congxia and CHEN Ming, op cit.

131 YI Chengchen, op cit.

132 YIN Hongwei, "Nujiang yuanzhumin manwan qujing" [Indigenous people from Nujiang/Salween River trying to learn lessons from Manwan hydropower project], *Nanfeng chuang* [South Reviews], Iss. 11, 2004, pp. 48–50.

133 Editorial, "Jiao ting Nujiang xiao shuidian juece guocheng keyi chuifan" [The decision process to discontinue small hydro schemes on Nujiang River sets a good example], *Diyi caijing ribao* [China Business News], 9 March 2016, p. A12.

134 QIE Jianrong, op cit.

135 CUI Xuan and HUANG Changcheng, op cit.

136 Ibid.

137 LIU Xiaolong et al., "Jizhong lianpian teshu kunnan diqu fupin kaifa Beijing xia de Nujiangzhou tuopin lujing" [Poverty reduction and development in contiguous poor areas: Path for Nujiang Prefecture], *Zhongg~~uo~~ong Yunnan shengwei dangxiao xuebao* [Journal of Yunnan Provincial Committee School of CPC], Vol. 13, No. 6, 2012, pp. 45–6.

138 ZHAI Chunyang, "Shuidian kaifai ye keyi na 'tuopin' shuoshi" ["Poverty reduction" can be used as a reason for hydropower development], *Zhongguo jingji shibao* [China Economic Times], 27 October 2005, p. 6.

139 TONG Zhifeng, op cit.

140 QU Geping, "Mingyu lishizhang zai qinghua daxue QIAN Yi yuanshi 80 huadan zhushou hui shang de zhici" [Honorary resident Qu Geping's speech at the 80th birthday celebration of Academician QIAN Yi from Tsinghua University], China Environmental Protection Foundation, 6 June 2016, online at www.cepf.org.cn/jjhdt/201606/t20160606_353640.htm.

141 YU Xiaogang and YANG Jiankun, "Shehui yingxiang pingjia shiye xia de Nujiang kaifa" [Social impact assessment and Nujiang development], *Zhongguo zhoukan* [China Weekly], Iss. 8, 2016, pp. 70–3.

142 MA Weihui, op cit.

143 PAN Congxia and CHEN Ming, op cit.

144 ZHANG Yang and ZHOU Shenbei, "Wo guo shuineng kaifa xieshang zhili tezheng yanjiu: yi nujiang shuineng kaifa weili" [Main features of governance and consultation in China's water resource development: case study of Nujiang], *Qiusuo* [Search], Iss. 5, 2007, p. 44.

145 YANG Zhigao, "Shuidian 2013 nian dahui zai Kunming juxing" [2013 Hydropower Conference held in Kunming], *Chuncheng wanbao* [Chuncheng evening news], 4 November 2013, p. A11.
146 XIA Zihang, "99 zuo shuidianzhan qiege 66 tiao zhiliu: qidi Nujiang cuiruo shengtai" [90 hydropower stations cut 66 tributaries: Unravelling Nujiang River's fragile ecology], *Meiri jingji xinwen* [National Business Daily], 23 September 2011, p. 14.
147 DENG Quanlun, op cit., p. 54.
148 ZHU Chunkui and SHEN Ping, "Xingdong zhe, ziyuan yu xingdong celue: Nujiang shuidian kaifa de zhengce wangluo fenxi" [Policy actors, resources and strategies: Policy network in Nujiang development], *Gonggong xingzheng pinglun* [Journal of Public Administration], Iss. 4, 2010, pp. 36–8; JIAN Guangzhou, op cit.
149 ZHAN Ling, op cit.
150 MA Weihui, op cit.
151 ZHENG Ting, "WANG Yongchen – na yipian jianghe de qing yu chou" [WANG Yongchen – love and sorrow for rivers], *Lüse zhongguo* [Green China], Iss. 21, 2013, pp. 46–7.
152 JIAN Guangzhou, op cit.
153 CCTV, op cit.
154 BAO Zhiheng, "Shuidian wu jutou geju Jiangshajiang" [Five hydropower giants carve up Jinshajiang River], *Dongfang zaobao* [Oriental Morning Post], 3 May 2012, pp. A16–17.
155 SU Xiaozhou et al., op cit.
156 FU Yuewen, "2015 zhongguo shuidian fazhan luntan" [2015 China Hydropower Development Forum], *Zhongguo nengyuan bao* [China Energy News], 9 February 2015, p. 16.
157 CCTV, op cit.
158 YANG Pingjian, "Ren yu zhi zheng nengfou zouxiang xiandai juece guocheng?" [Can human-fish competition be brought into modern decision-making process?], *Zhongguo huanjing bao* [China Environment News], 22 April 2015, p. 2.
159 CCTV, op cit.
160 WANG Yuye et al., "Bai zuo xiao shuidianzhan pohuai Shennongjia shengtai" [A hundred small hydropower stations undermine Shennongjia's ecology], *Chutian dushi bao* [Chutian metro daily], 15 August 2011, online at http://news.qq.com/a/20110815/000628.htm.
161 YANG Xiaohong, "Gaobie banteng de jianghe" [Bid farewell to galloping rivers], *Zhongguo caifu* [China Fortune], Iss. 5, 2013, pp. 36–8.
162 PENG Bo, "'Zhuangrang chao' yongxian: Yunnan san shuidianzhan dui wai zhuanrang" [Emerging "ownership transfer waves": Three of Yunnan's hydropower stations have already changed hands], *Yunnan jingji ribao* [Yunnan Economic Daily], 14 April 2011, p. A3.
163 LIAO Wangjie and REN Zhijun, "Shuidian ziyuan kaifa ying jianchi si you yuanze" [Hydropower development should be rational, controlled, orderly and useful], *Dangzheng yanjiu* [Studies on Party and Government], Iss. 4, 2015, p. 123.
164 ZHANG Kuixing, "Shuidian jianshe yinggai liji jiao ting 'da yuejin'" ["Great leap forward" in hydropower development should be stopped immediately], *Zhongguo shang bao* [China Business Herald], 28 June 2011, p. 2.
165 SU Wei, "Na xie yinsu zhiyue le shuidian kaifa?" [What factors restrict hydropower development?], *Zhongguo dianli bao* [China electricity news], 28 April 2016, p. 5.
166 LIN Chunting, "Xi dian dong song yuanyou liyi geju ying dapo" [West-to-east electricity transfer: The status quo interest pattern should be broken], *Diyi caijing ribao* [China Business News], 29 January 2014, p. A10.
167 HE Wu and A Pu, "Nujiang shen xia yimin de xianshi ganga" [Awkward realities of relocated Nujiang residents], *Zhongguo zhoukan* [China Weekly], Iss. 8, 2016, pp. 68–9.

168 GUI Junsong, op cit.
169 YANGZHOU Wanbao, op cit.
170 ZHANG Linhong et al., "Shuidian kaifa dui gefang sun yi yingxiang de fenxi" [Profit and loss analysis of affected parties in hydropower development], *Kunming yejin gaodeng zhuanke xuexiao xuebao* [Journal of Kunming Metallurgy College], Vol. 30, No. 1, 2014, pp. 38–44.
171 TIAN Canming et al., "Yunnan duan Jinshajiang shuidian yimin anzhi wenti tantao" [Resettlement issues in hydropower projects on Jingsha River in Yunnan], *Journal of Kunming University of Science and Technology (Social Sciences)*, Vol. 12, No. 2, 2012, p. 79.
172 LI Bo et al., op cit, p. 13.
173 HU Zhiqiang, "Zhongguo na qun shi nian zou jianghe de ren" [Stories of those Chinese who have travelled along China's rivers in the last 10 years], *Gonghui bolan* [A View of Labour Unions], Iss. 15, 2016, pp. 2–11.
174 XIE Yujuan, "Zhuihou de dahe" [Last river], *Jiemian xinwen* [JMedia], 23 December 2015, online at http://wemedia.ifeng.com/282574491739028/wemedia.shtml.
175 ZHANG Nan, "Kaifa shuidian shi weiyi de tuopin zhi lu ma?" [Is hydropower development the only way out of poverty?], *Zhongguo huanjing bao* [China Environment News], 13 July 2009, p. 1.
176 LIU Peiyuan, "Guangai daba bian shuidianzhan 300 mu shuitian cheng hantian" [Irrigation dams converted to hydropower plants and 300 acres of paddy fields turned into dry land], *Nan dao wanbao* [Nan Dao evening news], 14 June 2013, p. 6; CCTV, op cit.; CAO Lijun and LIU Pingchang, "Shuidian kaifa de shengtai buchang fangshi tantao" [Study of eco-compensation for hydropower development], *Shuili shuidian jishu* [Water Resources and Hydropower Engineering], Iss. 7, 2010, pp. 6–7; LIN Yu and DAI Ti, "Dianzhan yue jian yue duo qiongzhong yue qian yue qiong" [The more hydropower stations, the poorer the relocated masses], *Huanan xinwen* [South China news], 16 February 2006, p. 2.
177 LIU Yiman, "Jinshajiang de qingsu" [Jiangshajiang River pouring out its troubles], *Liaowang dongfang zhoukan* [Oriental Outlook], Iss. 24, 2012, pp. 12–25; HE Wu and A Pu, op cit.; YUE Yueguo, op cit.
178 LI Bo et al., op cit., p. 27; SHI Zhiliang et al., "Shuidian chenji duo nian jie li jian pai 'kai zha'" [Leveraging emission reduction to reopen the floodgate of hydropower development], *Jingji cankao bao* [Economic Information Daily], 20 September 2010, p. 6.
179 HE Wu and A Pu, op cit.
180 Ibid.
181 SUN Wenjuan, "Chongfen wajue shuidian 'zaoxue' gongneng" [Fully exploit "hematopoietic" function of hydropower development], *Xizang ribao* [Tibet Daily], 19 December 2016, p. 6.
182 HUAN Zhenli et al., "Changjiang shangyou shengtai baohu yu jingji fazhan zonghe gaige fanglue yanjiu" [Strategies and reforms for ecological protection and economic development of the upper Yangtze River], *Hubo kexue* [Journal of Lake Sciences], Vol. 29, Iss. 2, 2017, p. 260.
183 ZHAO Zigao, "Chong shen shuidian" [Revisiting issues related to hydropower], *Nengyuan* [Energy], Iss. 4, 2011, pp. 84–8; LIU Xiaoxing, "Shuidian yimin fan pin shui zhi guo?" [Who is to blame for hydro dam-induced migrants to fall back into poverty?], *Zhongguo huanjing bao* [China Environment News], 28 October 2009, p. 7.
184 HU Zhiqiang, op cit, p. 5.
185 HUO Xiaoguang et al., "Gaige, kuai ma jia bian wei xia an" [Reforms remain on a swift horse], *People's Daily*, 3 February 2017, p. 1; *International River*, "Big hydropower development approval and stakeholder analysis: A case study of the Nu River", *International River*, January 2016, p. 11; BAO Guangjing et al., "Nujing liuyu shuidian kaifa shehui jingji yingxiang fenxi" [Analysis of socio-economic effects of hydropower development along the Nujiang River], *Shuili shuidian keji jinzhan*

[Advances in Science Technolog~~ies~~y of Water Resources], Vol. 27, Iss. 6, 2007, pp. 11–12.

186 CCTV, op cit.

187 ZONG He, "Shuidian kaifa zichan shouyi naru fupin gaige shidian" [Pilot reform programmes to incorporate assets income from hydropower development into poverty alleviation], *Zhongguo nengyuan bao* [China Energy News]. 24 October 2016, p. 11.

188 LIN Chunting, op cit.

189 SHI Zhiliang et al., op cit.

190 HUANG Zhenli et al., op cit., p. 259.

191 LI Qing, op cit, p. 19.

192 HU Angang, "'Shi san wu' guihua: yinling lü se geming" ["13th Five-Year Plan": leading the green revolution], *Huanjing jingji* [Environmental Economy], Iss. ZA, 2016, pp. 25–6; WANG Tiechen, "Wo guo shuidian kaifa buru 'da shidai'" [China's hydropower development is entering "big time"], *Jingji ribao* [Economic Daily], 19 January 2016, p. 7.

193 CUI Xuan and HUANG Changcheng, op cit.

194 ZHANG Nan, op cit.

195 CUI Xuan and HUANG Changcheng, op cit.

196 The five major water systems are the Irrawaddy, Salween, Chao Phraya, Mekong, and Red Rivers. With the exception of the Chao Phraya, all of them flow out of China's Yunnan Province.

197 HONG Juhua and LUO Huasong, op cit., p. 31.

198 LI Qing, op cit., p. 20.

199 XIE Laihui, "Shi xi meiguo chongfan yatai de zhanlue 'ruan' weidu: Mekong quyu qihou hezuo de yiyi yu tiaozhan" ["Soft" side of US strategic pivot to the Asia Pacific: Significance and challenges of Mekong cooperation on climate change], *Journal of Liaoning University (Philosophy & Social Sciences)*, Iss. 1, 2014, p. 29.

200 FANG Jingjing, "Mekong ganliu shuidianzhan jianshe weihe pin re zhengyi?" [Why does building hydropower stations on mainstream Mekong repeatedly provoke controversies?], *Zhongguo-dongmeng yanjiu guancha* [China-ASEAN Research Observer], January 2015, pp. 151–2.

201 CAO Chunmiao and HU Tao, "Zhongguo qieye zai da Mekong ci quyu touzi huanjing lüzhi jiqi jianyi" [Problems and suggested improvements in Chinese outbound investors' performance of environmental responsibilities in the Greater Mekong Subregion], *Dongnanya zongheng* [Around Southeast Asia], No. 2, 2014, p. 73.

202 CAO Haili, op cit.

203 LI Qing, op cit., pp. 17–19.

204 XIE Kang and XIAO Jinghua, "Shipin anquan, shehui xitong shiling yu gonggong zhengce: jian lun chanye zhengce, fubai yu wumai zhili" [Food safety, social system failure and public policy: With references to industrial policy, corruption and smog control], *Journal of Beijing Jiaotong University (Social Sciences Edition)*, Vol. 16, No. 1, 2017, pp. 23–5.

205 SHI Qingling et al., "Wumai zhili zhong de 'zhengshixing lantian'" [Smog control and "political blue sky"], *Zhongguo gongye jingji* [China Industrial Economics], Iss. 5, 2016, pp. 40–56.

206 WANG Rengui, "Zhongguo qianjinyinuo 'tan paifang feng zhi'" ["Peaking carbon emission": China's solemn promise], *Liaowang* [Outlook Weekly], Iss. 49, 2014, p. 39.

207 SONG Guocheng, op cit., p. 53.

208 BI Liangliang, op cit., p. 81.

Index

Page numbers in italics refer to figures. Page numbers in bold refer to tables. Page numbers followed by "n" refer to notes.

Taylor & Francis Group
an **informa** business

Taylor & Francis eBooks

www.taylorfrancis.com

A single destination for eBooks from Taylor & Francis with increased functionality and an improved user experience to meet the needs of our customers.

90,000+ eBooks of award-winning academic content in Humanities, Social Science, Science, Technology, Engineering, and Medical written by a global network of editors and authors.

TAYLOR & FRANCIS EBOOKS OFFERS:

- A streamlined experience for our library customers
- A single point of discovery for all of our eBook content
- Improved search and discovery of content at both book and chapter level

REQUEST A FREE TRIAL

support@taylorfrancis.com

Routledge
Taylor & Francis Group

CRC Press
Taylor & Francis Group